Children in Custody Disputes

Anna Kaldal · Agnes Hellner · Titti Mattsson
Editors

Children in Custody Disputes

Matching Legal Proceedings to Problems

palgrave
macmillan

Editors
Anna Kaldal
Faculty of Law
Stockholm University
Stockholm, Sweden

Agnes Hellner
Faculty of Law
Stockholm University
Stockholm, Sweden

Titti Mattsson
Faculty of Law
Lund University
Lund, Sweden

ISBN 978-3-031-46300-6 ISBN 978-3-031-46301-3 (eBook)
https://doi.org/10.1007/978-3-031-46301-3

Cover credit: Romas_ph/Alamy Stock Photo

This Palgrave Macmillan imprint is published by the registered company Springer Nature Switzerland AG
The registered company address is: Gewerbestrasse 11, 6330 Cham, Switzerland

Paper in this product is recyclable.

Preface

This anthology is intended as a contribution to the rich academic discussion about custody disputes and children's rights. We have gathered researchers from different academic fields to discuss the topic from a procedural-law perspective. The aim is to cross academic boundaries and approach custody disputes using the collective experiences and perspectives of empirical, substantive, and procedural law. This would not have been possible without the engagement of the contributors to this edited volume. Therefore, our first and foremost thank you, is for those authors that have aided us with their input and tireless commitment.

The project is a collaboration between the Law Faculties of Lund University and Stockholm University; without their support, the project could not have reached its goal. We therefore thank Lund University for their financial support to cover open access costs, and two foundations at Stockholm University for their kind financial support: Stiftelsen Juridisk Fakultetslitteratur for language review; and Justitierådets Edward Cassels Stiftelse for a conference on the topic in Lund, as well as further support for language review and administrative assistance.

Furthermore, we would like to thank the peer reviewers for their invaluable comments on the manuscript. We also extend our thanks to language reviewers Peggy Oskarsson, Alex Moore, and research assistant and Ph.D. candidate Caroline Åvall. This book is published by Palgrave Macmillan as an open access publication. Our commissioned editor Josephine Taylor has provided valuable support and advice throughout the process.

Our hope is that this book will not only contribute to this area of study, but also encourage further research and discussions across academic and professional boundaries.

Stockholm, Sweden — Anna Kaldal
Stockholm, Sweden — Agnes Hellner
Lund, Sweden — Titti Mattsson
September 2023

Contents

Notes on Contributors

Anne Barlow is Professor of Family Law and Policy at the University of Exeter Law School, UK. She has a particular interest in family law and policy, including the regulation of adult relationships, such as: cohabitation and marriage, access to family justice, and the voice of the child in family disputes. Barlow also leads the interdisciplinary and international research network on Family, Regulation, and Society.

Thomas D. Barton is Emeritus Professor of Law at California Western School of Law, San Diego. He holds a Ph.D. from Cambridge University, UK, and a JD from Cornell University, US. Barton has published numerous articles about legal and political philosophy, legal sociology, and problem-solving, which exemplify his expansive knowledge of the social, historical, and intellectual contexts of law.

Maria Eriksson is Professor of Social Work at Marie Cederschiöld University, Sweden. Her research focuses on the effects of inequality on policy and practice relating to men's violence against women and children. Issues of parenthood and children's rights are central to her research. Eriksson has considerable experience as a senior lecturer in child and youth studies and is an associate professor in sociology at Uppsala University and a professor of social work at Mälardalen University.

Jan Ewing is Assistant Professor of Family Law at the University of Cambridge, UK. Her research involves family law and policy, particularly in strengthening relationships between couples. Her research focuses on out-of-court dispute resolution of private family-law disputes and family mediation services.

Trude Haugli is Professor of Law at the Faculty of Law, UiT—the Arctic University of Norway, Tromsø, Norway. She leads the research group on child law. Her research interests are the rights of the child, human rights, constitutional protection of children in Nordic countries, and child perspectives within legal science.

Rosemary Hunter is Professor of Law and Socio-Legal Studies at the University of Kent Law School, UK. She began her academic career in Australia, where she first taught at the University of Melbourne and then at Griffith University in Brisbane. In the UK, Hunter has spent time at Queen Mary University of London, and at University of Kent. Her research principally involves family law, feminist judging, and access to justice. Her research within family law investigates the different forms of out-of-court family dispute resolution, and family courts' handling of domestic abuse allegations.

Agnes Hellner is Senior Lecturer in Procedural Law at the Faculty of Law, Stockholm University, Sweden. Her research focuses on access to justice, comparative procedural law, and constitutional law dimensions of procedural law, such as the relationship between the courts and the legislature.

Anna Kaldal is Professor of Procedural Law at the Faculty of Law, Stockholm University, Sweden. Her main field of research is children in legal proceedings, child protection cases, custody cases, and criminal cases. She has a particular interest in evidence law and the interaction between different legal proceedings, especially in cases of domestic violence. Kaldal is one of the founder of The Stockholm Centre for the Rights of the Child.

Titti Mattsson is Professor of Public Law at the Faculty of Law, Lund University, Sweden. Her research focuses on legal, ethical, and human-rights issues within the social welfare system, including children's rights. Mattsson leads the Health Law Research Centre at Lund University.

Anna Norlén is Director and Vice-Chancellor at The Erica Foundation in Stockholm, Sweden. She is a licensed psychologist, licensed psychotherapist, and doctoral candidate at Karlstad University, Sweden. Concentrating on children who have experienced violence, Norlén has worked within social services, child and adolescent psychiatry, child and adolescent mental health services, and non-governmental organizations. Her research centres on Child Parent Psychotherapy (CPP), a trauma-focused treatment for children of preschool ages.

Anna Nylund is Professor of Procedural Law at the Faculty of Law, University of Bergen, Norway. Her current research includes alternative dispute resolution, family/child custody mediation, comparative civil procedure, and dispute resolution, and the Europeanization of civil procedure. She obtained her doctoral degree at the University of Helsinki.

Annika Rejmer is Doctor of Sociology of Law and Associate Professor at the Faculty of Law, Uppsala University, Sweden. Her research focuses on child rights, sociology of law, family law, alternative dispute resolution and domestic violence, with particular attention on high-conflict families of divorce, regarding issues of custody, residence, and contact with the child.

Randi Sigurdsen is Professor at the Faculty of Law, UiT—the Arctic University of Norway, Tromsø, Norway. Her research interests lie within child law and administrative law, particularly focusing on the rights of the child.

Anna Singer is Professor of Family Law at the Faculty of Law, Uppsala University, Sweden. Her research focuses on the rights of the child within the family and in society. She has served as a family-law expert in many public investigations and has written several books on children's rights.

List of Tables

1

Introduction: Matching Legal Proceedings to Problems in Custody Disputes

Anna Kaldal, Agnes Hellner, and Titti Mattsson

1.1 Background and Purpose: Matching Legal Proceedings to Problems

Many children have experienced being the object of legal disputes between their parents,[1] concerning their custody, residence, and

[1] Parental separation is predominantly a Western phenomenon. In the European Union, 17% of children live in a single parent household, see Anna Nylund, 'A Dispute Systems Design Perspective on Norwegian Child Custody in Mediation' in Anna Nylund, Kaijus Ervasti and Lin Adrian (eds), *Nordic Mediation Research* (Springer 2018). Joint physical custody (JPC), also referred to as shared parenting and shared residence—where a child lives with each parent for

A. Kaldal (✉) · A. Hellner
Faculty of Law, Stockholm University, Stockholm, Sweden
e-mail: anna.kaldal@juridicum.su.se

A. Hellner
e-mail: agnes.hellner@juridicum.su.se

T. Mattsson
Faculty of Law, Lund University, Lund, Sweden
e-mail: titti.mattsson@jur.lu.se

A. Kaldal et al. (eds.), *Children in Custody Disputes*,
https://doi.org/10.1007/978-3-031-46301-3_1

contact.[2] Research shows that parents battling in court over their children represent a risk factor, not only for children's health and development, but also for their own physical and mental health.[3] In addition, underlying causes such as abuse, neglect, or domestic violence can sometimes explain why parents struggle to legally obtain sole custody or limited contact.[4] Furthermore, custody disputes concern deeply emotional and intimate matters, involving relationships that will continue long after the legal proceedings have concluded. This illustrates the complexity of the problems underlying legal disputes concerning custody, residence, and contact. Thus, there are good reasons for preventing custody disputes or implementing legal proceedings that minimize the negative effects and optimize positive outcomes for children and their families.

---

at least 25–50% of the time after separation or divorce—is increasingly common in many Western societies, see Anja Steinbach, 'Children's and Parents' Well-Being in Joint Physical Custody: A Literature Review' (2019) 58(2) *Family Process* 353–369; Daisy JH Smeets and Stephanie Rap, 'Pedagogical Insights on Why and How to Involve Children', Wendy Schrama, Marilyn Freeman, Nicola Taylor and Mariëlle Bruning (eds), *International Handbook on Child Participation in Family Law* (Intersentia 2021); Mariëlle Bruning, Daisy Smeets and KGA Bolscher, 'Child Participation in Dutch Family Law and Child Protection Proceedings' in Mona Paré, Thierry Moreau, Mariëlle Bruning and Caroline Siffrein-Blanc (eds), *Children's Access to Justice: A Critical Assessment* (Leiden University Scholarly Publications 2022).

[2] In different legal systems, there are many variations of family law disputes between parents regarding their children. In this chapter the phrase 'custody disputes' will be used as a collective term that includes custody, residence and contact.

[3] Søren Sander, Jenna Marie Strizzi, Camilla S Øverup, Ana Cipric and Gert Martin Hald, 'When Love Hurts – Mental and Physical Health Among Recently Divorced Danes' (2020) 11 *Frontiers in Psychology*.

[4] Peter G Jaffe, Janet R Johnston, Claire V Crooks and Nicholas Bala, 'Custody Disputes Involving Allegations of Domestic Violence: Toward a Differentiated Approach to Parenting Plans' (2008) 46(3) *Family Court Review* 500–522; Paul R Amato, 'Research on Divorce: Continuing Trends and New Developments' (2010) 72(3) *Journal of Marriage and Family* 650–666; Kelly Musick and Ann Meier, 'Are both Parents Always Better than One? Parental Conflict and Young Adult Well-being' (2010) 39(5) *Social Science Research* 814–830; Fernada S Rossi, Amy Holtzworth-Munroe and Brittany N Rudd, 'Intimate Partner Violence and Child Custody' in Leslie Drozd, Michael Saini and Nancy Olesen (eds), *Parenting Plan Evaluations: Applied Research for the Family Court* (Oxford University Press 2016). See also, Anne Barlow, Rosemary Hunter and Jan Ewing, 'Mapping Paths to Family Justice: Resolving Family Disputes Involving Children in Neoliberal Times'; Annika Rejmer, 'Custody Disputes from a Socio-legal Perspective'; Maria Eriksson, 'Children's Participation and Perspectives in Family Disputes', all three in Anna Kaldal, Agnes Hellner and Titti Mattsson (eds), *Children in Custody Disputes: Matching Legal Proceedings to Problems* (Palgrave 2023).

The aim of this anthology is to explore how such legal proceedings in, and out-of-court, can be matched with the complex problems that are both caused by, and underlie such disputes. The anthology draws specifically on Nordic experiences of resolving custody disputes. However, the challenges are not unique to the Nordic legal systems: they exist across the world in various legal systems.

The twentieth century represented a paradigm shift in terms of how the interests and perspectives of the child are conceptualized in society at large. This ideological transformation is reflected in the UN Convention on the Rights of the Child (CRC), adopted by the UN General Assembly in November 1989. Today, the CRC is the most widely ratified human-rights treaty; it is part of a 'globalization of childhood' in the sense that it features an understanding of childhood, what a child is, and is presented as universal.[5] Since its adoption, the CRC has influenced custody-dispute legislation and practice on a global level.[6] The general principles of the best interests of the child (Article 3) and the right to participation (Article 12) play a prominent role in child custody conflicts. Article 3—pivotal to the whole convention—provides a general standard which underpins the rights set out in subsequent articles. The concept of the child's best interests is aimed at ensuring a holistic development of the child and embraces the child's physical, mental, spiritual, moral, psychological, and social development.[7]

Beyond being a substantive right, Article 3 is to be understood as a rule of procedure; assessing and determining the best interests of the child requires procedural guarantees. Therefore, applying the principle also sets a standard for a legal proceeding and requires, for example, a qualitative and individualized investigation of all relevant elements, if

[5] Anne Trine Kjørholt, 'Barn som samfunnsborgare—til barnets beste?' in Anne Trine Kjørholt (eds), *Barn som samfunnsborgare—til barnets beste?* (Universitetsforlaget 2010) 12.

[6] Michael Freeman, 'Why It Remains Important to Take Children's Rights Seriously' (2007) 15(5) *The International Journal of Children's Rights* 5–23.

[7] Committee on the Rights of the Child (CRC), *General comment no. 5 General measures of implementation of the Convention on the Rights of the Child*, (27 November 2003) CRC/GC/2003/527 para. 12; Michael Freeman, 'Article 3. The Best Interests of the Child' in André Alen, Johan Vande Lanotte, Eugeen Verhellen, Fiona Ang, Eva Berghmans and Mieke Verheyde (eds), *A Commentary on the United Nations Convention on the Rights of the Child* (Brill/Nijhoff 2007).

possible, by a multi-professional team—including the child's own view.[8] The importance of hearing the child and including the child's view is also covered by Article 12 and requires that the child is given the opportunity to express their views with respect to all matters that affect them, and the decision-maker must consider the child's view in accordance with their age and maturity.[9] The CRC thus sets certain standards for a legal proceeding concerning the best interests of the child and therefore also for custody dispute proceedings. However, it does not directly address custody-dispute proceedings; nor does the Committee on the Rights of the Child pursue the subject in more depth in its general comments.[10]

---

[8] CRC, *General comment no. 14 on the right of the child to have his or her best interests taken as a primary consideration (art. 3, para. 1)* (29 May 2013) CRC/C/GC/14 para. 6 (c). The principle is a dynamic concept that requires an assessment appropriate to the specific context. Para. 29 states that the principle applies to civil cases such as procedures concerning custody. The courts must provide for the best interests of the child to be considered in all such situations and decisions, whether of a procedural or substantive nature, and must demonstrate that they have effectively done so (para. 29). See also, Milka Sormunen, 'Understanding the Best Interests of the Child as a Procedural Obligation: The Example of the European Court of Human Rights' (2020) 20 *Human Rights Law Review* 745–768. In Swedish family law the best interests of the child are applied differently when the parents reach an agreement concerning custody of a child out-of-court with the support of the social services family law unit, and when the court decides in a custody dispute. In the first instance, the law states that an agreement should be accepted by the social services if it is '*not obvious that it is in conflict* with the best interests of the child' ('om det inte är uppenbart att avtalet är oförenligt med barnets bästa'), Swedish Children and Parent Code [Föräldrabalk] (1949:381) Chapter 6 Section 6 para. 2. If the parents do not agree, on the other hand, the court decision must be *according to* the best interests of the child. The reason behind this is that an agreement between the parents, in itself, is regarded as an important factor when assessing what is in the best interests of the child, and therefore can outdo other factors. Cf concerning the relation between CRC Article 3 and Article 12 in David Archard and Marit Skivenes, 'Balancing a Child´s Best interests and a Child´s Views' (2009) 17(1) *The International Journal of Children's Rights* 1–21.

[9] See further for this discussion: Laura Lundy, '"Voice" is not enough: conceptualising Article 12 of the United Nations Convention on the Rights of the Child' (2007) 2007 33(6) *British Educational Research Journal* 927–842; Mark Henaghan, 'Article 12 of the UN Convention on the Rights of Children: Where Have We Come from, Where Are We Now and Where to from Here?' (2017) 25(2) *The International Journal of Children's Rights* 537–552; Daly A, 'No Weight for "Due Weight"? A Children's Autonomy Principle in Best Interests Proceedings', *International Journal of Children's Rights* (2018) 26(1) *The International Journal of Children's Rights* 61–92.

[10] Divorce and separation is specified in CRC, *General Comment no. 12 The right of the child to be heard* (20 July 2009) CRC/C/GC/12 para. 15. According to the comment children have a right to be heard in any judicial or administrative proceedings that affects the child, such as court proceedings or mediation processes. The Committee emphasizes the importance of taking the child's view into account in custody disputes, CRC, *General Comment no. 12* paras. 32, 50 and 51.

In many legal systems, custody disputes are family-law disputes, and are resolved according to rules of civil procedure. The accusatory character of such proceedings has been argued as unsuitable for custody disputes. Framing a custody dispute as civil procedure can cause the parties' arguments to overshadow the investigation and assessment of the best interests of the child. It can also intensify and prolong the conflict between the parents.[11] With the aim of preventing court disputes, out-of-court dispute resolution proceedings have emerged within different national legal systems, with mediation being the most established concept.[12] However, research has shown that there are several challenges associated with these proceedings and they risk creating unwanted outcomes that are not in the best interests of the child. For instance, alternative dispute resolution mechanisms might fail to allow consideration of the child's own views. Power imbalances between the parties can have a negative impact on agreements regarding custody, and risk factors could be overlooked. In addition, research has noted a lack of a theoretical basis and the absence of educated professionals in the process.[13]

Applying the principle of the best interests of the child in a custody matter is a prognostic assessment that includes the identification of both short- and long-term consequences for the child.[14] Prognostic assessments also exist in other areas of law, such as medical law, migration law, and environmental law. A common feature of legal problems addressed in

[11] Jessica J Sauer, 'Mediating Child Custody Disputes for High Conflict Couples: Structuring Mediation to Accommodate the Needs & Desires of Litigious Parents' (2007) 7(3) *Pepperdine Dispute Resolution Law Journal* 501–533; Nylund (n 2). This is also discussed in Rejmer (n 4); Anna Singer, 'Out-of-court Custody Dispute Resolution in Sweden—A Journey Without Destination' and Anna Nylund 'Scandinavian Family Mediation: Towards a System of Differentiated Services?' , both in Anna Kaldal, Agnes Hellner and Titti Mattsson (eds), *Children in Custody Disputes: Matching the Legal Proceedings to the Problem* (Palgrave 2023).

[12] Sauer (n 11); Nylund (n 11).

[13] Nylund (n 11).

[14] CRC, *General comment no. 14* (n 8), para. 74, and CRC, General comment no. 7, para. 45; Freeman (n 6); Anna Kaldal, *Parallella processer. En rättsvetenskaplig studie av riskbesömningar I vårdnads- och LVU-mål*[A Legal Study of Risk Assessments in Custody and Child Protection Cases] (Jure 2010).

such assessments is that they are comparatively new to the legal system.[15] In legal scholarship, new theoretical approaches have emerged in relation to the assessment of future events and risks in legal proceedings. One such theoretical approach is proactive law, in which the law is seen as an instrument that can create success and foster sustainable relationships, rather than a constraint requiring compliance from companies and people.[16] Similarly, preventive law seeks to encourage new methods and concepts for how legal services can be organized to avoid conflict and disputes, with the goal of managing facts and events to avoid unwanted legal consequences.[17] Furthermore, Therapeutic Jurisprudence (TJ) studies the extent to which a legal rule or practice influences the psychological wellbeing of the person or persons affected by the rule or practice, and explores ways in which anti-therapeutic consequences can be reduced, and instead improve therapeutic consequences.[18]

Several of the abovementioned theories and concepts have connections with more established out-of-court resolution models, such as mediation. However, while mediation has a long tradition and roots in commercial-law conflicts, the proactive, preventive, and therapeutic law theories have emerged more recently and address a variety of legal problems. The emergence of the abovementioned theories indicates that new research methods and dispute resolution models might be needed in order to tackle new societal problems, and to achieve outcomes that are better adapted to the problem itself.

Given the challenges and complexities of custody-dispute proceedings, the present anthology relies on a comprehensive procedural-law approach that considers the emotional, personal, and intimate character of custody disputes, underlying causes, and the effects that such disputes can have on the health of both children and parents. Furthermore, it includes the substantive as well as the procedural international standards enshrined in

---

15 Cf Elizabeth Fisher, 'Risk and Environmental Law: A Beginner's Guide' in Benjamin J Richardson and Stepan Wood *Environmental Law for Sustainability* (Hart 2006) 97, 102.

16 Gerlinde Berger-Walliser and Kim Østergaard, *Proactive Law—in a Business Environment* (1st edn Tilst, DJØF Publishing, Jurist- og Økonomforbundets Forlag 2012) 16; Thomas D Barton, *Preventive Law and Problem Solving. Lawyering for the Future* (Vandeplas publishing 2009).

17 Barton (n 16).

18 David B Wexler, Michael L Perlin, Michel Vols, Pauline Spencer and Nigel Stobbs, 'Editorial: Current Issues in Therapeutic Jurisprudence' (2016) 16(3), *QUT Law Review* 1–3.

the CRC, and addresses the question of how legal proceedings in custody disputes can be adapted to the best interests of the child. The anthology presents both theoretical and empirical perspectives of custody disputes that account for the complexity of the issue. As a result, this anthology transcends disciplinary, institutional, and jurisdictional boundaries in search of new knowledge, with a view to exploring how legal proceedings, in and out-of-court, can be matched to the complex problems underlying these proceedings.

1.2 Setting the Scene—The Nordic Legal Systems and Swedish Law as an Example

Custody proceedings take different forms in different countries: the legal and institutional arrangements in place to tackle these conflicts have emerged in political and historical contexts specific to a particular state or tradition. However, across the world, the best interests of the child should now be the fundamental standard that permeate legal decision-making concerning the child. For this reason—and those relating to the nature and effects of custody disputes on health and long-term personal and emotional relationships—custody disputes present similar challenges in different legal systems.

The present book primarily draws on Nordic experiences—positive as well as negative—from in and out-of-court mechanisms as means of resolving custody disputes. However, the challenges addressed are by no means unique to Nordic legal systems. Rather, similar challenges exist in all states seeking to realize the best interests of the child in situations where the parents are involved in a deep conflict. Nevertheless, since in this book the Nordic legal systems and in particular Swedish law, serve as a context and an example of how such challenges are and have been addressed, it is worthwhile to briefly review some of the features of these legal systems.

Nordic societies and legal systems share some features that are central to the discussions and analyses of custody disputes and children in parental conflicts. One such feature is the basic historical relationship between the state and the individual, sometimes referred to as the *Nordic welfare model*—a system characterized by a strong state, or rather, a large and expensive public sector, with welfare benefits and services.[19] This system is defined as more family-oriented than child-oriented in the sense that children encompassed by the development of a strong welfare legislation, are not given a prominent or independent position in the law.[20] Such a system focuses on early prevention and support to the child and the child's family, rather than a more reactive approach, which characterizes a system focused on child protection. A family-oriented child-welfare system is primarily focused on support for the family as a whole, based on voluntary measures and collaboration as a first option and compulsory interventions as an exception. While there are organizational differences among the Nordic countries' systems, they can all be described as family-oriented child-welfare systems. This may explain why social services also generally play a role in custody disputes.[21] At the same time, a more recent focus on children's rights has moved these systems in a new direction. The ratification of the CRC, which has been incorporated into national law in all the Nordic countries except Denmark (though Denmark has ratified the Convention), imprints the procedural law applicable to parental conflicts of today and has played an important role in shifting to a more child rights-based perspective.[22] This has also

---

[19] Pia Letto-Vanamo 'Courts and Proceedings: Some Nordic Characteristics' in Laura Ervo, Pia Letto-Vanamo and Anna Nylund (eds), Rethinking Nordic Courts (Springer 2021) Ius Gentium: Comparative Perspectives on Law and Justice 90, 21, 23; Jaakko Husa, Kimmo Nuotio and Heikki Pihlajamäki 'Nordic Law—Between Tradition and Dynamism' in Jaakko Husa, Kimmo Nuotio and Heikki Pihlajamäki (eds), *Nordic Law – Between Tradition and Dynamism* (Intersentia 2007) 26–28; Susanna Johansson, Kari Stefansen, Elisiv Bakketeig and Anna Kaldal,'Implementing the Nordic Barnahus Model: Characteristics and Local Adaptions' in Susanna Johansson Kari Stefansen, Elisiv Bakketeig and Anna Kaldal (eds), *Collaborating Against Child Abuse Exploring the Nordic Barnahus Model* (Palgrave Macmillan 2017) 8; Gösta Esping-Andersen, 'The Three Worlds of Welfare Capitalism' (1990) *Cambridge Polity Press* 9–54.

[20] Johansson and others (n 19) 9.

[21] In Sweden and Finland, the child-welfare system is a part of a municipality's general social-services system; in Norway, Iceland, and Denmark, child welfare is regulated and organized as an independent body. See Johansson and others (n 19) 10.

[22] In the case of Norway and Finland, the obligation to respect the Convention on the Rights of the Child is enshrined in constitutional law. See further Trude Haugli, Anna Nylund, Randi

led to a greater focus on both children's right to participation and right to protection from violence and abuse.

Over the past couple of decades, gender equality has affected family law governing custody disputes in Nordic countries.[23] This has led to co-parenting, both in legislation and in society as a whole, as the norm in separated families. When both parents seek to take an active part in parenthood, it raises the bar with respect to what is required in terms of cooperation between them.[24] The emphasis on co-parenthood in law and society, and its consequences for custody disputes, is discussed in several chapters in the anthology.[25] Gender equality is also one of the reasons for a greater awareness of the existence of domestic violence. Research indicates that domestic violence (or alleged violence) is present in over 50% of litigated child custody cases in Sweden.[26]

Furthermore, in Nordic countries, the corporal punishment of children of all ages is always considered illegitimate and an act of violence. The bar is very low in this regard. Even if the legislation varies among Nordic countries, the attitude towards violence, in the legal sense, can be characterized as zero tolerance.[27] The growing awareness of the harm

---

Sigurdsen and Lena RL Bendiksen (eds), *Children's Constitutional Rights in the Nordic Countries* (Brill/Nijhoff 2019).

[23] Not least because the interpretation of the best interests of the child emphasizes the importance of both parents' participation in the child's life and upbringing. For example, Swedish legislation explicitly provides that the child has a right to a close and good relationship with both parents, and in most cases, it is considered that shared custody and even shared residence is in the best interests of the child. See Government Bill 2020/21:150 *Ett stärkt barnperspektiv i vårdnadstvister* [A Strengthened Child Rights Perspecitve in Custody Disputes].

[24] Johanna Schiratzki, 'Barnrättsperspektivet i vårdnadstvister—från domstolsförhandling till föräldraförhandling. Vad händer med barnets bästa?' (2022/23) (1) *Juridisk Tidskrift* 249.

[25] Anna Norlén, 'Children's health matters in custody conflicts—What do we know?' in Anna Kaldal, Agnes Hellner and Titti Mattsson (eds), *Children in Custody Disputes: Matching Legal Proceedings to Problems* (Palgrave 2023); Rejmer (n 4); Singer (n 11).

[26] The Swedish Gender Equality Agency, *Uppgifter om våld är inget undantag. Redovisning av kartläggning av uppgifter om våld eller andra övergrepp i mål om vårdnad, boende och umgänge*, Rapport 2022:1 [*Information on Violence is no Exception. Reporting of the Mapping of Data on Violence or other Abuse in Custody, Residence and Contact or Visitation*]; Eriksson (n 4).

[27] Johansson and others (n 19); Pernilla Leviner and Tiziana Sardiello, 'The Swedish Ban on Corporal Punishment of Children in a Multi-Cultural Context—Conflicting Logics in the Social Services' in Bernadette Saunders, Pernilla Leviner, and Bronwyn Naylor (eds), *Corporal Punishment of Children—Comparative Legal and Social Developments towards Prohibition and Beyond* (Brill/Nijhoff 2019).

caused by violence against children and exposure to domestic violence, as well as the strengthening of children's right to protection, has affected the legislation in criminal law, social welfare law, and family law concerning custody disputes. For example, it has led to legislation that identifies violence as a serious risk factor for children when assessing the best interests of the child and impacted the attentiveness and the notion of responsibility of public welfare authorities and the courts. Therefore, the conflict between the child's right to protection from violence and the child's right to a close relationship with his or her parents is often the core question in a high-conflict custody dispute. These issues are addressed from various perspectives by several authors contributing to this volume.[28]

As highlighted above, the aim to promote co-parenting and prevent parental conflicts from ending up in court has led to implementation of out-of-court resolution models to handle and prevent parental conflicts.[29] This has taken various approaches in Nordic countries, but a common feature is that achieving out-of-court solutions tends to be considered a goal in itself, beneficial to both children and parents. One reason for this is that bringing custody disputes before the court is believed to be associated with a risk of intensifying a parental conflict. Out-of-court dispute resolution is discussed in several contributions to the present work.[30]

Recent decades have seen an increased emphasis on children's rights through—for instance—the impact of the CRC. This is particularly the case for Article 12, which represents a view of children as competent agents who can participate in custody disputes. Under Swedish legislation, however, a child does not have the status of a party in custody cases. As a result, the discussion and the legislation concerning the child's right to participate in custody disputes has focused on alternative means of enabling the child to present their views. One challenge is finding a

[28] For example, Barlow, Hunter and Ewing (n 4); Rejmer (n 4); Eriksson (n 4); Norlén (n 25).

[29] Kirsikka Linnanmäki, 'Mediation and the Best Interests of the Child from the Child Law Perspective' in Nylund Kaijus Ervasti and Lin Adrian (eds), *Nordic Mediation Research* (Springer 2018) 209–222.

[30] Nylund (n 2); Singer (n 11). Barlow, Hunter and Ewing discuss this from a UK perspective in Barlow, Hunter and Ewing (n 4).

balance between protecting the child from being drawn into the parents' conflict, while still giving the child the opportunity to express their views, share experiences, and influence the decision. Even if children are increasingly being heard in custody disputes in Sweden and other Nordic countries, studies show that this is not always the case and that the views of children are not sufficiently considered in judicial decision-making.[31]

1.3 Structure of the Anthology

To fulfil the purpose set out above—to explore how legal proceedings in and out-of-court can be matched to the complex problems caused by, and underlying custody disputes—the present anthology brings together scholars and practitioners from different disciplines and areas of law. The contributions take historical, theoretical, and interdisciplinary perspectives and examine how the law is applied and affects children and parents involved.

In Chapter 2, ***Children's Health Matters in Custody Conflicts—What Do We Know?*** Licensed Psychologist and Psychotherapist, Anna Norlén, provides a literature review about the interrelationships between joint custody, interparental conflict, and the wellbeing of children. This is based on a selection of recent publications from child psychology and developmental research perspectives. Norlén points to various ways in which children are affected by long-standing parental conflicts and violence and uses this knowledge as a basis for identifying the type of support needed in each case. In particular, she highlights the need for allowing a child to express and explore their feelings. The chapter concludes that the means of effectively supporting children in custody conflicts must be further developed and researched and presents suggestions for supporting the mental health and wellbeing of children in custody conflicts.

[31] Kristin Skjørten and Kirsten Sandberg, 'Children's Participation in Family Law Proceedings' in Malcolm Langford, Marit Skivenes and Karl Harald Søvig (eds), *Children's Rights in Norway: An Implementation Paradox?* (Universitetsforlaget 2019); Eriksson (n 4).

In Chapter 3, ***Scandinavian Perspectives on Alternative Legal Proceedings in Custody Conflicts***, Anna Nylund, a professor of Procedural Law, maps and analyses the definition, purpose, and content of alternative legal proceedings in custody conflicts in Scandinavian legal systems. She discusses the fact that in Norway, Sweden, Denmark, and Finland, such proceedings take place both in court and through social services, and how there is a lack of coordination between the two instances. Expert mediators are involved in some of the proceedings, but the qualifications and methods used by the mediator are not yet defined. The conclusion is reached that the lack of clear content, role definition, and coordination results in alternative legal proceedings that do not sufficiently account for the rights and perspectives of the child.

In Chapter 4, ***Custody Disputes—A Socio-Legal Perspective***, Annika Rejmer, an associate professor of Sociology of Law, gives an in-depth analysis of high-conflict custody disputes in court. She discusses whether the Swedish legislation efficiently caters for children's rights and the best interests of the child in these disputes. Based on a qualitative and quantitative study of 33 Swedish court cases, this socio-legal contribution identifies and analyses the most common conflicts arising from family disputes, and whether the legal system is able to solve them. The author categorizes conflicts in custody disputes in two ways: conflicts of interest, and conflicts of value. The legal system is designed to deal with the former—concerning issues of residence, finance, time, and information. However, the system is not well-equipped to deal with the conflicts of value that dominate custody disputes: lack of childcare ability, cooperation difficulties, violence, threats and abuse, and access sabotage, among others. The author concludes that the best interests of the child remain insufficiently addressed in custody conflicts.

In Chapter 5, ***Children's Participation and Perspectives in Family Disputes***, Maria Eriksson, a professor of Social Sciences, examines how agency interventions in the lives of children involved in custody disputes, can become as child-centred and child-friendly as possible from a sociological point of view. The chapter is divided in two parts, the first focusing on child health in family disputes and the second on children's participation and perspectives. The results of several empirical studies of children in contact with family-law services are presented and their implications for policy and practice are identified. On a policy level, the author contends that boundaries between family-law proceedings and child welfare are dissolved. To reach that objective in practice, the issue of children's participation is connected to risk assessments and how to best communicate with children. The author explains how the principle of care and the principle of participation can be simplified and applied in practice to contribute to the child's sense of security and coherence. Eriksson further argues that children's participation can be enhanced by drawing on research of how to best communicate with the child. Finally, the contribution discusses children's agency beyond participation, noting that the children interviewed in one of the studies emphasized their right to decide for themselves.

In Chapter 6, ***Mapping Paths to Family Justice: Resolving Family Disputes Involving Children in Neoliberal Times***, Anne Barlow, a professor of Family Law and Policy, Rosemary Hunter, a professor of Law and Socio-Legal Studies, and Jan Ewing, a Doctor of Law, assess the extent to which the interests of the child are paramount in three types of out-of-court procedures in England and Wales. It is then discussed whether, in certain types of cases, the interests of the child are better protected through in-court procedures. The chapter is based on several empirical studies of families and mediators/lawyers involved in out-of-court procedures. The authors find that while out-of-court procedures generally are child-focused, it is less common that they are child-inclusive or that the voice of the child is reflected in the adult decision-making. Further, in the out-of-court procedure, 'child welfare' tends to be understood in terms of ongoing contact with both parents and co-parenting. Consequently, the protection of children from an abusive parent, risks being under-emphasized. In addition, concerns about children, in some instances, tend to be overshadowed by a problematic financial situation. Further, given there is growing evidence that many children would like to be consulted in out-of-court family dispute resolution, and that (where it is appropriate and safe), this can be a positive for children's wellbeing. Consideration is given to how current practice in family dispute resolution fits with the rights expressed in Article 12 CRC. In conclusion, the authors find a need for distinguishing different types of conflicts and adjusting procedures accordingly.

In Chapter 7, ***Out-Of-Court Custody Dispute Resolution in Sweden—A Journey Without Destination***, Anna Singer, a professor of Family Law, explores the development of out-of-court custody dispute resolution in custody conflicts in Swedish law and related legal scholarship. The chapter discusses the practical effects of Swedish family-law reforms and the continued efforts on behalf of the legislature, to avoid settlement of custody disputes by the courts. Mechanisms used to avoid the initiation of formal judicial proceedings are mapped, such as availability of cooperation talks (which can be initiated by both the parents themselves and by the court), mediation, and a mandatory information meeting. The author finds that the role of social services and the courts in custody disputes, as well as the responsibility they have towards one another and in relation to the parents, is not always clearly defined in the law. She further identifies a number of challenges relating to the application of the law in practice, for example, the appointment of an independent mediator, which is relied on in only 1–3% of cases. Finally, Singer argues that parents in custody disputes have problems that were not considered in the initial design of custody dispute processes: the Swedish out-of-court processes are too rigid in the sense that they only fit some of the families targeted and are not sufficiently adapted to the varying and often complex needs of a modern family.

In Chapter 8, ***Children's Health Matters in Custody Conflicts: Best Interests of the Child and Decisions on Health Matters***, Trude Haugli and Randi Sigurdsen, both professors of Law, address conflicts of interest that can arise when there are ongoing custody disputes and how legal instruments can be used to deal with a situation where parents disagree over a decision that must be taken concerning a child's health. When a child is younger than 16 years, their custodians must give consent regarding health matters. The child has a right, however, to be heard, and the custodians must act in the best interests of the child. Through the analysis of several potential scenarios, the authors discuss, from a Norwegian legal context, whether parents in conflict are in fact *able* to act in the best interests of the child, and whether the child's right to participation is respected. The authors conclude that the limited legal—or other—tools provided to parents and/or health institutions can lead to sole custody being the only way to solve the disagreement. The authors point out the dilemma in cases where the custody dispute or the parental conflict is the *reason* behind the child's need for treatment.

In Chapter 9, ***Challenges When Family Conflicts Meet the Law—A Proactive Approach***, Thomas D Barton, a professor of Law, analyses the prospective and therapeutic character of parental conflict from a proactive-law perspective, discussing whether and how legal proceedings could be adapted to it. The chapter starts with the premise that there is an interdependence of problems and procedures in the context of domestic relations legal issues and alternative dispute resolution mechanisms. For the author, attributes of domestic relations problems—especially child custody issues—do not fit well with the capabilities of traditional legal procedures. Yet this lack of fit between problem and procedure can be overcome and procedures improved. Using a proactive approach, the author identifies a need for acknowledging and incorporating different ways of speaking about domestic relations problems. He concludes that the legal system should supplement its traditional problem-solving methods with others.

Finally, in Chapter 10, ***Beyond the Horizon: Matching Legal Proceedings to the Problems in Custody Disputes***, Anna Kaldal, a professor of Procedural Law and Agnes Hellner, a senior lecturer of Procedural Law, draw on the findings of the previous chapters of the anthology to discuss how the challenge of matching legal proceedings to problems in custody disputes could be further addressed in the future. The first conclusion is that the nature of and inherent causes of custody conflicts, and how parent–child relationships, children's health, risk factors, and other aspects characterizing custody conflicts should be understood and considered in legal proceedings in and out-of-court. The second conclusion relates to the tensions between a private-law understanding of custody disputes and an understanding that relies on the best interests of the child as a starting point—especially when viewing the child as a rights-bearer. Tensions between legal structures that have been conserved, despite numerous legislative amendments, and more recently introduced legal objectives are discussed. The third conclusion relates to those challenges associated with guaranteeing the child's own procedural rights—particularly the right to participation. Respecting the child's right to participation ensures that the child is treated as a rights-bearer and active agent, with thoughts and ideas worth considering during decision-making. The fourth conclusion is that legal fragmentation which manifests in several ways in the law governing custody disputes and proceedings. Today, the best interests of the child is an international legal standard applicable in custody disputes, although it has been criticized for being vague. At the same time, national laws define the more precise content of the standard, with respect to both substantive and procedural law. The normative content of the law is thus defined on several levels of government. Furthermore, due to the complex nature of the conflicts underlying custody disputes, legal responses to the resulting problems take various forms and involve a wide range of agencies and courts—all with different mandates and investigational powers. The authors argue that in this legal landscape, it is essential to ensure that the application of the principle of the best interests of the child involves an individualized and knowledge-based assessment, one that integrates perspectives from several disciplines.

References

Amato P, 'Research on Divorce: Continuing Trends and New Developments' (2010) 72(3) *Journal of Marriage and Family* 650.

Archard D and Skivenes M, 'Balancing a Child's Best Interests and a Child's Views' (2009) 17(1) *The International Journal of Children's Rights* 1.

Barlow A, Hunter R and Ewing J, 'Mapping Paths to Family Justice: Resolving Family Disputes Involving Children in Neoliberal Times' in Kaldal A, Hellner A and Mattsson T (eds), *Children in Custody Disputes: Matching Legal Proceedings to Problems* (Palgrave 2023) 107.

Barton T D, *Preventive Law and Problem Solving. Lawyering for the Future* (Vandeplas publishing 2009).

Berger-Walliser G and Østergaard K, *Proactive Law—in a Business Environment* (1st edn Tilst, DJØF Publishing, Jurist- og Økonomforbundets Forlag 2012).

Bruning M, Smeets D and Bolscher KGA, 'Child Participation in Dutch Family Law and Child Protection Proceedings' in Paré M, Moreau T, Bruning M and Siffrein-Blanc C (eds), *Children's Access to Justice: A Critical Assessment* (Leiden University Scholar Publications 2022).

Committee on the Rights of the Child, *General comment no. 5 General measures of implementation of the Convention on the Rights of the Child* (27 November 2003) CRC/GC/2003/5.

Committee on the Rights of the Child, *General comment no. 12 The right of the child to be heard* (25 May–12 June 2009) CRC/C/GC/12.

Committee on the Rights of the Child, *General comment no. 14 on the right of the child to have his or her best interests taken as a primary consideration* (art. 3, para. 1) (1 February 2013) CRC/C/GC/14.

Eriksson M, 'Children's Participation and Perspectives in Family Disputes' in Kaldal A, Hellner A and Mattsson T (eds), *Children in Custody Disputes: Matching Legal Proceedings to Problems* (Palgrave 2023) 85.

Esping-Andersen G, 'The Three Worlds of Welfare Capitalism' (1990) *Cambridge Polity Press* 9.

Fisher E, 'Risk and Environmental Law: A Beginner's Guide' in Benjamin J Richardson and Stepan Wood *Environmental Law for Sustainability* (Hart 2006).

Freeman M, 'Why It Remains Important to Take Children's Rights Seriously' (2007) 15(5) *The International Journal of Children's Rights* 5.

Freeman M, 'Article 3. The Best Interests of the Child' in Alen A, Vande Lanotte J, Verhellen E, Ang F, Berghmans E and Verheyde M (eds), *A Commentary on the United Nations Convention on the Rights of the Child* (Brill/Nijhoff 2007).

Haugli T, Nylund A, Sigurdsen R and Bendiksen L R L (eds), *Children's Constitutional Rights in the Nordic Countries* (Brill/Nijhoff 2019).

Henaghan M, 'Article 12 of the UN Convention on the Rights of Children: Where Have We Come from, Where Are We Now and Where to from Here?' (2017) 25(2) *The International Journal of Children's Rights* 537.

Husa J, Nuotio K and Pihlajamäki H 'Nordic Law—Between Tradition and Dynamism' in Jaakko Husa, Kimmo Nuotio and Heikki Pihlajamäki (eds), *Nordic Law—Between Tradition and Dynamism* (Intersentia 2007) 1.

Jaffe P G, Johnston J R, Crooks C V and Bala N, 'Custody Disputes Involving Allegations of Domestic Violence: Toward a Differentiated Approach to Parenting Plans' (2008) 46(3) *Family Court Review* 500.

Johansson S, Stefansen K, Bakketeig E and Kaldal A, 'Implementing the Nordic Barnahus Model: Characteristics and Local Adaptions' in Johansson S, Stefansen K, Bakketeig E and Kaldal A (eds), *Collaborating Against Child Abuse Exploring the Nordic Barnahus Model* (Palgrave Macmillan 2017) 1.

Kaldal A, *Parallella processer. En rättsvetenskaplig studie av riskbesömningar I vårdnads- och LVU-mål* [A Legal Study of Riskassessments in Custody and Child Protection Cases] (Jure 2010).

Kjørholt T A, 'Barn som samfunnsborgare—til barnets beste?' in Kjørholt T A (eds), *Barn som samfunnsborgare—til barnets beste?* (Universitetsforlaget 2010) 11.

Letto-Vanamo P 'Courts and Proceedings: Some Nordic Characteristics' in Laura Ervo, Pia Letto-Vanamo and Anna Nylund (eds), *Rethinking Nordic Courts* (Springer 2021) *Ius Gentium: Comparative Perspectives on Law and Justice* 90 21.

Leviner P and Sardiello T, 'The Swedish Ban on Corporal Punishment of Children in a Multi-Cultural Context—Conflicting Logics in the Social Services' in Bernadette Saunders, Leviner P, and Naylor B (eds), *Corporal Punishment of Children—Comparative Legal and Social Developments towards Prohibition and Beyond* (Brill/Nijhoff 2019).

Linnanmäki K, 'Mediation and the Best Interests of the Child from the Child Law Perspective', in Nylund A, Ervasti K and Adrian L (eds), *Nordic Mediation* (Springer 2018).

Lundy L, '"Voice" is not enough: conceptualising Article 12 of the United Nations Convention on the Rights of the Child' (2007) 33(6) *British Educational Research Journal* 927.

Musick K and Meier A, 'Are both Parents Always Better than One? Parental Conflict and Young Adult Well-being' (2010) 39(5) *Social Science Research* 814.

Norlén A, 'Children's Health Matters in Custody Conflicts—What do we know?' in Kaldal A, Hellner A and Mattsson T (eds), *Children in Custody Disputes: Matching Legal Proceedings to Problems* (Palgrave 2023) 21.

Nylund A, 'A Dispute Systems Design Perspective on Norwegian Child Custody Mediation' in Nylund A, Ervasti K and Adrian L (eds), *Nordic Mediation Research* (Springer 2018) 9.

Rejmer A, 'Custody Disputes from a Socio-legal Perspective' in Kaldal A, Hellner A and Mattsson T (eds), *Children in Custody Disputes: Matching Legal Proceedings to Problems* (Palgrave 2023) 67.

Rossi FS, Holtzworth-Munroe A and Rudd B N, 'Intimate Partner Violence and Child Custody' in Leslie Drozd, Michael Saini and Nancy Olesen (eds), *Parenting Plan Evaluations: Applied Research for the Family Court* (Oxford University Press 2016) 346.

Sander S, Strizzi M J, Øverup C S, Cipric A and Hald G M, 'When Love Hurts—Mental and Physical Health Among Recently Divorced Danes' (2020) *Frontiers in Psychology* 11.

Sauer J J, 'Mediating Child Custody Disputes for High Conflict Couples: Structuring Mediation to Accommodate the Needs & Desires of Litigious Parents' (2007) 7(3) *Pepperdine Dispute Resolution Law Journal* 501.

Schiratzki J, 'Barnrättsperspektivet i vårdnadstvister—från domstolsförhandling till föräldraförhandling. Vad händer med barnets bästa?' (2022/23) 1 Juridisk Tidskrift 249.

Singer A, 'Out-of-court Custody Dispute Resolution in Sweden—A Journey Without Destination' in Kaldal A, Hellner A and Mattsson T (eds), *Children in Custody Disputes: Matching Legal Proceedings to Problems* (Palgrave 2023) 129.

Skjørten K and Sandberg K, 'Children's Participation in Family Law Proceedings' in Langford M, Skivenes M and Søvig K H (eds), *Children's Rights in Norway: An Implementation Paradox?* (Universitetsforlaget 2019) 300.

Smeets D J H and Rap S, 'Pedagogical Insights on Why and How to Involve Children' in Schrama W, Freeman M, Taylor N and Bruning M (eds), *International Handbook on Child Participation in Family Law* (Intersentia 2021) 41.

Sormunen M, 'Understanding the Best Interests of the Child as a Procedural Obligation: The Example of the European Court of Human Rights' (2020) 20 *Human Rights Law Review* 745.

Steinbach A, 'Children's and Parents' Well-Being in Joint Physical Custody: A Literature Review' 2019 58(2) *Family Process* 353.

Swedish Government Bill 2020/21:150 *A Strengthened Child Rights Perspective in Custody Disputes.*

Wexler D B, Perlin M L, Vols M, Spencer P and Stobbs N, 'Editorial: Current Issues in Therapeutic Jurisprudence' (2016) 16(3), *QUT Law Review* 1.

2

Children's Health Matters in Custody Conflicts—What Do We Know?

Anna Norlén

2.1 Introduction

Family patterns, gender equality, female rights, and the possibilities of raising children as a single parent have changed and developed in many countries over the last few decades. More children than ever before are experiencing parental divorce or separation, and custody conflicts are also on the rise. Understanding the implications of divorce for children is vital for parents, professionals, and researchers, with a growing interest in the matter of joint custody and its effects on the lives of children.

In many Western countries, the everyday life of divorced parents and their children is increasingly characterized by joint custody, shared parenting, and shared residence for children. These practices are gaining acceptance as a post-divorce solution for families and are promoted by legislation in many countries, although they are far more common

A. Norlén (✉)
The Erica Foundation, Stockholm, Sweden

A. Kaldal et al. (eds.), *Children in Custody Disputes*,
https://doi.org/10.1007/978-3-031-46301-3_2

in northern European countries such as Sweden and Norway.[1] Many studies have investigated how such arrangements relate to children's general adjustment, wellbeing, mental health, and development. To briefly summarize, the studies show that while both positive and negative outcomes have been found for parents and children, most children seem to gain from joint custody, yet it cannot be regarded as a one-size-fits-all solution.[2]

However, the impact of post-divorce interparental conflict on children in the context of joint custody or custody conflict is rarely the subject of empirical investigations, even though parents, children, and professionals often assume and report that such conflict has a negative effect on children's wellbeing. These circumstances are sometimes a delicate and time-consuming question for the practitioners, clinicians, and courts involved in the processes designed to find workable solutions for children and parents following divorce. The conditions of joint custody that facilitate or interfere with the wellbeing of children are complex matters that should be identified, explored, and conceptualized in more detail.[3] Implications for preschool-aged children are of particular interest, since these children are known to be more vulnerable to stressors such as parental conflict and particularly influenced by changes in everyday environment. Additionally, there is a need to elaborate on strategies and

---

[1] Emma Fransson, Anders Hjern and Malin Bergström, 'What Can We Say Regarding Shared Parenting Arrangements for Swedish Children?' (2018) 59(5) *Journal of Divorce & Remarriage 349–358*; Lara Augustijn, 'The Relation Between Joint Physical Custody, Interparental Conflict, and Children's Mental Health' (2021) *Journal of Family Research* 613–636.

[2] Malin Bergström, Emma Fransson, Bitte Modin, Marie Berlin, Per A Gustafsson, and Anders Hjern, 'Fifty Moves a Year: Is There an Association Between Joint Physical Custody and Psychosomatic Problems in Children?' (2015) 69(8) *Journal of Epidemiology and Community Health* 769–774; Linda Nielsen, 'Joint Versus Sole Physical Custody: Outcomes for Children Independent of Family Income or Parental Conflict' (2018) 15(1) *Journal of Child Custody* 35–54; Amandine Baude, Sylvie Drapeau, Véronique Lachance and Hans Ivers, 'Adjustment of Children in Joint Custody and Associated Variables: A Systematic Review' (2019) 16(4) *Journal of Child Custody* 313–338.

[3] Gordon T Harold and Ruth Sellers, 'Annual Research Review: Interparental Conflict and Youth Psychopathology: An Evidence Review and Practice Focused Update' (2018) 59(4) *The Journal of Child Psychology and Psychiatry* 374–402.

instruments for the evaluation of risks for the wellbeing and development of children, and the tools used to ensure that the voices of children are heard in the context of custody conflict.[4]

This chapter aims to provide a brief overview of available empirical knowledge regarding the relationships of joint custody, interparental conflict, and the wellbeing of children, based on a selection of recent publications from child psychology and developmental research findings on or discussing the associations of these perspectives. A further aim is to highlight suggestions for supporting the mental health and wellbeing of children in custody conflicts.

2.2 Joint Custody and Implications for Children

Many studies have shown that divorce is associated with lower levels of general wellbeing for parents and children. However, the reactions and implications associated with divorce are found to be quite varied. A common perspective among researchers and clinicians is that although divorce might be followed by disruption and crisis, most individuals—both children and parents—can adjust over a couple of years. However, as reflected in the rising number of studies on the subject, the increase of joint custody arrangements for children has stimulated interest in whether these circumstances mitigate or worsen the impact of divorce for children. The existing body of research focuses on the wellbeing of children and parents living in these circumstances. Several meta-analyses and research reviews have been published that contribute valuable knowledge and overview.[5]

---

[4] Harold and Sellers (n 3); Augustijn (n 1); Tommie Forslund, Pehr Granqvist, Marinus H van Ijzendoorn and Avi Sagi-Schwartz, 'Attachment Goes to Court: Child Protection and Custody Issues' (2022) 24(1) *Attachment & Human Development* 1–52.

[5] Paul R Amato, 'The Consequences of Divorce for Adults and Children' (2000) 62(4) *Journal of Marriage and Family* 1269–1287; Paul R Amato, 'Research on Divorce: Continuing Trends and New Developments' (2010) 72(3) *Journal of Marriage and Family* 650–666; Baude and others (n 2) 349–358; Harold and Sellers (n 3) 374–402; Anders Hjern, Stine Kjaer Urhoj and Malin Bergström, 'Early Social Determinants and Family Relationships Predict Parental Separation and Living Arrangements Thereafter' (2020) 110(1) *Acta Peaediatrica* 247–254; Anja

Based on empirical findings and practical experiences, there seems to be a consensus that most children benefit from joint custody. However, while this arrangement is broadly supported, the empirical evidence does not provide a clear picture. One major issue is the background and characteristics of parents involved in joint custody who choose to participate in studies. It has been noted that these parents are more likely to have:

- High levels of education
- High socio-economic status
- Low levels of interparental conflict
- A low degree of psychiatric problems
- High levels of active paternal parenting pre-divorce
- Close residence to each other after divorce.

Accordingly, the positive findings that support joint custody should be understood in this context.[6] In short, joint custody is more likely to be applied—and more likely to succeed—when the parents have a good chance of cooperating. Consequently, their children will benefit from such conditions.

Joint custody and shared residence not only enable children to maintain close relationships with both parents, but also increase the child's access to psychological, social, and economic resources from two caregivers. Several studies focusing on general mental health, self-esteem, and degree of stress and adjustment, show that children in joint custody are better adjusted than children in sole physical custody.[7] The results also

Steinbach, 'Children's and Parents' Wellbeing in Joint Physical Custody: A Literature Review' (2019) 58(2) *Family Process* 353–369.

[6] Anja Steinbach, 'Children's and Parents' Wellbeing in Joint Physical Custody: A Literature Review' (2019) 58(2) *Family Process* 353–369.

[7] Malin Bergström and others (n 2) 769–774; Emma Fransson, Sara Brolin Låftman, Viveca Östberg, Anders Hjern and Malin Bergström, 'The Living Conditions of Children with Shared Residence—The Swedish Example' (2017) 11(3) *Child Indicators Research* 861–883; Nielsen (n 2) 35–54; Anders Hjern, Stine Kjaer Urhoj, Emma Fransson, and Malin Bergström, 'Mental Health in Schoolchildren in Joint Physical Custody: A Longitudinal Study' (2021) 8 *Children* 473.

confirm that children can develop and maintain secure attachment relationships to several caregivers and benefit from access to more than one 'safe haven'.[8]

In cases of joint custody, stronger bonds between fathers and children have been shown, when compared with traditional, sole (mothers') physical custody. However, the association between father-child contact and wellbeing of children was found to be dependent on the degree of paternal involvement *before* divorce. According to some findings, only when the father's pre-divorce degree of involvement was medium to high, could the positive effects of children's wellbeing be noticed post-divorce. Hence, it was assumed that post-divorce arrangements reflect the quality of pre-divorce relations and that active fathers are more likely to practice joint custody.[9]

2.3 Joint Custody and Implications for Parents

Parents' wellbeing is the strongest mediator for the wellbeing of children; thus, when trying to understand post-divorce implications for children, it is relevant to explore the implications for parents when it comes to separation and arrangements of joint custody. However, this area has been studied far less than the perspective of children, there is a lack of consensus in research and an ongoing discussion among experts.[10] Advocates for shared physical custody argue that this arrangement decreases interparental conflict and strengthens gender equality structures. Those who disagree highlight findings that show conflict can linger and even escalate post-divorce, as joint custody challenges parents' flexibility, planning opportunities, and ability to cooperate continuously as the needs of their children change according to development and age. Interparental conflict might also interfere with child-parent relationships and evoke

[8] Forslund and others (n 4).

[9] Steinbach (n 6).

[10] Ibid.

emotional insecurity. Experiencing interparental conflict may cause children to feel afraid, insecure, and caught between parents. Interparental conflict can also negatively affect caregiving capacities and increase the risk of children being drawn into conflicts. In addition, the proper function of the joint arrangement entails financial costs (for example, for double sets of children's furniture, clothing, and other items) and preferably close residence.

Parents with joint physical arrangements report being more satisfied compared to those with sole custody. Fathers are more likely to be satisfied, while the satisfaction of mothers decreases with higher incidence of interparental conflict, safety concerns for children and oneself, and court-imposed arrangements.[11] Other studies show that poor parental adjustment after divorce is associated with conflict between ex-spouses. Parents in conflict with joint custody have more concerns regarding their children's and their own safety. A recent Swedish qualitative study revealed that most parents were pleased with the joint arrangements, with the clear exception of couples experiencing ongoing conflict.[12] Finding a new partner appears to be beneficial for divorced individuals, as it is associated with better general adjustment and, in many cases, improved financial situations.[13]

While most children gain from joint custody and shared residence, it is obvious that the model and practical arrangements must be tailored to

---

[11] Judy Cashmore, Patrick Parkinson, Ruth Weston, Roger Patulny, Gerry Redmond, Lixia Qu, Jennifer Baxer Marianne Sitek Tomaz and Ilan Katz, *Shared Care Parenting Arrangements Since the 2006 Family Law Reforms: Report for the Australian Government Attorney-General's Department Sydney* (Social Policy Research Centre, University of New South Wales 2010); Malin Bergström, Emma Fransson, Anders Hjern, Lennart Köhler, and Thomas Wallby, 'Mental Health in Swedish Children Living in Joint Physical Custody and Their Parents' Life Satisfaction: A Cross-Sectional Study' (2014) 55(5) *Scandinavian Journal of Psychology* 433–439.

[12] Rae Kaspiew, Kelly Hand, and Lixia Qu, *Evaluation of the 2006 Family Law Reforms* (Australian Institute of Family Studies 2009); Malin Bergström, Anna Sarkadi, Anders Hjern, and Emma Fransson, 'We Also Communicate Through a Book in the Diaper Bag—Separated Parents' Ways to Coparent and Promote Adaptation of Their 1–4-Year Olds in Equal Joint Physical Custody' (2019) 14(4) *PLOS ONE*.

[13] Kaspiew and others (n 12); Steinbach (n 6).

the complex combination of needs of the individual child and parental conditions. There is no such thing as a 'one-size-fits-all' solution when it comes to joint custody.[14]

2.4 The Interrelationships of Joint Custody, Interparental Conflict, and the Wellbeing of Children

It is well known that intense and chronic conflict in any form, verbal or physical, between parents is a major stressor that negatively affects children's mental health and wellbeing. When interparental conflicts occur frequently and with intensity, the risk increases for negative outcomes in children. Despite these clear indications, only a few studies have investigated how post-divorce interparental conflict is related to the wellbeing and mental health of children in the context of joint custody. However, there are studies that show the combination of high levels of post-divorce conflict and joint custody, is strongly related to negative implications for wellbeing and mental health in children. These results have contributed to the assumption that joint custody, in the context of high-level conflict, has the potential to be harmful.[15]

In a recent research review, Harold & Sellers summarize the developmental areas in children shown to be negatively affected by interparental conflict within intact households and/or parental separation/divorce[16]:

- **Sleep**—Disturbances in sleep patterns in children are assumed to indicate impact of stress on neurobiological function. Sleep problems that emerge early tend to persist in later development.
- **Externalizing**—Symptoms of aggression, conduct problems, and temper tantrums are the most common outcomes in studies of impact of interparental conflict for children.

---

[14] Augustijn (n 1); Harold and Sellers (n 3).

[15] Augustijn (n 1); Steinbach (n 6).

[16] Harold and Sellers (n 3).

- **Internalizing**—Symptoms of withdrawal, inhibition, low self-esteem, anxiety, depression, and suicidality are associated with ongoing conflicts between parents.
- **Academic performance**—Deficits in attention, perception processes, general academic outcomes, and classroom problems.
- **Social and interpersonal relationships**—Negative impact on social and interpersonal skills, social competence, and problem-solving. Increased level of parent–child conflict.
- **Physical health**—Reduced physical growth, fatigue, abdominal stress, and headaches. Increased risk behaviour, including tobacco use, substance abuse, and early sexual activity.

Harold & Sellers conclude that parental conflict is an early risk factor that elevates the probability for development of child psychopathology.[17] They suggest an integrated and dynamic framework to organize understanding of the interplay of interparental conflicts and parenting processes with neurobiological, psychological, cognitive, and emotional processes in the child. This model can guide practitioners in assessment and establishment of targets for intervention.

Despite the problematic findings, professionals and researchers still disagree whether joint custody can be the best solution—even for high-conflict parents. Existing studies are methodologically, contextually, and conceptually heterogeneous and of varying quality. Moreover, some studies show little or no increase of negative effects for children as a result of post-divorce interparental conflicts. The contradictory results are interpreted to mean that the benefit of having access to both parents could outweigh the costs of conflict-related stress for children. This is assumed to be particularly valid when the quality of parenting is 'good enough'. Further, there are differing opinions concerning whether children are exposed to less or more conflict when living in shared residence *and* with high levels of parental conflict. Finally, other findings show that children who experience above-average degrees of interparental conflict have about the same levels of mental health problems as children living

[17] Harold and Sellers (n 3).

in sole physical custody. These results might indicate that the custodial arrangement is not the main issue, but rather the parents' ability to manage divorce and co-parenting.[18]

Obviously, further research is needed to improve our understanding of these diverse associations. The degree of child exposure to interparental conflict and the features of conflict must be investigated, as well as how implications of conflict relate to age, developmental level, gender, and other characteristics of the child and the overall context.[19] Perspectives of risk should be carefully evaluated, because stress and adversities during early years can have long-term implications for future general development in children. The developing brain is especially vulnerable to stress, particularly for children up to about seven years of age.[20]

2.5 Preschool-Aged Children, Joint Custody, and Interparental Conflict

The suitability of joint custody for preschool-aged children, especially those under the age of four, is a subject of disagreement and debate among experts and researchers. Limited empirical evidence has been presented for how infants, toddlers, and young children are affected by shared residence. Questions about overnight stays, time cycles of visitation, and separation are specifically discussed, as well as this age group's need for stability and continuity in relationships and everyday routines.[21]

Based on the central significance of attachment theory and the emphasis on quality of interaction between young children and parents, there is an urgent need for thorough evaluation of custodial and residential arrangements for preschoolers. The recommendations from most

---

18 Nielsen (n 2); Baude and others (n 2); Steinbach (n 6); Augustijn (n 1).

19 Harold and Sellers (n 3).

20 Christine Heim and Charles B Nemeroff, 'The Role of Childhood Trauma in the Neurobiology of Mood and Anxiety Disorders: Preclinical and Clinical Studies' (2001) 49(12) *Biological Psychiatry* 1023–1039; Tenah K A Hunt, Kirsten S Slack and Lawrence M Berger, 'Adverse Childhood Experiences and Behavioral Problems in Middle Childhood' (2017) 67 *Child Abuse & Neglect* 391–402.

21 Forslund and others (n 4).

attachment theory researchers and clinicians concerning preschool children, are that children's regular attachment relationships are of crucial importance and should be supported whenever possible, while longer separations should be avoided. Further, researchers emphasize that the capacity of children to develop simultaneous secure attachment relationships must be ensured.[22]

A recent study of the living arrangements of three-year-old children in Sweden, showed that those living with joint custody after divorce had better mental health than children living with only one parent. However, when accounting for co-parent quality, child mental health was very similar across the different arrangements, including cases of children living in intact families.[23]

Divorce and separation during the first years of childhood are substantial, stressful circumstances at a delicate time for both children and parents. Hence, it should be acknowledged that parenting in this context is challenging, and temporary support might be required to enhance adjustment to new family structures and circumstances. Stress affects parental sensitivity, which in turn, is predictive of the development of attachment relations; it also affects parenting skills and emotional availability. The emotional quality of parent–child relationships during the divorce process can affect child adjustment after divorce.

In cases of a less involved, non-resident parent and questions of visits and possibly overnight stays, the current advice is to arrange the situation with great flexibility and ample opportunity for the child and non-resident parent to adjust gradually to each other. It is recommended that, the younger the child, the shorter the time cycles of separation from the regular caregiver. It is also emphasized that attachment is one of several aspects of child-parent relationships. Current contact and visitation, including the opportunity to be involved in care and play, can

[22] Ibid.

[23] Malin Bergström, Raziye Salari, Anders Hjern, Robin Hognäs, Kersti Bergqvist and Emma Fransson, 'Importance of Living Arrangements and Coparenting Quality for Young Children's Mental Health After Parental Divorce: A Cross-sectional Survey' (2020) 5 *BMJ Paediatrics Open* 2021.

support child development, and contribute to the foundation of a secure future child-parent relationship.[24]

Attachment theory and research is often applied by professionals (such as social workers, child protection services, and courts) in different settings, for example, to evaluate and provide testimony regarding custody questions in family court. Unfortunately, misconceptions in this regard are common and sometimes result in misapplications of knowledge. A policy paper on attachment perspectives in child protection and custody issues was recently published by a considerable number of attachment researchers.[25]

The policy paper emphasizes three attachment principles to improve practice:

- Children's need for familiar and non-abusive caregivers;
- The continuity of good-enough care; and
- Children's access to a network of attachment relationships.

2.6 Supporting Children Living with Interparental Custody Conflict

Child-rights organizations, (such as, the Children's Welfare Foundation and Save the Children), have highlighted the many complex challenges for children experiencing high interparental conflict in the context of joint custody, and the importance of meeting the specific needs of these children. The significance of evaluating safety for children and parents and careful assessment of information concerning violence in this context is emphasized.[26]

---

[24] Forslund and others (n 4).

[25] Ibid.

[26] See for example, Save the Children, Mellan stolarna. Barn som har utsatt för våld och inte får hjälp – Ett dubbelt svek (2022) https://www.raddabarnen.se/globalassets/dokument/rad--kunskap/arbetar-for-barn/rapport_mellanstolarna.pdf accessed 15 May 2023 and Children's Welfare Foundation https://allmannabarnhuset.se/vart-arbete/barn-i-vardnadstvister-separationer/ accessed 15 May 2023.

There is an evident need for further development of risk assessment tools in this area. Adult intimate-partner violence, violence and abuse towards children, and general developmental risks for children must be addressed.[27] Additionally, robust knowledge about how the experiences and opinions of children can be systematically collected in investigation and assessment are not available. Guidelines for professionals about questions such as the age at which children should be involved in these matters and available models for child interviews are still lacking. Children's right to raise their voices, to be listened to and involved in practical solutions after divorce are often overlooked. Existing qualitative child interview studies suggest that it is more important than ever for children with adverse experiences in their families, such as abuse, neglect, and violence, to be able to express their will and opinions directly to investigators, social workers, and courts.[28]

Studies have found a dose-response relationship regarding children of divorce: the number of adversities to which children are exposed, is a predictor of their ability to adjust after the divorce. Stressful events such as moving to a new location, changing preschools or schools, or separation from friends and relatives seem to be especially disruptive. Repeated and extensive changes are particularly stressful. Hence, minimizing the number of stressful events and making thorough, stepwise preparations can help children adapt.[29]

Other factors that can facilitate children's adjustment include the use of active coping skills, that is, supporting a child's problem-solving capacity, encouraging them to seek social and emotional support, and enhancing self-regulation strategies in stressful and emotional situations. Strategies can be encouraged in the home as well as in cooperation

---

[27] Jennifer E. McIntosh, Yvonne Well and Jamie Lee, 'Development and Validation of the Family Law DOORS' (2016) 28(11) *Psychological Assessment 1516–1522*; Ole Hultmann and Anders Broberg, 'Riskbedömningsintervjuer med förövare av partnervåld och våld mot barn – en litteraturgenomgång' in Appendix 2 in Anders Broberg, Ulf Axberg, Maria Eriksson and Ole Hultmann (eds), *Utveckling av bedömningsmetoder för barn som utsatts för våld i sin familj. Rapport från en fortsättningsstudie* (University of Gothenburg, Department of Psychology 2018).

[28] Bren Neale, 'Dialogues with Children. Children, Divorce and Citizenship' (2002) 9(4) *Childhood* 445–475; Maria Eriksson and Elisabeth Näsman, *När barn som upplevt våld möter socialtjänsten – om barns perspektiv, delaktighet och giltiggörande* (Stockholm: Gothia 2011).

[29] Amato, 'The Consequences of Divorce for Adults and Children' (n 5); Amato 'Research on Divorce: Continuing Trends and New Developments' (n 5).

with preschool and school staff. The significance of peer interaction, social support from contact with friends, teachers, siblings, and parents can facilitate adaptation post-divorce. However, empirical knowledge regarding these circumstances is still limited.[30]

Several supportive programmes for children experiencing divorce have been developed. Most of them offer age-appropriate information and psychoeducation about divorce and the opportunity to explore, express, and understand emotional reactions associated with the approaching changes. Although the programmes have not been systematically evaluated to any great degree, they seem to be beneficial and appreciated by many children. Information regarding specific interventions for children experiencing complex circumstances, such as, interparental conflicts, joint custody, shared residence, and visitation are lacking in the scientific literature.

Experts and other adults often emphasize that children experiencing divorce and interparental conflict might need, and gain from, therapeutic interventions. This option is not always readily available; mental-healthcare services often assign lower priority to problems in children related to what can be considered as mainly parental problems. While this might be the case, numerous clinical examples demonstrate how exposure to problematic divorce, interparental conflict, and (in some cases) violence, trigger and exacerbate psychological and psychiatric problems in children. Among clinicians, it is also known that in children, severe problems originating from other sources can be suppressed or disguised by interparental conflict.

Working with children and parents in the context of joint custody and interparental conflict can be challenging. Parents might not realize that they or their child need support or therapy; they might see no need to promote the perspectives of the child, or the co-parent could be resistant to the idea.[31] Because the autonomy of children is limited,

[30] Amato, 'The Consequences of Divorce for Adults and Children' (n 5); Amato 'Research on Divorce: Continuing Trends and New Developments' (n 5).

[31] Leezah Hertzmann, Mary Target, David Hewison, Polly Casey, Pasco Fearon and Dana Lassri, 'Mentalization-Based Therapy for Parents in Entrenched Conflict: A Random Allocation Feasibility Study' (2016) 53(4) *Psychotherapy* 388–401; Leezah Hertzmann, Susanna Abse, and Mary Target, 'Mentalization-Based Therapy for Parental Conflict—Parenting Together; An

the therapist must treat the matter of child privacy with great care. Agreements concerning information and transparency must be clarified with all parties involved, including the authorities responsible for child protection and child welfare—to assure a trustful cooperation with the therapist. Children might not always have the capacity to grasp complex situations, but they have the right and are often able to contribute thoughts, opinions, and ideas about how their everyday life and important relationships should be arranged.

Interventions specifically targeting parents and children living in the context of joint custody and interparental conflict are still rare, but some initiatives are under way to design tailored support and preventive approaches. Some programmes focus on parents of intact households or in the context of separation; others address domestic violence. Family therapy models use various approaches, mainly systemic and psychoeducational, and conflict mediation is often offered. Children participate in some of the interventions, but the dominating idea seems to be that children will benefit from improved parental support—an assumption that requires more investigation, and study of other dimensions of effects. Although most programmes are poorly evaluated, parents often appreciate them.[32]

Recently, a mentalization-based programme for parents in entrenched conflicts over their children was developed and assessed in a pilot study.[33] The model aims to reduce hostile conflicts between parents and mitigate the damaging effects of interparental conflict on children. The primary focus of mentalization-based interventions is about making sense of the feelings experienced by each parent, particularly how negative assumptions about the other parent's intentions can lead to anger, misunderstandings, and conflict. Further, the intervention highlights the perspective of the child, and how children can communicate their needs.

Intervention for Parents in Entrenched Post-separation Disputes' (2017) 31(2) *Psychoanalytic Psychotherapy* 195–217.

[32] Harold and Sellers (n 3).

[33] Hertzmann and others, 'Mentalization-based Therapy for Parents in Entrenched Conflict: A Random Allocation Feasibility Study' (n 31); Hertzmann and others, 'Mentalisation-Based Therapy for Parental Conflict—Parenting Together; an Intervention for Parents in Entrenched Post-separation Disputes' (n 31).

This approach is assumed to develop the capacity to regulate the intense effects in the context of separation and distress and reduce impulsive and destructive behaviours. The results of the pilot study were promising and parents taking part in the intervention reported fewer feelings of stress and depression, less expressed anger towards their ex-partner, and improvements in their children's emotional and behavioural difficulties.

2.7 Conclusions

Research and experience show that no post-divorce custody and residential arrangement exists to suit all children and parents. Arrangements must be tailored to the individual needs of children and parents and modified as children's relationships with parents develop, and as child developmental status and parents' circumstances change. The quality of co-parenting has been shown to be a key determinant of child mental health for children with divorced parents, which shows why tailored parental support is central. This requires flexibility and cooperation from parents, professionals, the courts—and children.

Available research and evaluation show that many aspects and interrelationships of custody arrangements remain unidentified, and several central questions remain unanswered. Most important is the need to explore the voices and experiences of children who have dealt with interparental conflicts, joint custody, and shared residence. Qualitative and longitudinal studies must be made to understand children's opinions, needs, hopes, and thoughts derived from living in various divorce-related circumstances. The effects of relationships with friends, siblings, relatives, and foster parents in the context of joint custody and interparental conflict also warrant detailed evaluation. Available knowledge and research about implications of adversities, stress, and trauma for children—particularly the youngest and most vulnerable—must be better integrated into services. In addition, it is important to develop effective models for safe and secure visitation between children and non-resident parents, as well as efficient support for children who are reluctant to have contact with a parent. Finally, children's exposure to different forms of violence requires improved assessment and understanding. Flexible strategies for strengthening child safety that do not involve removing children from parents' care or disrupting relationships—unless absolutely necessary—must be developed in close cooperation with the individual child and the caregivers.

References

Augustijn L, 'The Relation Between Joint Physical Custody, Interparental Conflict, and Children's Mental Health' (2021) *Journal of Family Research* 613.

Amato P R, 'The Consequences of Divorce for Adults and Children' (2000) 62(4) *Journal of Marriage and Family* 1269.

Amato P R, 'Research on Divorce: Continuing Trends and New Developments' (2010) 72(3) *Journal of Marriage and Family* 650.

Baude A, Drapeau S, Lachance V and Ivers H, 'Adjustment of Children in Joint Custody and Associated Variables: A Systematic Review' (2019) 16(4) *Journal of Child Custody* 313.

Bergström M, Fransson E, Hjern A, Köhler L and Wallby T, 'Mental Health in Swedish Children Living in Joint Physical Custody and Their Parents' Life Satisfaction: A Cross-Sectional Study' (2014) 55(5) *Scandinavian Journal of Psychology* 433.

Bergström M, Fransson E, Modin B, Berlin M, Gustafsson P A and Hjern A, 'Fifty Moves a Year: Is there an Association Between Joint Physical Custody and Psychosomatic Problems in Children?' (2015) 69(8) *Journal of Epidemiology and Community Health* 769.

Bergström M, Sarkadi A, Hjern A and Fransson E, 'We also Communicate Through a Book in the Diaper Bag—Separated Parents' Ways to Coparent and Promote Adaptation of Their 1–4-Year-Olds in Equal Joint Physical Custody' (2019) 14(4) *PLOS ONE* 1.

Bergström M, Salari R, Hjern A, Hognäs R, Bergqvist K and Fransson E, 'Importance of Living Arrangements and Coparenting Quality for Young Children's Mental Health After Parental Divorce: A Cross-sectional Survey' (2020) *BMJ Paediatrics Open* 2021;5.

Cashmore J, Parkinson P, Weston R, Patulny R, Redmond G, Qu L, Baxter, J, Rajkovic, M Sitek, Tomaz and Katz, I, 'Shared Care Parenting Arrangements Since the 2006 Family Law Reforms: Report for the Australian Government

Attorney-General's Department Sydney' (Social Policy Research Centre, University of New South Wales 2010).

Children's Welfare Foundation, (2022) https://allmannabarnhuset.se/vart-arbete/barn-i-vardnadstvister-separationer/ accessed 15 May 2023.

Daly A, 'No Weight for "'Due Weight"? A Children's Autonomy Principle in Best Interests Proceedings' (2018) 26(1) *International Journal of Children's Rights* 61.

Eriksson M and Näsman E, *När barn som upplevt våld möter socialtjänsten – om barns perspektiv, delaktighet och giltiggörande* (Gothia 2011).

Fransson E, Hjern A and Bergström M, 'What Can We Say Regarding Shared Parenting Arrangements for Swedish Children?' (2018) 59(5) *Journal of Divorce & Remarriage* 349.

Fransson E, Brolin Låftman S, Östberg V and Hjern A, 'The Living Conditions of Children with Shared Residence—The Swedish Example' (2017) 11(3) *Child Indicators Research* 861.

Forslund T, Granqvist P, van Ijzendoorn M and Sagi-Schwartz A, 'Attachment Goes to Court: Child Protection and Custody Issues' (2022) 24(1) *Attachment & Human Development* 1.

Gordon T, Sellers H and Sellers R, 'Annual Research Review: Interparental Conflict and Youth Psychopathology: An Evidence Review and Practice Focused Update' (2018) 59(4) *The Journal of Child Psychology and Psychiatry* 374.

Heim C and Nemeroff C B, 'The Role of Childhood Trauma in the Neurobiology of Mood and Anxiety Disorders: Preclinical and Clinical Studies' (2001) 49(12) *Biological Psychiatry* 1023.

Hertzmann L, Abse S, Target M, Glausius K, Nyberg V and Lassri D, 'Mentalization-based Therapy for Parents in Entrenched Conflict: A Random Allocation Feasibility Study' (2016) 53(4) *Psychotherapy* 388.

Hertzmann L, Abse S, Target M, Glausius K, Nyberg V and Lassri D, 'Mentalisation-based Therapy for Parental Conflict—Parenting Together; an Intervention for Parents in Entrenched Post-separation Disputes' (2017) 31(2) *Psychoanalytic Psychotherapy* 195.

Hjern A, Kjaer Urhoj S, and Bergström M and Nybo Andersen A M, 'Early Childhood Social Determinants and Family Relationships Predict Parental Separation and Living Arrangements Thereafter' (2020) 110(1) *Acta Peaediatrica* 247.

Hjern A, Kjaer Urhoj S, Fransson E and Bergström M, 'Mental Health in Schoolchildren in Joint Physical Custody: A Longitudinal Study' (2021) 8 *Children* 473.

Hultmann O and Broberg A, 'Riskbedömningsintervjuer med förövare av partnervåld och våld mot barn – en litteraturgenomgång' in Appendix Axberg U, Broberg A, Eriksson M, Hultmann O and Iversen C, Utveckling av bedömningsmetoder för barn som utsatts för våld i sin familj' Rapport från en fortsättningsstudie (Göteborgs universitet, Psykologiska institutionen 2018).

Hunt T, Slack K S and Berger L M, 'Adverse Childhood Experiences and Behavioral Problems in Middle Childhood' (2017) 67 *Child Abuse & Neglect* 391.

Kaspiew R, Weston R, Moloney L, Hand K and Qu L, *Evaluation of the 2006 Family Law Reforms* (Australian Institute of Family Studies 2009).

McIntosh J, Well Y and Lee J, 'Development and Validation of the Family Law DOORS' (2016) 28(11) *Psychological Assessment* 1516.

Neale B, 'Dialogues with Children. Children, Divorce and Citizenship' (2002) 9(4) *Childhood* 455.

Nielsen L 'Joint Versus Sole Physical Custody: Outcomes for Children Independent of Family Income or Parental Conflict' (2018) 15(1) *Journal of Child Custody* 247.

Save the Children, Mellan stolarna. Barn som har utsatt för våld och inte får hjälp – Ett dubbelt svek (2022) https://www.raddabarnen.se/globalassets/dokument/rad--kunskap/arbetar-for-barn/rapport_mellanstolarna.pdf accessed 15 May 2023.

Steinbach A, 'Children's and Parents' Wellbeing in Joint Physical Custody: A Literature Review' (2019) 58(2) *Family Process* 353.

3

Nordic Family Mediation: Towards a System of Differentiated Services?

Anna Nylund

3.1 Introduction to Family Mediation and Diverse Family Needs

The Nordic welfare-state paradigm frames parental disputes during and after divorce, and the dissolution of domestic partnerships, primarily as disagreements regarding care arrangements for custody, residence, and visitation. Since both parents are expected to support themselves with (full-time) employment—and considering that education and health-care are practically free of charge for children and young people—maintenance and other economic issues are of limited importance. In accordance with the prevailing gender-equality paradigm, parents are presumed to possess roughly equal and adequate parenting capacity.[1]

[1] See Anna Kaldal, Agnes Hellner and Titti Mattsson, 'Introduction: Matching Legal Proceedings to Problems in Custody Disputes' in Anna Kaldal, Agnes Hellner and Titti Mattsson (eds), *Children in Custody Disputes: Matching Legal Proceedings to Problems* (Palgrave 2023).

A. Nylund (✉)
Faculty of Law, University of Bergen, Bergen, Norway

A. Kaldal et al. (eds.), *Children in Custody Disputes*,
https://doi.org/10.1007/978-3-031-46301-3_3

Consequently, most parents are expected to agree on care arrangements without requiring assistance from lawyers or other professionals, and only a small percentage of families file for court proceedings.[2]

Despite the dominance of out-of-court services, legal scholarship has generally been disinterested in them. One likely reason is that out-of-court services belong to the realm of social (family) services and not the justice system; lawyers are generally not involved in any capacity, either as mediators or legal counsel. Although recent reforms with Nordic out-of-court mediation aim at reducing litigation, thus making out-of-court mediation in practice part of the civil justice system,[3] the reforms have not stimulated much interest among lawyers. Moreover, few scholars have specialized in mediation and alternative dispute resolution, and so, the dispute resolution aspects of the system are only weakly rooted in mediation theory. Lawyers could also be disinterested because parents are implicitly construed as rational persons with good parenting capacity and the ability to agree on outcomes that are in the best interests of the child. Hence, the parents mainly need help to reorient themselves to the needs and wishes of their children, and to acquire post-separation parenting and conflict resolution skills, not legal assistance. These assumptions disregard the inability of some parents to meet the standards of ideal parenting, particularly in the aftermath of divorce, and the fact that some parents abuse or neglect their children.[4] Legal scholarship seems oblivious to the fact that even when the outcome is voluntary, and not imposed on the parents, mediation is a decision-making process with profound legal implications.

---

[2] There are no exact statistics available; the figure is around 10–15%, see for example, Ann-Sofie Bergman and Annika Rejmer, 'Parents in Child Custody Disputes: Why Are They Disputing?' (2017) *Journal of Child Custody* 134–150; Anna Nylund, 'A Dispute System Design Perspective on Norwegian Child Custody Mediation' in Anna Nylund, Kaijus Ervasti and Lin Adrian (eds), *Nordic Mediation Research* (Springer 2018) 15.

[3] For example, in Norway, Norwegian Government Official Report 2019:20 En styrket familietjeneste. En gjennomgang av familieverntjenesten [A stronger family service. A review of the family welfare service] and in Sweden, Swedish Government Official Report 2017:6 Se barnet! [See the Child!].

[4] Elisabeth Gording Stang, 'Når vi ikke får gehør i rettsapparatet har vi tapt på vegne av barnet' in Karl Harald Søvig, Sigrid Eskeland Schtz and Ørnulf Rasmussen (eds), *Undring og erkjennelse. Festskrift til Jan Fridthjof Bernt 70 år* (Fagbokforlaget 2013).

There is an increased awareness that some parents abuse their children or partners[5] and that some parents neglect their children because of their insufficient parenting capacity. Additionally, some families experience high levels of conflict—repeated, persistent, and intense conflicts.[6] Research indicates that high conflict levels and risk of abuse or neglect occur simultaneously in many families, which reduces the quality of parenting,[7] and has repercussions for the health and wellbeing of children.[8] Moreover, the (perceived) lack of adequate parenting capacity is often itself a source of conflict.[9] Research suggests that high conflict and child neglect are not evenly distributed throughout the population. These phenomena are more prevalent in multicultural families (that is, families where one or both parents or a child are born abroad), families with a low socio-economic status, and families where the child or a

5 A recent Swedish report discovered that child abuse, or allegations of it, was present in 67% of litigated child custody cases, The Swedish Gender Equality Agency, *Uppgifter om våld är inget undantag. Redovisning av kartläggning av uppgifter om våld eller andra övergrepp i mål om vårdnad, boende och umgänge*, Rapport 2022:1 [Information on Violence Is No Exception. Reporting of the Mapping of Data on Violence or Other Abuse in Custody, Residence and Contact or Visitation] 8–9.

6 The term *high conflict* is widely used, but it lacks a clear definition, see for example, Shayne R Anderson, Stephen A Anderson, Kristi L Palmer, Matthew S Mutchler and Louisa K Baker, 'Defining High Conflicts' (2010) *The American Journal of Family Therapy 11–27*. For an overview of research attempting to define the term, see Maren Sand Helland and Ingrid Borren, *Foreldrekonflikt; identifisering av konfliktnivåer, sentrale kjennetegn og risikofaktorer hos høykonfliktpar* (Nasjonalt folkehelseinstitutt 2015) 17–22.

7 For example, Bergman and Rejmer (n 2); Fritz Leo Breivik and Kate Mevik, *Barnefordeling i domstolen. Når barnets beste blir barnets verste* (Universitetsforlaget 2012); Wenke Gulbrandsen, 'Foreldrekonflikter etter samlivsbrudd: En analyse av samspill og kilder til det fastlåsende' (2013) *Tidsskrift for norsk psykologforening* 538–551.

8 For example, Paul R Amato, 'The Consequences of Divorce for Adults and Children' (2002) *Journal of Marriage and the Family* 5–24; Janet Johnston, Vivienne Roseby and Kathryn Kuehnle, *In the Name of the Child—A Developmental Approach to Understanding and Helping Children of Conflicted and Violent Divorce* (Springer 2009); Ann-Sofie Bergman and Annika Rejmer, '"Det är klart att barnen blir lidande": om barns mående när föräldrar är i vårnadstvist' (2017) *Socialmedisinsk tidskrift* 437–446.

9 For example, Judy Cashmore and Patrick Parkinson, 'Reasons for Disputes in High Conflict Families' (2011) *Journal of Family Studies* 186–203; Marian Ådnanes, Gry Mette D Haugen, Heidi Jensberg, Tonje Lossius Husum and Minna Rantalaiho, 'Hva karakteriserer vanskelige saker i foreldremekling, og er meklingsordningen godt nok tilpasset?' (2011) 39 *Fokus på Familien 86–115*.

parent has a disability or serious long-term illness.[10] These insights challenge the assumptions in which the Nordic family mediation system—thus far—has been rooted. In this chapter, the term 'high conflict' encompasses all permutations of persistent, intense conflict, abuse, and child neglect.[11]

In this text, Nordic family mediation systems and their processes are analysed with a thorough reading of regulation and policy documents (such as preparatory works and guidelines), using the lens of family mediation and dispute-system design theory. The examination focuses on three issues:

1. A look at the organization of the Nordic systems, in terms of the processes available, their target groups, and the organizational framework of family mediation.
2. Whether and how the quality of mediation is expressed and what mechanisms are available to ensure sufficient quality of mediation, such as, ethical standards and adequate mediator training.
3. Whether adequate mediation processes have been developed to address the needs of high-conflict families.

The analysis begins by defining family mediation processes and the mechanisms for ensuring quality (Section 3.2). It then discusses whether and when family mediation is an appropriate service for high-conflict families (Sect. 3.2.1). The second step examines current Nordic family mediation systems and their processes in the light of the standards and definitions set forth in the first step. Section 3.3 presents the family mediation systems in Nordic countries by giving an overview of the processes available in each country and how these are organized. In Sect. 3.3.2, the nature and content of each mediation process are discussed, like whether all the processes fall within the scope of mediation, and describing the content and target group for each process. The important question

[10] Swedish Government Official Report 2017:6 Se barnet! (n 3) 117–118.

[11] See also, Annika Rejmer, 'Custody Disputes from a Socio-Legal Perspective' in Anna Kaldal, Agnes Hellner and Titti Mattsson (eds), *Children in Custody Disputes: Matching Legal Proceedings to Problems* (Palgrave 2023).

here is, whether these systems include processes designed to help high-conflict families. Section 3.3.3 presents the Nordic countries' standards and mechanisms that focus on ensuring sufficient quality in the process and outcome. Finally, Sect. 3.4 offers some concluding observations.

3.2 Family Mediation as a Quality Process

3.2.1 Defining Family Mediation Processes

Mediation is often used as an umbrella term that encompasses a range of dispute resolution processes, 'whereby parties attempt to reach an amicable settlement of their dispute with the assistance of a third person or persons ("the mediator") lacking the authority to impose a solution upon the parties to the dispute'.[12] This definition, which will be used in this chapter, includes diverse forms of mediation practice, often labelled facilitative, evaluative, transformative, and therapeutic mediation.[13]

Family mediation has dual roots: one in the legal context, the other in the family therapy or family services context. Legal family mediation emphasizes the legal and economic aspects of parenthood, and the goal is that parents resolve conflicts and cooperate in a 'business-like' manner.[14] Counselling family mediation focuses on the intra- and inter-personal processes in the family, and the concept that addressing these issues is the key to resolving conflicts.[15] Therapeutic family mediation, a subgroup

[12] Singapore Convention on Mediation Art 2 nr 3. This is approximately the same definition as in, for example, Vibeke Vindeløf, *Reflexive Mediation: With a Sustainable Perspective* (Steven Harris, transl.) (DJØF Publishing 2012) 52.

[13] For example, Robert A Baruch Bush and Sally Ganong Pope, 'Transformative Mediation: Changing the Quality of Family Conflict Interaction' (2002) 3 *Pepperdine Dispute Resolution Law Journal* 67–96; Randolph L Lowry, 'Evaluative Mediation'; Marsha Klein Pruett and Janet R Johnston, 'Therapeutic Mediation with High-Conflict Parents: Effective Models and Strategies'; Bernard Mayer, 'Facilitative Mediation', all in Jay Folberg, Ann L Milne and Peter Salem (eds), *Divorce and Family Mediation: Models, Techniques, and Applications* (The Guilford Press 2004).

[14] O J Coogler, *Structured Mediation in Divorce Settlement: A Handbook for Marital Mediators* (Lexington Books 1978).

[15] See, for example, John M Haynes, *Divorce Mediation: A Practical Guide for Therapists and Counselors* (Springer 1981).

of counselling mediation, is a process designed for high-conflict families.[16] Moreover, hybrids of the two approaches can be found, often as co-mediation in which one mediator is a lawyer and the other is a family counsellor or therapist.[17] One variant could be characterized as educative,[18] in that the mediator primarily educates the parents in post-divorce co-parenting skills, recognizing and acting upon the needs of their children, while letting the parents negotiate on their own.

Although mediation is both a broad term and a flexible process, it must still be delimited from other processes. If mediation is to serve families with various needs, each procedure under the umbrella of family mediation must be defined to help families find the procedure that matches their needs, that is, to 'fit the forum to the family fuss'.[19] If families are unable to understand the contents of the various mediation procedures or find a process that is appealing to them, they might reject mediation based on a misguided perception.[20]

Without a clear definition, setting quality standards for mediation and making mediators accountable for their services is difficult, or even impossible. Research on the Finnish family mediation system revealed that the professionals working as family mediators lacked a clear conception regarding the main rationale of the system and their role as mediators.[21] Mediators cannot receive adequate training unless the role is

---

[16] Pruett and Johnston (n 13).

[17] Erin R Archerd, 'Evaluating Mediation's Future' (2020) *Journal of Dispute Resolution* 31–60.

[18] Ellen A Waldman, 'Identifying the Role of Social Norms in Mediation: A Multiple Model Approach' (1996) *Hastings Law Journal* 703–769.

[19] John Lande and Gregg Herman, 'Fitting the Forum to the Family Fuss: Choosing Mediation, Collaborative Law, or Cooperative Law for Negotiating Divorce Cases' (2004) *Family Court Review* 280–291.

[20] Vaula Haavisto, 'Developing Family Mediation in Finland: The Change Process and Practical Outcomes' in Anna Nylund, Kaijus Ervasti and Lin Adrian (eds), Nordic *Mediation Research* (Springer 2018) 44; Norwegian Government Official Report 2019:20 En styrket familietjeneste [A stronger family service] (n 3) 114–116; Swedish Government Bill 2020/21:150 Ett stärkt barnrättsperspektiv i vårdnadstvister [A Strengthened Child Rights Perspective in Custody Disputes] 55–56.

[21] Haavisto (n 20) 43–46; Vaula Haavisto, Marina Bergman-Pyykkönen and Synnöve Karvinen-Niinikoski, *Perheasioiden sovittelun uudet tuulet* (Suomen sovittelufoorumi ry 2014).

clearly defined, and inadequate training is believed to decrease the quality of family mediation.[22]

A coherent family mediation system requires a clear definition of each process in the system.[23] Otherwise, the system is neither comprehensive nor coherent, creating a risk that families will not find a process that matches their needs; indeed, as a society, we risk devoting resources to redundant or inadequate services while, in some families, conflicts escalate due to lack of access to appropriate services.

When mediation is regarded as a process connected to skills required in certain professions, rather than a separate process, it is likely to be guided by the standards of that profession.[24] Mediators are likely to prefer and practice, consciously or unconsciously, a model that reflects their respective profession and training: lawyers practise legal mediation, social workers favour counselling mediation, and family therapists opt for therapeutic mediation. Although some skills overlap, each process requires adequate training in addition to the professional training and skills that lawyers, family therapists, and social workers have acquired during their studies and work. In social services, parents are often referred to as 'clients', which implies that the parents are unable to identify their needs and the alternatives available to them.[25] Hence, the professional is the expert who designs the process and is in the position to determine what will be the best outcome. This view conflicts with the basic tenets of mediation. Similarly, therapists serving as mediators risk over-emphasizing the therapeutic dimensions of the dispute.[26] Moreover, mediation is an independent area of expertise that requires

---

22 Swedish Government Official Report 2017:6 Se barnet! (n 3) 257–259; Haavisto (n 20) 44–45.

23 Lisa Blomgren Amsler, Janet K Martinez and Stephanie E Smith, *Dispute System Design. Preventing, Managing, and Resolving Conflict* (Stanford University Press 2020) 22–38.

24 Cf. Marian Roberts, *Mediation in Family Disputes. Principles of Practice* (3rd edn, Ashgate 2008) 12–27; Lisa Parkinson, *Family Mediation: Appropriate Dispute Resolution in a New Family Justice System* (2nd edn, Family Law 2012) 23–34 and 119–140.

25 Roberts (n 24) 15.

26 Inger Kristin Heggdalsvik, 'Fastlåste foreldrekonflikter: En analyse av familieterapeuters skjønnsutøvelse i saker med høy konflikt' (2020) *Fokus på familien* 74–95.

specific training and skills.[27] If mediators do not receive specific mediation training, they risk falling back on their original professional role and delivering a less-than-optimal process, with potentially detrimental effects.

Self-determination is a hallmark of mediation[28]: the process is intended to ensure that parents make informed, rational decisions regarding their children, while the mediator's role is to put the parents in a position to make these decisions and refrain from making decisions directly or indirectly on behalf of the parents. A common problem with mediation is that the mediator becomes the de facto decision-maker, that is, the mediator directly or indirectly pressures the parents to adopt a specific outcome. Research suggests that many parents feel that the mediator or the other parent pressures them to agree to care arrangements that are not in the best interests of the child or to which the parent cannot commit.[29] The risk of coercion increases when mediation is made mandatory, mediators are directly or indirectly rewarded for producing settlements, and the mediator has multiple roles in the process.[30]

Poorly defined services are particularly problematic when the mediator has multiple roles, as in family mediation.[31] Both the best interests

---

27 For example, Nancy Welsh, 'Do You Believe in Magic? Self-Determination and Procedural Justice Meet Inequality in Court-Connected Mediation' (2017) *Southern Methodist University Law Review* 721–762; Karoline Angvik Ipsen, 'Meklere som lekmenn eller meklere som profesjonelle aktører?' (2008) *Kart og plan* 240, 246; Roberts (n 24) 12–27; Alison Taylor, *The Handbook of Family Dispute Resolution: Mediation Theory and Practice* (San Francisco 2002) 104–179.

28 For example, Jacqueline Nolan-Haley, 'Does ADR's Access to Justice Come at the Expense of Meaningful Consent' (2018) *Ohio State Journal on Dispute Resolution* 373–383.

29 For example, Nancy A Welsh, 'You've Got Your Mother's Laugh: What Bankruptcy Mediation Can Learn from the Her/History of Divorce and Child Custody Mediation' (2009) *American Bankruptcy Institute Law Review* 427, 454–458; Sandra J Perry, Tanya M Marcum and Charles R Stoner, 'Stumbling Down the Courthouse Steps: Mediator' Perceptions of the Stumbling Blocks to Successful Mandated Mediation in Child Custody and Visitation' (2010) *Pepperdine Dispute Resolution Law Journal* 441–465.

30 Forrest S Mosten, 'Institutionalization of Mediation' (2004) 42(2) *Family and Conciliation Court Review* 297–298; Marian Roberts, 'Family Mediation: The Development of the Regulatory Framework in the United Kingdom' (2005) 22(4) *Conflict Resolution Quarterly* 509–526, observing how the law defines success even in out-of-court mediation; Welsh (n 29) 438–441; Camilla Bernt, 'Custody Mediation in Norwegian Courts: A Conglomeration of Roles and Processes' in Anna Nylund, Kaijus Ervasti and Lin Adrian (eds), Nordic *Mediation Research* (Springer 2018) 105–132, 127–128.

31 Bernt (n 30).

of the child and the aim of settlement promote role conflicts in family mediation. When and how must the mediator intervene if there is reason to believe that the interests of the child are endangered? What information do the families need regarding this aspect? Although settlement is the goal, mediator performance should be measured using other indicators. At best, however, family mediation is a process where parents receive help to adjust from the role of ex-partners to co-parents and adapt care arrangements to the changing needs of their family.[32]

3.2.2 (When) Is Mediation an Appropriate Service for All Families?

Mediation is not a panacea. When a parent lacks adequate parenting capacity or is abusive, the mediated agreement could be contrary to the interests of the child. Spousal abuse in all its forms—physical, emotional, psychological, economic, and sexual—can also diminish the ability of a parent to make rational, child-centred decisions. In these cases, too, mediation is not likely to be an appropriate method for dispute resolution. If the mediator believes that the parents are not capable of making an agreement that is in the best interests of their child, the mediator should end the process—not decide on behalf of the parents or pressure the parties to accept an agreement. The mediation process lacks a system for gathering information and enabling the parties to argue their cases. Thus, the outcome that a mediator imposes or suggests can be based on erroneous assumptions. Incorporating elements that would enable the mediator to act as an 'adjudicator' runs counter to the nature of the

[32] For example, Renee Thørnblad, Astrid Strandbu and Anita Salamonsen, 'Hvordan påvirker barns deltakelse foreldremekling? Barns deltakelse som mål og middel' (2019) *Barn* 67–80; Lovise Grape, Renee Thørnblad and Bjørn Helge Handegård, 'Children Sharing Preferences on Contact and Residence Arrangements in Child-Inclusive Family Mediation in Norway' (2021) 29(1) *The International Journal of Children's Rights* 31–53.

mediation process and would thus diminish or even eradicate the qualities that make mediation a process that enhances self-determination and creative, collaborative problem-solving.[33]

Since mediation can be detrimental for high-conflict families, many countries have implemented screening tools to identify families with intimate partner violence, severe mental health issues, and so forth, as well as to determine distinct dispute resolution processes to fit the needs of these families.[34] The broad spectrum of needs in high-conflict families adds to the complexity of creating appropriate services for them.[35] Moreover, many countries have also introduced auxiliary services such as courses and support groups specifically for certain types of families, such as multicultural families or families with a child that has health-related problems.[36] Some families might benefit from therapeutic interventions; families who grapple with poverty and unemployment could find interventions that encompass social services to be helpful, while other families would be better aided with a combination of child-welfare services and services for divorcing families. Ideally, services for high-conflict families would be multi-professional and customized to the needs of each family.

[33] For example, Anna Nylund, 'Alternative Dispute Resolution, Justice and Accountability in Norwegian Civil Justice' in Xandra Kramer, Betül Kas and Erlis Themeli (eds), *Frontiers in Civil Justice: Privatisation, Monetisation and Digitisation* (Edward Elgar 2022) 81–100.

[34] For example, Pruett and Johnston (n 13) 92–111; Patrick Parkinson, *Family Law and the Indissolubility of Parenthood* (Cambridge University Press 2011) 184–185 and 190; Amy G Applegate, Connie J Beck, Jeannie M Adams, Fernanda S Rossi, and Amy Holtzworth-Munroe, 'Preparing Mediators to Mediate Cases Reporting High IPV in a Randomized Controlled Trial: The Importance of a Mediation Manual, Training, and Consultation' (2021) 59(4) *Family Court Review* 725–740.

[35] For example, Grethe Nordhelle, *Høykonflikt. Utvidet forståelse og håndtering via mekling* (Universitetsforlaget 2016) 23–39.

[36] For example, Thomas D Barton, 'Challenges When Family Conflicts Meet the Law—A Proactive Approach' in Anna Kaldal, Agnes Hellner and Titti Mattsson (eds), *Children in Custody Disputes: Matching Legal Proceedings to Problems* (Palgrave 2023); Marsha Kline Pruett, Jonathan Alschech and Talia Feldscher, 'The Family Resolutions Specialty Court (FRSC): An Evidence-Informed Court-Based Innovation' (2021) 59(4) *Family Court Review* 656–672.

3.3 Nordic Family Mediation

3.3.1 Nordic Family Mediation Systems

Although the boundaries between the services are not clear, all of the Nordic countries have specific, divorce-related services that can be conceptualized as a three-tier system: services for all families during the early stages of divorce, services for families needing (or desiring) assistance to resolve their disputes, and mandatory pre-filing services—that is, taking part in 'mediation' is a prerequisite for filing a court case. As Table 3.1 shows, there is no uniform Nordic system.

The Danish system has services for each tier, the Norwegian system has services for early divorce families and pre-filing; Sweden has services for families seeking help and a new pre-trial service, while Finland only has services for families who actively seek help. Denmark has the most diversified system, featuring multiple processes for families with various needs and preferences.

Since March 2022, when Sweden introduced mandatory pre-filing information talks (*informationssamtal*),[37] the systems of all Nordic countries (except Finland) follow a model with mandatory pre-filing

Table 3.1 Nordic family mediation/dispute resolution systems, m = mandatory, v = voluntary

	Early divorce families	Dispute resolution	Pre-filing
Denmark	Counselling (v)	Mediation (v) Expert counselling (v)	Family mediation (m) Expert assessment (m)
Finland	–	Child welfare supervision (v) Family mediation (v)	–
Norway	Family mediation (m)	–	Family mediation (m)
Sweden	–	Cooperation talks (v)	Information talks (m)

[37] Swedish Children and Parent Code [Föräldrabalk] (1949:381) Chapter 6 Section 17c and Social Services Act [Socialtjänstlag] (2001:453) Chapter 5 Sections 3 and 3a.

services.[38] The rationale for mandatory information sessions in Sweden is the low usage of the voluntary cooperation talks process (*samarbetssamtal*) and an increasing number of court cases.[39] Norway and Finland are outliers: Norway requires all divorcing families with children under the age of 16 to attend mediation, and Finland offers only voluntary services.

Denmark and Finland have two parallel services for families. Parents can select the service that they believe will best serve their preferences and perceived needs. In Danish pre-filing cases, the parents are assigned either to family mediation or to an expert assessment, according to the results of a screening conducted at intake.[40]

Denmark and Norway have implemented screening processes at intake to identify families experiencing violence, substance abuse, and parental mental disorders, and thus the risk of child neglect and abuse.[41] Unlike Denmark, the Norwegian screening process is not reflected in statutory law or official guidelines; nor is it described on the Family Counselling Services website. The need for screening is also recognized in Sweden, but screening is not regulated.[42]

Ostensibly, it appears that no Nordic country has implemented a mediation process specifically designed for high-conflict families; however, in practice, the Norwegian system operates with three forms

---

[38] Danish Parental Responsibility Act [Forældreansvarslov] Section 31 and Norwegian Children Act [Lov om barn og foreldre] 8 April 1981 no 7 Section 51.

[39] Swedish Government Official Report 2017:6 Se barnet! (n 3) 138–139. For a discussion on cooperation talks, see Anna Singer 'Out-of-Court Custody Dispute Resolution in Sweden—A Journey Without Destination' in Anna Kaldal, Agnes Hellner and Titti Mattsson (eds), *Children in Custody Disputes: Matching Legal Proceedings to Problems* (Palgrave 2023).

[40] Danish Family Law House Act [Lov om familieretshuset] Sections 5 to 9. Family Law House Instruction Sections 3.2 and 3.3. An example of the questionnaire can be found at: https://familieretshuset.dk/media/1320/foraeldremyndighed.pdf accessed 10 May 2023.

[41] For example, Norwegian Directorate for Children, Youth and Family Affairs (Barne-, ungdoms- og familiedirektoratet), *Årsrapport 2020 Barne-, ungdoms- og familiedirektoratet* [Yearbook 2020 Directorate for Children, Youth and Family Affairs] 40; Thomas Hugaas Molden, Gro Ulset and Melina Røe, *Kvalitet i familievernet Ansattes vurderinger av betingelser for et faglig godt tjenestetilbud* [Quality in Family Care Employees' Assessments of Conditions for a Professionally Good Service Offer] (NTNU Samfunnsforskning 2019) 18–20.

[42] Swedish Government Bill 2020/21:150 Ett stärkt barnrättsperspektiv i vårdnadstvister (n 20) 62–63; Swedish Government Official Report 2017:6 Se barnet! (n 3) 327 ff.

of mediation—so-called A, B, and C mediations.[43] Based on the intake screening, families who need limited assistance are directed to A mediation; families with low to medium levels of conflict are directed to B mediation; and high-conflict families are encouraged to attend C mediation, which consists of a mixture of interventions including family and group therapy.

In Denmark and Norway, auxiliary services such as conversation groups for children and young people experiencing divorce, informational videos, information booklets, and courses for families with specific needs (for example, family members with disabilities or serious illnesses, or who require anger-management training), are offered as a complement to mediation.[44] Families can also use these services independently of mediation.

The organization of Nordic family mediation is as diverse as the range of processes. Denmark and Norway have centralized services located within entities that partly specialize in family mediation. In Denmark, the Agency of Family Law (*familieretshuset*), a specialized administrative body, is the apex body of the family justice system. In addition to providing family dispute resolution service, it hears cases involving (among other things) adoption, paternity, and guardianship. Norway also has a centralized service in the Family Mediation Service (*familievernet*, literally family protection), which offers family counselling and therapy in addition to mediation services, and is part of social services. The Finnish and Swedish systems are organized by municipalities or counties. In Sweden, the local social service (*socialtjänsten*) delivers the services. In Finland, Child-Welfare Supervisors (*lastenvalvoja/barnatillsyningsman*), whose main task is to assist parents with agreeing on maintenance, and family counselling services (*perheneuvola/familjerådgivning*) are municipal services. In addition to the public services, alternatives are also offered by private providers and churches.

43 Norwegian Government Official Report 2019:20 En styrket familietjeneste (n 3) 113.

44 The Agency of Family Law Familjeretshuset, Cooperation course [Samarbejdskursus] https://familieretshuset.dk/forloeb-og-tilbud/forloeb-og-tilbud/samarbejdskursus and Norwegian Directorate for Children, Youth and Family Affairs, Courses and group guidance at the family welfare office [Kurs og gruppeveiledning hos familievernet] https://www.bufdir.no/Familie/Familievernet/Kurs_og_gruppeveiledning_hos_familievernet accessed 25 February 2022; Norwegian Government Official Report 2019:20 En styrket familietjeneste 95–98.

The centralized organization of family mediation services in Denmark and Norway coincides with tiered services and systematic use of intake screening to identify families where there is a risk of child abuse or neglect, and high conflict levels. Denmark uses processes with well-defined target groups, and the systems are clearly tiered according to the severity of the conflict level in the family, whereas in the other Nordic countries, the relationship of the various services is less clear.

3.3.2 Nordic Family Mediation Processes

Danish, Finnish, Norwegian, and Swedish legislation provide concordant definitions of family mediation: it is a process that assists parents with agreeing on care arrangements,[45] which is concordant with mediation theory. The only exception is Finnish child-welfare supervision, for which no unequivocal purpose is stated. The organizations that are responsible for providing family mediation divide their processes into five groups, presented on their websites and promotional literature.

The first group can be characterized as counselling family mediation—that is, the main intervention informs and educates the parents on applicable rules and regulations, children's needs during and after divorce, and teaching co-parenting and conflict-resolution skills. These processes include the Danish counselling session (*rådgivnings- og afklaringssamtale*), which is for newly separated families,[46] and expert counselling (*børnesagkyndig rådgivning*).[47] The Norwegian A and B mediations also

[45] Danish Family Law House Act of 27 December 2018 no 1702 Section 21, Finnish Marriage Act [Avioliittolaki/Äktenskapslag] no 411 of 16 April 1987 Sections 20–23a, Norwegian Children Act Section 52, and the Swedish Children and Parent Code Chapter 6 Sections 17c and 17a, Social Service Act Chapter 5 Section 3, and Information Talks Act [Lag om informationssamtal] (2021:530) Section 7.

[46] The Agency of Family Law, 'Tilbud til brudteamiliarr' https://familieretshuset.dk/forloeb-og-tilbud/forloeb-og-tilbud/tilbud-til-brudte-familier accessed 25 February 2022; The Agency of Family Law, 'Når vi behandler din sag' https://familieretshuset.dk/forloeb-og-tilbud/forloeb-og-tilbud/naar-vi-behandler-din-sag accessed 25 February 2022.

[47] The Agency of Family Law, 'Børnesagkyndig rådgivning' https://familieretshuset.dk/forloeb-og-tilbud/forloeb-og-tilbud/boernesagkyndig-raadgivning accessed 25 February 2022.

fall into this category.[48] These services are suitable as universal services for all families who want guidance during or after separation.

The second group focuses on dispute resolution and decision-making, that is, legal family mediation. Danish conflict mediation (*konfliktmægling*)[49] and the mandatory Danish pre-filing family mediation *(familjemægling)*[50] belong in this group. Finnish family mediation can also be placed in this category.[51] These processes are suitable when the parents have adequate parenting capacity but might need a structured process to be able to make good decisions.

The third group could be labelled therapeutic family mediation. Norwegian C mediation (which is also called procedure mediation, *prosessmekling*) falls into this category because therapeutic interventions are a primary feature. This type of mediation is suitable for those high-conflict families who need assistance to deal with underlying emotional and relational issues before they proceed to decision-making.

The fourth group uses procedures with an undefined approach. The Finnish child-welfare supervision process and Swedish cooperation talks belong to this category because the techniques and approaches used are not described.[52] It is unclear what the process entails, and the intensity of disputes for which it is designed, is not defined.

Finally, the fifth group includes processes that do not involve decision-making. Danish expert assessment *(familieretlig udredning)* is for families where the child is at risk of abuse or serious neglect. It is designed to

---

[48] Norwegian Directorate for Children, Youth and Family Affairs, 'Mekling ved samlivsbrudd' https://bufdir.no/Familie/Samlivsbrudd/mekling_og_avtale/Mekling/ accessed 25 February 2022. See also, Rundskriv Q-02/2008 Mekling etter ekteskapsloven og barneloven, comment to Section 1, and Ådnanes and others (n 9).

[49] The Agency of Family Law, 'Konfliktmaegling' https://familieretshuset.dk/forloeb-og-tilbud/forloeb-og-tilbud/konfliktmaegling accessed 25 February 2022.

[50] The Agency of Family Law, 'Familjemæglin' https://familieretshuset.dk/forloeb-og-tilbud/forloeb-og-tilbud/familiemaegling accessed 25 February 2022.

[51] Terveyden ja Hyvinvoinnin Laitos, 'Perheasioiden sovittelu' https://thl.fi/fi/web/lapset-nuoret-ja-perheet/sote-palvelut/perheoikeudelliset-palvelut/perheasioiden-sovittelu accessed 25 February 2022.

[52] For example, Soite, https://www.soite.fi/sv?page_id=lastenvalvoja accessed 25 February 2022; Family Law and Parental Support Authority, 'Vad är ett samarbetssamtal?' https://www.mfof.se/vardnad-boende-och-umgange/information-for-foraldrar/vad-ar-samarbetssamtal.html accessed 25 February 2022; Singer (n 39).

provide an expert report on the care situation of the child.[53] The Swedish information talks aim to educate parents regarding the potential repercussions of court proceedings and the available alternatives.[54] Hence, these processes cannot be called mediation, although they might have important functions in the family mediation or family justice system.

Denmark has the broadest range of mediation services for low- to medium-conflict families. They can choose between counselling and dispute resolution approaches to mediation, and between early preemptive services and services once conflicts have happened. It should be noted that the Danish system has only a single process for high-conflict families, known as expert assessment, which serves to identify abuse and neglect and funnel those families to court proceedings. Although there are courses designed for specific groups of (high-conflict) families, there are no therapeutic processes available; this is an outspoken policy choice,[55] and probably reflects the fact that the Agency of Family Law is embedded within the justice system, not the welfare systems.

Although Norwegian Family Counselling Services formally have only a single process, in practice it has three processes as explained above, all of which follow a counselling or therapeutic approach. This is not surprising, considering that the Family Counselling Services provide couples and family therapy services to the general population,[56] and the methods are drawn from psychological research.[57] Family mediation belongs in the realm of family services, which is reflected in the mediation process, in that the mediators emphasize maintaining the therapist-client relationship in high-conflict cases.[58] The screening at intake serves to funnel some families to court, while C mediation and courses

[53] The Agency of Family Law, 'Familieretlig udredning' https://familieretshuset.dk/forloeb-og-tilbud/forloeb-og-tilbud/familieretlig-udredning accessed 25 February 2022.

[54] Swedish Government Bill 2020/21:150 Ett stärkt barnrättsperspektiv i vårdnadstvister (n 20) 55.

[55] The Agency of Family Law Instruction VEJ no 9404 of 26 June 2020 pt 8.1.

[56] Norwegian Directorate for Children, Youth and Family Affairs, *Barn i familievernet.* Familievernets skriftserie 1/2011 8–10.

[57] For example, Peder Kjøs, *Obligatorisk foreldremekling i høykonfliktsaker. En kvalitativ studie* (Department of Psychology, University of Oslo 2016) 52–56.

[58] This fact is not manifested in policy documents, but it is latently present as an assumption that the mediators apply a therapeutic lens to the mediation process, see for example,

for specific populations, are attempts to provide for the needs of high-conflict families. As in Denmark, the mediation services also offer courses designed to meet the needs of high-conflict families.

The Finnish and Swedish systems are less diversified or well-defined. The decentralized organization of mediation services probably contributes to this situation. There are no services specifically for high-conflict families. From a dispute-system design perspective, these systems are unsatisfactory because the content of the processes and their target groups are not adequately defined and the relationship between the processes is unclear. To some extent this applies to the Norwegian system also, because the three-tiered mediation system is not formalized and is opaque to those who do not know the system well.

The family mediation systems in Nordic countries mainly consist of processes that can be characterized as mediation but also include some processes that do not fulfil the criteria of mediation; in addition, some processes are ill-defined, which renders them incomprehensible. Only the Danish system has services that are openly intended for high-conflict families, while similar services in the Norwegian system are available, but somewhat perplexing. Interestingly, the Danish and Norwegian systems are situated in different organizations—the former in the justice system, and the latter in the family therapy system—which also affects the type of services available. The Danish system does not explicitly offer therapeutic services, while the Norwegian system is embedded in a family-therapy approach.

3.3.3 Quality Standards in Nordic Family Mediation

We have limited information regarding the quality of Nordic family mediation. One reason is that although the outspoken goal of family mediation is to help parents agree on care arrangements, the rationale is to reduce the workload of the courts. The mediation process, the role of the mediation, and the criteria for success vary depending on the

---

Heggdalsvik (n 26); Kjøs (n 57); Hilde Kåstad, Kjersti Halvorsen and Vibeke Samsonsen, 'Standardisering og profesjonelt skjønn i høykonfliktmekling: En kvalitativ undersøkelse av mekleres erfaringer med prosessmekling i høykonfliktsaker' (2021) *Fokus på familien* 285–302.

mediation model used. Still, reading Nordic regulation and policy documents through the lens of family mediation theory, reveals the striking absence of references to the extensive international body of research regarding both the mediation process and mediator interventions, as well as ethical and regulatory challenges. These circumstances are likely to have repercussions on the quality of the process and outcome, mediation process development, training of mediators, accountability of mediators and the organizations that provide mediation services, the perception of mediation among potential users, and so forth.

As discussed above,[59] Finnish family mediators believe that the lack of clear definitions for family mediation goals, the nature of the mediation process, and the role of the mediator, reduces the quality of mediation and hinders development of mediation methods and mediator training. Additionally, it renders adequate management of mediation quality impossible. Two Norwegian government-appointed committees have recommended a clearer demarcation between therapeutic and counselling services on the one hand, and services for separated families on the other, to enhance the quality of services.[60] They also proposed that the system of three types of mediation should be formalized.[61] This approach resonates with the idea of a system that consists of distinct processes that are designed for different target groups and stages of separation.

Mediation still seems to be considered primarily as an auxiliary to other professions and to family services, not a discrete service that requires specific skills. This is reflected in requirements for mediation training; only in Norway are mediators required to have some training,[62] and even there, the length and scope of the training is not regulated.

---

[59] See text accompanying footnotes 20 and 21.

[60] Norwegian Government Official Report 2019:20 En styrket familietjeneste (n 3) 87; Norwegian Government Official Report 2020:14 Ny barnelov – Til barnets beste [A new Children's Act—In the Best Interest of the Child] 288.

[61] Norwegian Government Official Report 2019:20 En styrket familietjeneste (n 3) 119–121; Norwegian Government Official Report 2020:14 Ny barnelov—Til barnets beste (n 60) 238.

[62] Norwegian Decree on Mediation in Matters Related to the Marriage Act and Children Act of 18 December 2006 no 1478 [Forskrift om mekling etter ekteskapsloven og barneloven] Section 4.

Danish and Swedish regulations imply that mediation training is important, but it is not unequivocally required.[63] The Finnish rules require no mediation training; it is sufficient that the child-welfare supervisor is a social worker or has other suitable training.[64] Nordic countries would probably benefit from training and professional standards. At present, the Danish system appears to be in the best position to develop such rules and programmes because it has five distinct processes, and the services are centralized. The Association of Family and Conciliation Courts' Model Standards of Practice for Family and Divorce Mediation[65] could serve as a model for the other Nordic countries to ensure appropriate mediator skills for promoting child-friendly mediation processes and outcomes, distinct definitions of processes, and identification and management of ethical and professional challenges.

Pressure to settle is seldom discussed in policy documents on family mediation in Scandinavia; nor is this aspect addressed in family mediation regulation. As discussed above,[66] institutional constraints—for example, mediators not having adequate time in each mediation or mediators being (indirectly) rewarded for settlement, as well as personal and professional biases, such as therapist-mediators over-emphasizing the value of maintaining the client-therapist relationship—could obscure the mediation process. While mediation is usually considered superior to litigation, an excessive belief in the advantages of mediation could lead a mediator to be overconfident regarding the capacity of the parents to act according to the best interests of the child, and thus to overlook signs of an insufficient parenting capacity. Currently, no mechanisms are in place in Nordic countries to monitor whether families feel pressured to settle. Nor have mechanisms been implemented for addressing mediator pressure, such as cooling-off periods or complaint systems.

---

63 Danish Family Law House Act Section 1 para. 4; Swedish Government Bill 2020/21:150 Ett stärkt barnrättsperspektiv i vårdnadstvister (n 20) 78–79.

64 Finnish Social Services Act [Sosiaalihuoltolaki/Socialvårdslag] 30.12.2014/1301 Section 27a.

65 Association of Family and Concillation Courts, 'Model Standards of Practice for Family and Divorce Mediation' https://www.afccnet.org/Portals/0/PDF/ModelStandardsOfPracticeForFamilyAndDivorceMediation.pdf?ver=ykuc9AnD6m4jf9IZs4PhkQ%3D%3D accessed 11 January 2023.

66 See text accompanying footnotes 24–30.

The lack of clarity in these processes could also reduce their appeal in the eyes of potential users. Although mediation is mandatory in Norway, many families have not used the services beyond the first mandatory hour-long session.[67] However, the introduction of the C-track for high-conflict families has made mediation more attractive for this group.[68] This illustrates the importance of clear designation of processes.

Considering the complexity of problems that high-conflict families face, these families would probably benefit from a system consisting of multi-professional services that can be combined to fit the needs of each family. While the Nordic mediation systems have become more diversified, services intended for high-conflict families are still fragmented and underdeveloped. Progress has been made, notably in Denmark and Norway, where the centralized organization of family mediation services appears to facilitate the process, and in Norway, where the devising of better services for high-conflict families has been a priority for several years.[69] These efforts have been fruitful, yet there is still significant need for further improvement.

3.4 Conclusions

Nordic family mediation systems have taken a leap forward during the past decade. Danish family mediation and dispute resolution have undergone transformational shifts towards differentiation, more accurately defined services, and increased child participation. With Norway and (to some extent) Sweden following suit. Differentiation could make the services more attractive to parents and more compatible with the needs of each family, and thus also more likely to provide processes and outcomes that are in the best interests of the child. Services targeted at the diverse group of high-conflict families have also emerged: screening for abuse and other challenges, the development of a specific mediation

[67] Norwegian Government Official Report 2019:20 En styrket familietjeneste (n 3) 114.

[68] Norwegian Directorate for Children, Youth and Family Affairs *Årsrapport 2020* 40; Norwegian Government Official Report 2019:20 En styrket familietjeneste (n 3) 114.

[69] Norwegian Directorate for Children, Youth and Family Affairs, for example (n 56) (n 41).

process, and auxiliary services that can be combined with mediation or used separately.

Despite the developments, the Nordic systems are still incomplete; indeed, they are far from comprehensive and well-designed. To improve the system, Nordic family mediation needs solid theoretical foundations and should be firmly based on dispute-system design theory. Additionally, rigorous empirical studies are required to test whether the new models help families manage their conflicts, make better care arrangements, and give voice and choice to children—or whether the outcomes will largely be the same. Research on user satisfaction, compliance with mediated agreements, the impact of mediation on conflict levels and conflict resolution, and other related aspects is sorely needed. Measures to monitor and (when needed) reduce pressure to settle must also be implemented. More research is required to understand how the institutional design of mediation (that is, centralized vs. decentralized services, mediation as part of the social services or justice system) influences the mediation process and its long-term outcomes, and how best to coordinate—and when appropriate, combine—family, therapeutic, and dispute resolution services.

References

Ådnanes M, Haugen M G D, Jensberg H, Husum T L and Rantalaiho M, 'Hva karakteriserer vanskelige saker i foreldremekling, og er meklingsordningen godt nok tilpasset?' (2011) Fokus på Familien 86.

Agency of Family Law Instruction VEJ no 9404 of 26 June 2020.

Amato P R, 'The Consequences of Divorce for Adults and Children' (2002) *Journal of Marriage and the Family* 1269.

Anderson S R, Andersin S A, Palmer K L and Mutchler M S, 'Defining High Conflicts' (2011) *The American Journal of Family Therapy* 11.

Angvik Ipsen K, 'Meklere som lekmenn eller meklere som profesjonelle aktører?' (2008) Kart og plan 240.

Archerd E R, 'Evaluating Mediation's Future' (2020) *Journal of Dispute Resolution* 31.

Applegate A G, Beck C J, Adams J M, Rossi F S and Holtzworth-Munroe A, 'Preparing Mediators to Mediate Cases Reporting High IPV in a Randomized Controlled Trial: The Importance of a Mediation Manual, Training, and Consultation' (2021) 59(4) *Family Court Review* 725.

Barton T D 'Challenges When Family Conflicts Meet the Law—A Proactive Approach' in Kaldal A, Hellner A and Mattsson T (eds), *Children in Custody Disputes: Matching Legal Proceedings to Problems* (Palgrave 2023) 169.

Baruch Bush R A and Ganong Pope S, 'Transformative Mediation: Changing the Quality of Family Conflict Interaction' (2002) 3 *Pepperdine Dispute Resolution Law Journal* 53.

Bergman A-S and Rejmer A, 'Parents in Child Custody Disputes: Why Are They Disputing?' (2017) *Journal of Child Custody* 134.

Bergman A-S and Rejmer A, '"Det är klart att barnen blir lidande": om barns mående när föräldrar är I vårnadstvist' (2017) *Socialmedisinsk tidskrift* 437.

Bernt C, 'Custody Mediation in Norwegian Courts: A Conglomeration of Roles and Processes' in Nylund A, Ervasti K and Adrian L (eds), *Nordic Mediation Research* (Springer 2018) 105.

Blomgren Amsler L, Martinez J K and Smith S E, *Dispute System Design: Preventing, Managing, and Resolving Conflict* (Stanford University Press 2020).

Breivik F L and Mevik K, *Barnefordeling i domstolen. Når barnets beste blir barnets verste* (Universitetsforlaget 2012).

Cashmore J and Parkinson P, 'Reasons for Disputes in High Conflict Families' (2011) *Journal of Family Studies* 186.

Coogler O J, *Structured Mediation in Divorce Settlement: A Handbook for Marital Mediators* (Lexington Books 1978).

Finnish Institute for Health and Welfare 'Perheasioiden sovittelu' https://thl.fi/fi/web/lapset-nuoret-ja-perheet/sote-palvelut/perheoikeudelliset-palvelut/perheasioiden-sovittelu accessed 25 February 2022.

Gording Stang E, 'Når vi ikke får gehør i rettsapparatet har vi tapt på vegne av barnet' in Søvig K H, Eskeland Schütz S and Rasmussen Ø (eds), *Undring og erkjennelse. Festskrift til Jan Fridthjof Bernt 70 år* (Fagbokforlaget 2013) 665.

Grape L, Thørnblad R and Handegård B H, 'Children Sharing Preferences on Contact and Residence Arrangements in Child-Inclusive Family Mediation in Norway' (2021) 29(1) *The International Journal of Children's Rights* 31.

Gulbrandsen W, 'Foreldrekonflikter etter samlivsbrudd: En analyse av samspill og kilder til det fastlåsende' (2013) *Tidsskrift for norsk psykologforening* 538.

Haynes J M, *Divorce Mediation: A Practical Guide for Therapists and Counselors* (Springer 1981).
Haavisto V, 'Developing Family Mediation in Finland: The Change Process and Practical Outcomes' in Nylund A, Ervasti K and Adrian L (eds), *Nordic Mediation Research* (Springer 2018) 41.
Haavisto V, Bergman-Pyykkönen M and Karvinen-Niinikoski S, *Perheasioiden sovittelun uudet tuulet* (Suomen sovittelufoorumi ry 2014).
Heggdalsvik I K, 'Fastlåste foreldrekonflikter: En analyse av familieterapeuters skjønnsutøvelse i saker med høy konflikt' (2020) 48 *Fokus på familien* 74.
Helland M S and Borren I, *Foreldrekonflikt; identifisering av konfliktnivåer, sentrale kjennetegn og risikofaktorer hos høykonfliktpar* (Nasjonalt folkehelse-institutt 2015).
Hugaas Molden T, Ulset G and Røe M, *Kvalitet i familievernet Ansattes vurderinger av betingelser for et faglig godt tjenestetilbud* (NTNU Samfunns-forskning 2019).
Johnston J, Roseby V and Kuehnle K, *In the Name of the Child—A Developmental Approach to Understanding and Helping Children of Conflicted and Violent Divorce* (Springer 2009).
Kline Pruett M, Alschech J and Feldscher T, 'The Family Resolutions Specialty Court (FRSC): An Evidence-Informed Court-Based Innovation' (2021) 59(4) *Family Court Review* 656.
Kaldal A, Hellner A and Mattsson T, 'Introduction: Matching Legal Proceedings to Problems in Custody Disputes' in Kaldal A, Hellner A and Mattsson T (eds), *Children in Custody Disputes: Matching Legal Proceedings to Problems* (Palgrave 2023) X.
Kjøs P, *Obligatorisk foreldremekling i høykonfliktsaker. En kvalitativ studie* (Department of Psychology, University of Oslo 2016).
Kåstad H, Halvorsen K and Samsonsen V, 'Standardisering og profesjonelt skjønn i høykonfliktmekling: En kvalitativ undersøkelse av mekleres erfaringer med prosessmekling i høykonfliktsaker' (2021) *Fokus på familien* 285.
Lande J and Herman G, 'Fitting the Forum to the Family Fuss: Choosing Mediation, Collaborative Law, or Cooperative Law for Negotiating Divorce Cases' (2004) *Family Court Review* 280.
Lowry R L, 'Evaluative Mediation' in Folberg J, Milne A L and Salem P (eds), *Divorce and Family Mediation: Models, Techniques, and Applications* (The Guilford Press 2004) 72.

Mayer B, 'Facilitative Mediation' in Folberg J, Milne A L and Salem P (eds), *Divorce and Family Mediation. Models, Techniques, and Applications* (The Guilford Press 2004) 29.

Mosten F S, 'Institutionalization of Mediation' (2004) 42(2) *Family and Conciliation Court Review* 292.

Nolan-Haley J, 'Does ADR's Access to Justice Come at the Expense of Meaningful Consent' (2018) *Ohio State Journal on Dispute Resolution* 373.

Nordhelle G, *Høykonflikt. Utvidet forståelse og håndtering via mekling* (Universitetsforlaget 2016).

Norwegian Government Official Report 2019:20 En styrket familietjeneste.

Norwegian Government Official Report 2020:14 Ny barnelov – Til barnets beste.

Norwegian Decree on Mediation in Matters Related to the Marriage Act and Children Act of 18 December 2006 no 1478 (Forskrift om mekling etter ekteskapsloven og barneloven).

Norwegian Directorate for Children, Youth and Family Affairs, *Årsrapport 2020 Barne-, ungdoms- og familiedirektoratet*.

Norwegian Directorate for Children, Youth and Family Affairs, *Barn i familievernet.* Familievernets skriftserie 1/2011.

Nylund A, 'A Dispute System Design Perspective on Norwegian Child Custody Mediation' in Nylund A, Ervasti K and Adrian L (eds), *Nordic Mediation Research* (Springer 2018) 9.

Nylund A, 'Alternative Dispute Resolution, Justice and Accountability in Norwegian Civil Justice' in Kramer X, Kas B and Themeli E (eds) *Frontiers in Civil Justice: Privatisation, Monetisation and Digitisation* (Edward Elgar 2022) 81.

Parkinson L, *Family Mediation: Appropriate Dispute Resolution in a New Family Justice System* (2nd edn, Family Law 2012).

Parkinson P, *Family Law and the Indissolubility of Parenthood* (Cambridge University Press 2011).

Perry S J, Marcum T M and Stoner C R, 'Stumbling Down the Courthouse Steps: Mediators' Perceptions of the Stumbling Blocks to Successful Mandated Mediation in Child Custody and Visitation' (2010) *Pepperdine Dispute Resolution Law Journal* 441.

Pruett M and Johnston J R, 'Therapeutic Mediation with High-Conflict Parents: Effective Models and Strategies' in Folberg J, Milne A L and Salem P (eds), *Divorce and Family Mediation. Models, Techniques, and Applications* (The Guilford Press 2004).

Rejmer A, 'Custody Disputes from a Socio-Legal Perspective' in Kaldal A, Hellner A and Mattsson T (eds), *Children in Custody Disputes: Matching Legal Proceedings to Problems* (Palgrave 2023) 67.

Roberts M, 'Family Mediation: The Development of the Regulatory Framework in the United Kingdom' (2005) 22(4) *Conflict Resolution Quarterly* 509.

Roberts M, *Mediation in Family Disputes: Principles of Practice* (3rd edn, Ashgate 2008).

Singer A, 'Out-of-Court Custody Dispute Resolution in Sweden—A Journey Without Destination' in Kaldal A, Hellner A and Mattsson T (eds), *Children in Custody Disputes: Matching Legal Proceedings to Problems* (Palgrave 2023) 129.

Soite, https://www.soite.fi/sv?page_id=lastenvalvoja accessed 25 February 2022.

Swedish Government Bill 2020/21:150 Ett stärkt barnrättsperspektiv i vårdnadstvister [A Strengthened Child Rights Perspective in Custody Disputes].

Swedish Government Official Reports 2017:6 Se barnet! [See the Child!].

Swedish Family Law and Parental Support Authority, 'Vad är ett samarbetssamtal?' https://www.mfof.se/vardnad-boende-och-umgange/information-for-foraldrar/vad-ar-samarbetssamtal.html accessed 25 February 2022.

Vindeløf V, *Reflexive Mediation: With a Sustainable Perspective* (Steven Harris, transl.) (DJØF publishing 2012).

Taylor A, *The Handbook of Family Dispute Resolution: Mediation Theory and Practice* (Jossey-Bass 2002).

Thørnblad R, Strandbu A and Salamonsen A, 'Hvordan påvirker barns deltakelse foreldremekling? Barns deltakelse som mål og middel' (2019) *Barn* 67.

Waldman E A, 'Identifying the Role of Social Norms in Mediation: A Multiple Model Approach' (1996) *Hastings Law Journal* 703.

Welsh N, 'Do You Believe in Magic? Self-Determination and Procedural Justice Meet Inequality in Court-Connected Mediation' (2017) *Southern Methodist University Law Review* 721.

Welsh N A, 'You've Got Your Mother's Laugh: What Bankruptcy Mediation Can Learn from the Her/History of Divorce and Child Custody Mediation' (2009) *American Bankruptcy Institute Law Review* 427.

Swedish Gender Equality Agency, *Uppgifter om våld är inget undantag. Redovisning av kartläggning av uppgifter om våld eller andra övergrepp i mål om vårdnad, boende och umgänge* Report 2022:1.

4

Custody Disputes From a Socio-Legal Perspective

Annika Rejmer

4.1 Introduction

This article's objective is to explore whether court proceedings are suited to serve children's best interests in high-level custody conflicts. The research question to be answered is whether Swedish laws regulating custody, residence, and visitation can contribute to the resolution of custody disputes in the best interests of the child. A socio-legal perspective applies, grounded in empirical data collected by a method of triangulation, of legal dogma, and qualitative and quantitative social-science method. Results are analysed based on theoretical concepts such as low-level and high-level conflicts, and conflicts of interest and value, norm, gender, class, and health. The conclusion is that the legal system is not adapted to the nature of parents' conflict or their ability to serve the best interests of their child, which results in court decisions that cannot either.

A. Rejmer (✉)
Faculty of Law, Uppsala University, Uppsala, Sweden

A. Kaldal et al. (eds.), *Children in Custody Disputes*,
https://doi.org/10.1007/978-3-031-46301-3_4

4.2 Background

Since 2000, and over the last two decades, lawsuits addressing custody, residence, and visitation have steadily increased in Sweden.[1] In an effort to reverse this trend, there has been legislative reform, and alternative handling methods introduced. Despite these measures, however, and with the exception of the pandemic period when the number of cases stopped growing and even decreased, custody cases are still on the rise.[2] By the age of 17, 33% of children will have experienced parental separation,[3] while 6% will also have experienced a parental battle in court over custody, residence, and visitation.[4] In addition, almost half of these children will have experienced repeated litigation—indicating that the courts have limited powers to serve children's best interests in custody disputes.[5]

4.3 Aim

With reference to the background presented above, this article aims to explore the nature of custody disputes, and whether Swedish legislation is adapted to ensure children's best interests in cases of parental conflicts regarding custody, residence, and visitation.

---

[1] Swedish National Council for Crime Prevention, 'Domstolsstatistik 2001' [Court Statistics, Official Statistics of Sweden 2001], Rapport 2002:15, https://bra.se/download/18.123055341 31e173a7f180001909/1371914735698/2002_15_domstolsstatistik_2001.pdf accessed 9 May 2023; Domstolsverket, Court Statistics, Official Statistics of Sweden 2021 https://www.dom stol.se/contentassets/65a838e5ba2a42418f57b1c39ef389ab/court_statistics_2021.pdf/ accessed 9 May 2023.

[2] Court Statistics, Official Statistics of Sweden 2021 (n 1).

[3] Court Statistics, Official Statistics of Sweden 2020, Family Statistics 2020, https://www. domstol.se/globalassets/filer/gemensamt-innehall/styrning-och-riktlinjer/statistik/2021/court_sta tistics_2020.pdf/ accessed 9 May 2023.

[4] Court Statistics, Official Statistics of Sweden 2020 (n 3).

[5] Swedish Government Official Reports 2017:6 Se barnet! [See the Child!] 464.

4.4 Method

The empirical data presented here was collected in the socio-legal research project: *High-Conflict Families of Divorce—A Survey of Parents, Their Custody Dispute and an Impact Analysis of Three Handling Models.*[6] Using a combination of legal dogmatic and social-science methods including quantitative and qualitative studies, qualitative methods contribute to a visualization of the argumentation from both parents and professionals, while quantitative methods provide an overview and demonstrate patterns.

The qualitative studies consist of a content analysis of 33 randomly chosen district court case files, including 33 summons applications, 28 statements of defence from parents, 26 rapid information inquiries (*snabbupplysningar*), and 4 social services (*socialtjänsten*) family-law unit custody investigations (*vårdnadsutredning*). The documents represent the authorities' views on the conflict. To include the parents' view, the content analyses were supplemented with in-depth interviews from 48 randomly chosen parents who were involved in a high-level custody dispute.[7]

To obtain background information regarding parents in custody disputes and to search for patterns, a quantitative content analysis was conducted on 413 summons applications and 33 district court acts. To include parents' perspectives, the content analysis was supplemented with a survey to which 202 parents responded. Participating parents were parties in ongoing, high-level custody disputes in a representative sample of district courts.[8] A drop-out analysis revealed that primarily middle-class parents of Swedish origin participated in the survey.

The results from the quantitative studies were processed statistically, while the results from the qualitative studies were processed hermeneutically. The results were also compared with applicable law to determine the extent to which legislation fulfils children's best interests in custody

---

[6] Granted by the Swedish research council.

[7] Cf Göran Bergström and Kristian Boréus, *Textens mening och makt: metodbok i samhällsvetenskaplig text- och diskursanalys* (2nd edn, Studentlitteratur 2005).

[8] Cf Peter Esaiasson, *Metodpraktikan: konsten att studera samhälle, individ och marknad* (3rd edn, Norstedts Juridik 2007).

disputes from a parental perspective. Traditional legal dogmatic method, legislative history, and case law were used to explore applicable law. The results of the comparison were analysed using such theoretical concepts as: low- and high-level conflict, conflicts of interest and value, norms, class, gender, health, and violence.

4.5 Custody Disputes—A Conflict of Interest and Values, or Passivity and Activity?

Under Swedish law, custody disputes are brought before the district court. Family law provides that the court has an obligation to align its judgement with the best interests of the child. Therefore, the court can go beyond the claims of the parties and investigate the case more extensively than in other civil cases. In practice, the investigation is normally carried out by the social services, which assist the court by conducting investigations upon request.

Legislation on courts' handling of conflicts originates in resolving conflicts of interest between parties. However, most of these cases include elements of both conflicting interests and conflicting values.[9] A conflict of values originates from differing opinions about facts and values. Usually, it is difficult for one of the parties to impose a change of opinion on the other; therefore, a third party—such as a court—must decide how to solve value-based conflicts.[10] Conflict of interest is about opposing demands on a scarce resource, and is usually resolved through mediation and compromise because neither of the parties is willing to risk a total loss.[11] Custody disputes are categorized as a conflict of interest when the parents disagree on matters relating to time with, care of, and information about the child, and as a conflict of values when parents disagree on what is best for their child and question the other party's parenting ability.

---

[9] Vilhelm Aubert, *Continuity and Development in Law and Society* (Norwegian University Press 1989) 95–96.

[10] Annika Rejmer, 'Vårdnadstvist—en kontraproduktiv genusbias?' in Mattias Dahlberg (eds), *Genuskritiska frågor inom juridiken* (Iustus 2018) 89.

[11] Aubert (n 9) 90–104.

The empirical results show that it is not sufficient to simply analyse custody disputes as a conflict of interest and values. Half of the examined summons' applications can be characterized as low-level conflicts.[12] These situations usually arise when one parent is passive in exercising joint custody, which makes it legally impossible for the other parent to change residence with the child, obtain a passport for the child, choose schools, and meet the child's health and medical care needs.[13] In these conflicts, sole custody is the only solution for creating a functioning everyday life for the child. Low-level custody disputes are unlikely to increase the negative impact on the child and are usually handled as administrative cases by the court.

The remaining cases involve high-level conflict. The parties actively pursue the matter and obtain support from legal representation, and the suit often results in appeals and repeated litigation; this has a negative impact on the child. High-level custody disputes apply predominantly to underlying, value-based conflicts about parties' ability to parent or cooperate due to drug problems, mental disorders, or domestic violence.[14]

To sum up, half of all custody disputes are actively pursued and can be characterized as long-lasting, high-level conflicts about values, and thus increase the probability of a negative impact on parties' children.[15]

4.6 Parents in High-Level Custody Disputes

Concepts such as norms and gender can be used to analyse the behaviour and actions of parents engaged in high-level conflicts on custody disputes rooted in their disagreement about values. When considering gender,

[12] n = 413 summons applications.

[13] The Swedish Children and Parent Code [Föräldrabalken] (1949:381) Chapter 6 Section 11.

[14] Annika Rejmer, *Vårdnadstvist: en rättssociologisk studie av tingsrätts funktion vid handläggning av vårdnadskonflikter med utgångspunkt från barnets bästa* [Custody Disputes: A socio-legal study of the role of district courts in the handling of custody disputes with the child's best interest as a base] (Department of Sociology, Lund University 2003); Ann-Sofie Bergman and Annika Rejmer, 'Parents in Child Custody Disputes: Why are they Disputing?' (2017) 14(1) *Journal of Child Custody 134–150*.

[15] Bergman and Rejmer (n 14).

it is interesting to note that the Swedish political definition of gender equality is 60/40%.[16] The concept of gender relates to social-behavioural expectations placed on mothers and fathers and is created by day-to-day interplay and practice; it is constantly reproduced and creates social norms regarding acceptable characteristics, behaviours, and actions of mothers and fathers.[17] Formal norms are created in a politically authoritative order. Social and legal norms do not necessarily correspond to each other but can exist side-by-side in society.[18]

The results of conducted empirical studies show that mothers (60%) are more often the initiators of court proceedings in high-level custody disputes. They sue for sole custody, residence, and a limitation of visitation for fathers. Fathers (40%) sue for sole custody, joint custody, residence, and extended visitation. Based on the claims studied here, it seems that mothers seek to minimize fathers' contact with and influence over joint children, while fathers seek to maintain contact and involvement with joint children. Differences in legal and social norms can explain the results; only 6% of mothers and 1% of fathers obtain sole custody.[19] Joint custody is assumed to be in the best interests of the child and has become the legal and social norm.[20] The child's residence and visitation, however, is not gender-equal. For instance, 60% of children with separated parents live full-time or mostly with their mothers, and only 10% live with their fathers, while 30% have an alternate residence.[21]

[16] Government Bill 1978/79:175 med förslag till lag om jämställdhet mellan kvinnor och män i arbetslivet, m.m. [with a proposal for a law on equality between women and men in worklife].

[17] Raewyn Connell, *Gender and Power Society, the Person and Sexual Politics* (Polity Press 1987); Anthony Giddens and Karen Birdsall, *Sociologi* (3rd edn, Studentlitteratur 2003); Annika Rejmer, Vårdnadstvist—en kontraproduktiv genusbias? in Dahlberg M [ed], *Genuskritiska frågor inom juridiken* (Iustus 2018).

[18] Hans Hydén, *Sociology of Law as the science Norm* (1st edn, Routledge 2022) 91–128.

[19] Court Statistics, Official Statistics of Sweden 2020 (n 3).

[20] Governmental Bill 2020/21:150 Ett stärkt barnrättsperspektiv i vårdnadstvister [A Strengthened Child Rights Perspective in Custody Disputes] 70.

[21] Statistics Sweden 2018, 'När tre av tio barn bor växelvis' [When Nearly Three out of Ten Children have Shared Residence] https://www.scb.se/hitta-statistik/statistik-efter-amne/levnadsforhallanden/levnadsforhallanden/undersokningarna-av-levnadsforhallanden-ulf-silc/pong/statistiknyhet/barns-boende-2016-2017/ accessed 9 May 2023.

The social norm for female caregivers still dictates the organization of the divided family.[22]

The empirical studies of court case files show that high-level custody disputes are also a matter of class, when the concept of class is defined in terms of education and income.[23] Viewed from this perspective, most of the parents involved in custody disputes are working-class.[24] The results indicate that these parents usually have complex, problematic life conditions rooted in immigration and assimilation, unemployment, health problems, abuse,[25] and violence that increase the socio-economic vulnerability of the family.[26]

It is interesting to note, however, that one-third of Swedish parents in high-level custody conflicts are middle-class.[27] Unlike working-class parents, they are often eager to participate in interview studies and surveys; therefore, knowledge about middle-class parents in custody disputes is in-depth and extensive. Among these parents, there is an over-representation of adult children of divorce. A majority of parents have experience of growing up with separated parents in conflict and sporadic or no contact with the non-resident or non-custodial parent.[28] The results indicate that half of the middle-class parents in high-level custody disputes repeat their own parents' patterns of dealing with conflicts—and that to some extent—custody disputes are a socialized behaviour.

From a health perspective (defined as a lack of perceived ill health), most middle-class parents in a high-level conflict state in interviews

[22] Thomas Johansson, 'Part-time Fatherhood —Everyday Life, Masculinity and Marginalization' in Margareta Bäck-Wiklund and Thomas Johansson (eds), *The Network Family* (2nd ed, Natur & Kultur 2012), Chapter 4; Rejmer (n 17).

[23] To define class, Erikson's, Goldthorpes and Portocareros classification includes white-collar/middle-class and working class, 2014. Maria Eriksson, John H Goldthorpe and Lucienne Portocarero, 'Classification (EGP)' in Alex C Michalos (ed), *Encyclopedia of Quality of Life and Wellbeing Research* (Springer 2014).

[24] Maria Eriksson, John H Goldthorpe and Lucienne Portocarero, *Intergenerational class mobility and the convergence thesis: England, France and Sweden* (Swedish institute for social research 1983).

[25] n = 33 30% of the parents have problems with addiction.

[26] n = 33 acts from six district courts in the Stockholm area.

[27] n = 413 lawsuits from six district courts in the Stockholm area.

[28] n = 202 survey.

and surveys that they are dealing with additional life crises in connection with the custody dispute. They have experienced reorganization at work, unemployment, accidents, personal health issues, or the illness or death of relatives.[29] The results also show that almost all middle-class parents experience increased levels of stress due to the conflict, often accompanied by depression, anxiety, and sleep disorders.[30]

Furthermore, a majority state they suffer from diagnosed illnesses and disabilities. In addition to somatic diagnoses, 14% of mothers state that they have been diagnosed with mental health problems, while the corresponding proportion among fathers is 5%. Moreover, 10% of parents state that they suffer from a disability that affects their everyday life.[31] Additionally, 5% of the parents state they have a neuropsychiatric diagnosis, which is an overrepresentation compared with the occurrence in the adult Swedish population (3%).[32] The result likely underestimates the situation; 16% of the parents state that their children have a neuropsychiatric diagnosis, which is typically a hereditary disability.[33] According to the survey and interview study, few of the middle-class parents consider themselves as having problems with addiction.

The Istanbul Convention—Action against violence against women and domestic violence[34] provides a definition of violence that covers acts of physical, sexual, psychological, and economic violence between family members. Based on that definition, all investigated high-level custody

---

[29] Rejmer (n 14) 203–213.

[30] n = 202 survey, sleep disorder= 40%.

[31] n = 202 survey.

[32] Swedish National Board of Health and Welfare 2019, 'Konsekvenser för vuxna med diagnosen adhd kartläggning och analys' [Consequences for Adults Diagnosed with ADHD Mapping and Analysis] https://www.socialstyrelsen.se/globalassets/sharepoint-dokument/artikelkatalog/ovrigt/2019-6-21.pdf accessed 9 May 2023.

[33] Swedish National Board of Health and Welfare 2019, 'Behov av nationella kunskapsstöd inom området neuropsykiatriska funktionsnedsättningar' [Need for National Knowledge Support in the Field of Neuropsychiatric Impairments].

https://www.socialstyrelsen.se/globalassets/sharepoint-dokument/artikelkatalog/ovrigt/2019-6-25.pdf accessed 9 May 2023.

[34] Council of Europe, Istanbul Convention Action Against Violence Against Women and Domestic Violence.

disputes involve some kind of violence.[35] Mothers[36] were primarily subjected to physical violence, while fathers were subjected to psychological violence, and their children were exposed to a long-lasting parental conflict with a negative impact for life.[37]

To sum up, the results indicate that the underlying causes of high-level conflicts are—to some extent—class-related. Working-class parents are turning to the courts more often than middle-class families, due to a complex life situation and socio-economic vulnerability, while middle-class parents seem to struggle with the socialized behaviour of interparental conflict, life crises, and ill health.

4.7 Custody Dispute—A Question of Paradigm?

The social phenomenon of custody disputes emerged in the latter half of the 1970s as an effect of Sweden's political goal of gender equality, and several political measures were taken in this regard. It became much easier for women to earn wages and become self-sufficient. An expansion of the welfare state created jobs for women. The government also reformed legislation on child custody and visitation, with gender-neutral provisions that increased opportunities to initiate custody disputes in court. Furthermore, new provisions were introduced to enable joint custody for divorced parents. The idea was that fathers would take their share

---

[35] n = 202 survey, n = 33 act study, n = 48 interview study.

[36] n = 202 60% of mothers and 30% of fathers in high-level disputes experience physical violence, while 76% of fathers and 30% of mothers experience psychological violence.

[37] Johan B Kelly and Robert E Emery, 'Children's Adjustment Following divorce: Risk and Resilience Perspectives' (2003) 52(4) *National Council on Family Relations* 352–362; Kim Leon, 'Risk and Protective Factors in Young Children's Adjustment to Parental Divorce: A Review of Research' (2003) 52(3) *National Council on Family Relations* 258–270; Janet Johnston, Vivienne Roseby, and Kathryn Kuehnle, *In the Name of the Child—A Developmental Approach to Understanding and Helping Children of conflicted and Violent Divorce* (Springer 2009); James W Stewart, 'Symptoms of Emotional Damage to Children of High-conflict Divorce' in James W Stewart (eds), *The Child Custody Book: How to Protect your Children and Win your Case* (Impact Publisher 2000).

of parental responsibility, thus allowing mothers to work and be self-sufficient, but the legislation did not address any specific concerns about parenting ability.[38]

Sweden's ratification of the Convention on the Rights of the Child (CRC) contributed to a shift in the family-policy paradigm from an objective of increased gender equality to realizing children's rights and best interests. This paradigm shift influenced several legislative reforms. In 1991, the provisions of the Social Services Act were reformed, assigning social services an explicit responsibility to follow up those cases where children were exposed to custody disputes.[39] Nevertheless, an evaluation by the National Board of Health and Welfare shows that Swedish social services do not conduct follow-ups. One reason could be, that according to the law, guardians must consent to a follow-up.[40] In 1993, the court was obliged to take into account the risk of children being abused, illegally abducted or detained, or otherwise harmed, when considering the best interests of the child in custody disputes.[41] The provision is designed to identify parents who pose a risk to their child. Evaluations show that risk assessments carried out, both by the social services family-law units and the district courts, vary in content due to different methods and definitions of risk. The social services' starting point is a social-science perspective, while the court assesses the matter from a legal perspective.

In 1998, the legislator stated that the best interests of the child should be paramount in determining all matters of custody, residence, and visitation, and that joint custody was to be considered the best solution for children—irrespective of the parents' relationship. The reform contributed to a redefinition of a custody dispute, shifting it from a conflict of interest to a conflict of values.[42] The court's main task was now changed to determining which parent could serve the child's best interests.

---

[38] Rejmer (n 10).

[39] Swedish Government Bill 1990/91:8 om vårdnad och umgänge [on Custody and Contact].

[40] Swedish Government Official Reports 2017:6 (n 5) 294.

[41] To harmonize with Article 11 and 19, CRC.

[42] Rejmer (n 14) 203–213.

The latest legal reform of the courts assessment of the child's best interests in custody disputes dates from 2020, when the CRC was incorporated into Swedish law.[43] The best interests of the child shall be a guide in accordance with the provisions of both the Children and Parent Code and the CRC, but these instruments are not fully harmonized. According to the Children and Parent Code, authorities must provide for the best interests of the child, while Article 3 CRC stipulates a primary consideration and Article 18 CRC provides that parents as well as authorities are obliged to ensure the best interests of the child.[44]

In summary, despite Sweden's ratification of the CRC, the paradigm shift in Swedish legislation has not yet been completed. Implementation of the CRC deficiencies consist of material but foremost procedural provisions. There seems to be a lack of holistic perspective with its handling; a validation of the legislation to secure a coherent normative system that can ensure the best interests of the child in custody disputes.[45]

4.8 Procedural Law—An Overlooked Legal Aspect

Since Sweden ratified the CRC, legislative work has focused on adapting the substantive provisions of the law, while the procedural provisions have been overlooked.

The handling of custody disputes in court follows Swedish civil-law procedure.[46] The district court's primary task is to get parents to agree, through mediation, on the child's best interests and ratify the agreement in a judgement—with 65% of custody disputes resolved in agreement.[47]

---

43 Swedish Government Bill 2017/18:186 Inkorporering av FN:s konvention om barnets rättigheter [Incorporation of the UN Convention on the Rights of the Child].

44 Swedish Government Official Reports 2020:63 Barnkonventionen och svensk rätt [The Convention on the Rights of the Child and Swedish law].

45 Rejmer (n 10).

46 Code of Judicial Procedure [Rättegångsbalken] (1942:740) Chapter 42.

47 Swedish Government Official Reports 2017:6 (n 5) 172.

The documentation that the courts use to determine the best interests of the child consists of information from the social services.

If it is not possible to achieve an agreement, the district court must ensure that the custody case is sufficiently investigated[48] and that a judgement is based on what is best for the child. At the request of the district court, the social services' family-law unit contributes documentation for assessing the child's best interest. If necessary, the district court can request a rapid information inquiry to make interim decisions or initiate a custody investigation.[49]

To fulfil its investigative obligation, the social services' family-law unit has the legal support to take on investigative measures. Investigators can search three different registries: authority registries, records of suspected offenders, and criminal records. Personal information and information on measures taken are included when parents or their new partners are registered in the authorities' registries. If parents or their new partners appear in the criminal registry, the family court can obtain information about whether the parents or their partners are suspected of a crime and if they have committed crime abroad.[50] In addition, the criminal registry offers investigators information about whether the parents or their partners appear in judgements, decisions, and criminal injunctions, and whether they have been given compulsory care for substance abuse (and therefore have not been subject to criminal prosecution). The registry also contains information about whether the parents are subject to a restraining order.[51] The registries are kept for statistical purposes and do not address a child's rights or best interests, or adults' parenting skills; therefore, the information must be interpreted and placed in the context of custody disputes.

Furthermore, since 1 July 2021, the social services' family-law unit has the right to speak with children without guardians' consent.[52] It is still questionable if the provisions of the Children and Parent Code harmonize with Article 12 CRC, which provides the right of children

[48] Children and Parent Code Chapter 6 Section 19 para. 1.

[49] Children and Parent Code Chapter 6 Section 19 para. 1 and Section 20 paras. 1 and 2.

[50] On records of suspected offenders [Lag om misstankeregister] (1998:621) Sect. 4.3.

[51] Act on Criminal Record [Lag om belastningsregister] (1998:620) Section 4.3.

[52] Government Bill 2020/21:150 (n 20).

to be heard in all matters affecting them. Investigators at the family-law unit decide on the individual child's right to be heard, not the parents. According to the Children and Parent Code, the child does not yet have an independent right to receive information or to be heard in custody disputes.

Parents decide which investigative measures the family-law unit may take; for example, parents must consent to investigative interviews and home visits. The parents' consent is also required in the selection of reference persons with a professional relation to the child, such as teachers, and to allow investigators access to the child's and parents' medical records. Any non-parent guardian in the matter must also consent to allow investigators access to the child's medical records. Thus, as custodians, parents control what information the family-law unit can see and thereby the extent to which value-based conflicts can be investigated. At the same time, the proceedings[53] lack incentives for parents to be open about their problems. Such information could be used against them during the trial, and this aspect is characterized by a risk perspective[54] rather than a supportive service perspective as stipulated in Article 18 CRC.

4.9 Can the Court Fulfil the Best Interests of the Child in High-Level Custody Disputes?

The results of empirical studies show that custody disputes are not homogeneous in character. A better understanding of parental conflicts requires a categorization into low- and high-level conflicts. Low-level conflict disputes are unlikely to have further negative impact on children, but high-level conflict disputes are lengthy and harmful to children and can be categorized as either a conflict of interest or conflict of values.

Conflicts of interest usually involve issues of visitation, child support, and information about the child, and are often mediated and resolved

53 Code of Judicial Procedure Chapter 42.

54 Children and Parent Code Chapter 6 Section 4.2a.

through compromise. Conflicts of values concerning parenting skills are more difficult to resolve; this can be explained by parents' refusal to consent to a reasonable investigation of value-based conflicts or insufficient investigation of accusations regarding the other parent's personal problems or lack of parenting ability.

Can Swedish legislation satisfy children's best interests in custody disputes? The dogmatic investigation of applicable law shows that children's rights can be fulfilled through the district courts' application of the CRC, which is also Swedish law. On the other hand, the Children and Parent Code—a law that specifically regulates custody, residence, and visitation—should be reformed to harmonize with CRC.

The empirical results show that current provisions do not allow sufficient investigation of the target group's need for support. They also show that the handling of these disputes must be developed to meet the needs of the target group. Mediation, agreements, and judgements cannot eliminate underlying problems such as poverty, ill health, abuse, violence, or parents' disabilities.

The results indicate that custody disputes are a complex phenomenon, requiring inter-professional management to meet parents' specific needs, so they can in turn fulfil their children's best interests. Current legislation does not allow inter-professional handling of custody disputes; therefore, the law should be reformed, primarily in the context of custody disputes, to ensure children's best interests.

References

Aubert V, *Continuity and Development in Law and Society* (Norwegian University Press 1989).

Bergman A-S and Rejmer A, 'Parents in Child Custody Disputes: Why are they Disputing?' (2017) 14(2–3) *Journal of Child Custody* 134.

Bergström G and Boréus K, *Textens mening och makt: metodbok i samhällsvetenskaplig text- och diskursanalys* (2nd edn Studentlitteratur 2005).

Connell R, *Gender and Power: Society, the Person and Sexual Politics* (Polity Press 1987).

Erikson R, Portocarero L and Goldthorpe J, *Intergenerational Class Mobility and the Convergence Thesis: England, France and Sweden*, Swedish institute for social research (Stockholm 1983).

Erikson R, Goldthorpe J and Portocarero L, 'Classification (EGP)' in Michalos A C (ed), *Encyclopedia of Quality of Life and Wellbeing Research* (Springer 2014).

Esaiasson P, *Metodpraktikan: konsten att studera samhälle, individ och marknad* (3rd edn, Norstedts Juridik 2007).

Giddens A and Birdsall K, *Sociologi* (Studentlitteratur 2003).

Hydén H, *Sociology of Law as the Science of Norms* (1st edn, Routledge 2021).

Johansson T, 'Part-time Fatherhood—Everyday Life, Masculinity and Marginalization' in Bäck-Wiklund M and Johansson T (eds), *The Network Family* (Natur & Kultur 2012)

Johnston J, Roseby V and Kuehnle K, *In the Name of the Child—A Developmental Approach to Understanding and Helping Children of conflicted and Violent Divorce* (Springer 2009).

Kelly J and Emery R, 'Children's Adjustment Following Divorce: Risk and Resilience Perspectives' (2003) 52(4) *National Council on Family Relations* 352.

Leon K, 'Risk and Protective Factors in Young Children's Adjustment to Parental Divorce: A Review of the Research' (2003) 52(3) *National Council on Family Relations* 258.

Official statistics of Sweden Court statistics 2020 (domstol.se) accessed 16 May 2023.

Official statistics of Sweden Court statistics 2021—Official statistics of Sweden, available at www.domstol.se accessed 16 May 2023.

Rejmer A, *Vårdnadstvister: en rättssociologisk studie av tingsrätts funktion vid handläggning av vårdnadskonflikter med utgångspunkt från barnets bästa* (Lund University, Department of Sociology 2003).

Rejmer A, Vårdnadstvist—en kontraproduktiv genusbias? in Dahlberg M [ed], *Genuskritiska frågor inom juridiken* (Iustus 2018).

Rejmer A, 'Kan rättssociologi bidra till att vidareutveckla rättsdogmatiken?' in Banakar R, Dahlstrand K, and Ryberg-Welander L (eds), *Festskrift till Håkan Hydén* (Juristförlaget i Lund 2018).

Statistics Sweden *Nära tre av tio barn bor växelvis* (2018) https://www.scb.se/hitta-statistik/statistik-efter-amne/levnadsforhallanden/levnadsforhallanden/undersokningarna-av-levnadsforhallanden-ulf-silc/pong/statistiknyhet/barns-boende-2016-2017/ accessed 4 September 2023.

Statistics Sweden *Children and their Families* (2022) https://www.scb.se/en/finding-statistics/statistics-by-subject-area/living-conditions/living-conditions/children-and-their-families/ accessed 10 May 2023.
Stewart J W, 'Symptoms of Emotional Damage to Children of High-conflict Divorce' in Stewart J W (ed) *The Child Custody Book: How to Protect your Children and Win your Case* (Impact Publisher 2000).
Swedish National Board of Health and Welfare *Konsekvenser för vuxna med diagnosen adhd* (2019) https://www.socialstyrelsen.se/globalassets/sharepoint-dokument/artikelkatalog/ovrigt/2019–6–21.pdf accessed 10 May 2023.
Swedish National Board of Health and Welfare *Behov av nationella kunskapsstöd inom området neuropsykiatriska funktionsnedsättningar* (2019). https://www.socialstyrelsen.se/globalassets/sharepoint-dokument/artikelkatalog/ovrigt/2019-6-25.pdf accessed 10 May 2023.
Swedish National Council for Crime Prevention Official statistics of Sweden Court statistics. https://bra.se/download/18.12305534131e173a7f180001909/1371914735698/2002_15_domstolsstatistik_2001.pdf accessed 9 May 2023.
Swedish Government Bill 1978/79: 175 med förslag till lag om jämställdhet mellan kvinnor och män i arbetslivet m.m.
Swedish Government Bill 1990/91:8 Om vårdnad och umgänge.
Swedish Government Bill 2017/18:186 Inkorporering av FN:s konvention om barnets rättigheter.
Swedish Government Bill 2020/21: 150 Ett stärkt barnrättsperspektiv i vårdnadstvister
Swedish Government Official Reports 2017:6 Se barnet!
Swedish Government Official Reports 2020:63 Barnkonventionen och svensk rätt.

5

Children's Participation and Perspectives in Family Disputes

Maria Eriksson

5.1 Introduction

Every year in Sweden, over 60,000 children experience parental separation or divorce.[1] That number is equivalent to almost 4% of the children who were living with both of their parents at the beginning of the year. It has also become more common in recent years that the child's parents have never lived together.[2] Currently, approximately 25% of children in Sweden have parents who live apart. In 2020, 21,000 children had parents that went through cooperation talks (*samarbetssamtal*)—a form of mediation—offered by local authority social services (*socialtjänsten*), to resolve conflicts regarding their children. Almost 7,000 children

[1] Statistics Sweden 2021 (Child and Family Statistics 2021) www.scb.se accessed 6 February 2023.

[2] Statistics Sweden 2013, 'Barn, föräldrar och separationer: Utvecklingen under 2000-talet' [Children, Parents and Separations Trends of the 21st Century], Demographic Reports 2013:1.

M. Eriksson (✉)
Marie Cederschiöld University, Stockholm, Sweden

A. Kaldal et al. (eds.), *Children in Custody Disputes*,
https://doi.org/10.1007/978-3-031-46301-3_5

were subject to a social services investigation in a legal dispute regarding custody, residence, or visitation.[3] According to a previous estimate by the Swedish National Board of Health and Welfare (*Socialstyrelsen*), about 14% of children who experience parental separation become the subject of a legal dispute regarding custody, residence, or visitation.[4]

What do we know about the situation of children involved in such processes? How can agency interventions into the lives of children involved in family disputes become as child-centred and child-friendly as possible? This chapter is divided in two parts, focusing on child health matters in family disputes, and on children's participation and perspectives, respectively. The first part draws on the results from a study of multidisciplinary 'Collaboration Teams' developed to assist families in conflictual separations, and the results from a national evaluation study of children exposed to violence against their mothers. In this first part, the need for dissolving boundaries between family-law proceedings and child-welfare/child protection policy and practice is demonstrated. The second part of the chapter draws on previous academic debates on approaches to vulnerable children, and a study of children's views on child participation in family-law proceedings. A 'dual approach' to children in difficult life situations is outlined, wherein children are regarded as both in need of adult protection and care, and as competent actors with rights to participation. It is argued that it is vital to connect risk assessments and ways of communicating with children to the issue of children's participation. Implications for policy and practice are discussed throughout and in a concluding section.

---

[3] Family Law and Parental Support Authority 2021, Statistics on Family Law 2020, www.mfof.se accessed 29 September 2021.

[4] National Board of Health and Welfare 2011, *Familjerätten och barnet i vårdnadstvister: uppföljning av hur 2006 års vårdnadsreform slagit igenom i socialtjänstens arbete* [Social Services and Child in Custody Disputes: A Follow-up of the Effects of the 2006 Reform of the Children and Parents Code] 2011. Statistics from 2021 indicate the number of children who have become the subject of a legal dispute in more recent years; according to these statistics, 18% (12,612 children) of 66,000 experiencing parental separation were included in retrieval of information requests by the court in 2021, Family Law and Parental Support Authority 2021, Statistics on Family Law 2020, www.mfof.se and Statistics Sweden 2021, Child and family statistics 2021, www.scb.se both accessed 6 February 2023.

5.2 Children's Health Matters in Family Disputes

Like many other Western countries, Swedish policy and law assume shared parenting and a high degree of parental cooperation after separation or divorce. Since the 1970s, a string of changes to both family law (for example, the Swedish Children and Parent Code) and welfare law (like the Social Services Act) have aimed to reduce conflict between parents and encourage out-of-court agreements regarding visitation, custody, and children's residence. At the time of writing, it is possible for parents to use the municipal social services to make formal agreements with the same legal status as a court order, and the social services are obliged to offer cooperation talks—the Swedish version of mediation—to non-cohabiting parents who want help to resolve conflicts regarding their children.[5] However, some parents still end up in court over disputes about visitation, custody, or residence. Previous research shows that conflicts between parents can have detrimental effects on children's health and wellbeing.[6] However, not much is known about what agencies dealing with family disputes can do to secure the health and wellbeing of the children they encounter. The first step here is to explore the level of health issues and other problems among children in contact with such agencies.

[5] On this notion, see further Anna Nylund, 'Nordic Family Mediation: Towards a System of Differentiated Services?' in Anna Kaldal, Agnes Hellner and Titti Mattsson (eds), *Children in Custody Disputes: Matching Legal Proceedings to Problems* (Palgrave 2023) and Anna Singer, 'Out-of-court Custody Dispute Resolution in Sweden—A Journey without destination' in Anna Kaldal, Agnes Hellner and Titti Mattsson (eds), *Children in Custody Disputes: Matching Legal Proceedings to Problems* (Palgrave 2023).

[6] Brian D'Onofrio and Robert Emery, 'Parental Divorce or Separation and Children's Mental Health' (2019) 18(1) *World Psychiatry* 100–101. See also Anna Norlén, 'Children's Health Matters in Custody Conflicts—What Do We Know?' in Anna Kaldal, Agnes Hellner and Titti Mattsson(eds), *Children in Custody Disputes: Matching Legal Proceedings to Problems* (Palgrave 2023).

5.2.1 Problems Displayed by Children Involved With Early Intervention and Prevention Agencies

To improve services and prevent legal disputes between parents, the Swedish Ministry of Social Affairs tasked the Children's Welfare Foundation Sweden to discover whether a coordinated multidisciplinary 'Collaboration Team' could provide meaningful assistance to families in conflictual separations.[7] Between 2014 and 2017, collaboration teams, designed to prevent or mitigate conflicts between parents and promote effective parental cooperation were formed in four medium-sized municipalities and one city in Sweden. The development work was evaluated by two research teams: one focusing on the collaboration process,[8] and the other focusing on (a) the wellbeing of children and parents; (b) the experiences of children and parents in their contacts with the collaboration teams; and (c) the support that families received or were offered. The project also examined data about families in contact with the teams.[9]

Basic socio-economic data was gathered about 115 children and 118 parents from 69 families in contact with the teams, and about 454 children in a reference group, whose parents were seeking help through mediation from the respective local authority. Data about the children and parents in contact with the collaboration teams was also gathered through various other measures, including a self-assessment questionnaire from the structured risk detection model 'Family law detection

7 Maria Eriksson and Marianne Gabrielsson, 'Supporting Children and Parents in Sweden through Collaboration Teams' (2019) 57(3) *Family Court Review* 362–367.

8 Berth Danermark and Ulrika Englund 'Utvärdering av Allmänna Barnhusetsocialt Samverkansteam – stöd till barn med föräldrar i konflikt' [Evaluation of the Children's Welfare Foundation's Project Collaboration Team – Support for Children with Parents in Conflict] in *Slutrapport Samverkansteam – för stöd till barn och föräldrar i samband med separation* [Final Report Collaboration Team – for Support to Children and Parents in the Context of Separation] Children's Welfare Foundation Sweden (2018) 145–166; Berth Danermark and Ulrika Englund 'Samverkan – förutsättningar och utfall – en kompletterande och avslutande analys' [Collaboration – Prerequisites and Outcomes – A Complementary and Final Analysis] in *Final Report Collaboration Team – for Support to Children and Parents in the Context of Separation*, Children's Welfare Foundation Sweden] (2018) 36–51.

9 Maria Eriksson, Linnea Bruno, and Marie-Louise Klingstedt, 'Samverksansteam: Barns och föräldrars situation och upplevelser' [Co-operation teams: Children' and Parents' Situation and Experiences] in *Final report. Collaboration Team – to Support Children and Parents in the Context of Separation*, Children's Welfare Foundation Sweden (2018); Eriksson and Gabrielsson (n 7).

of overall risk screen' (FL-DOORS).[10] This dataset contains 101 questionnaire responses from 58 mothers and 43 fathers. This screening and assessment tool was used to assess the children's and parents' situation and their need for support or protection. The tool, which focuses on risks from a broad perspective—including the risk of the child's development being damaged by everything from a lack of care to a risk of abduction, violence, suicide, and murder-suicide—is divided into 10 target areas based on research knowledge about the factors that may pose risks for families who are undergoing separation. In their first contact with the teams, parents reported signs of stress and worry displayed by their children during the previous six months (Tables 5.1 and 5.2).

Table 5.1 The number of indications of stress and worry displayed by children under six years during the last six months, reported by mothers and fathers (percent)

	Mother	Father
No problems	20	50
1 problem	27	22
2–3 problems	33	28
Total (*n*)	30	18

Table 5.2 The number of indications of stress and worry displayed by children seven years and older during the last six months, reported by mothers and fathers (percent)

	Mother	Father
No problems	7	24
1 problem	10	18
2–3 problems	32	36
4–5 problems	42	21
Missing (%)	*10*	*0*
Total (*n*)	41	33

[10] Jennifer E McIntosh, Yvonne Well, and Jamie Lee '*The FL-DOORS Detection of Overall Risk Screen Framework*', Attorney-General's Department (2012), Canberra, Australia 2012; Jennifer E McIntosh, Yvonne Well, and Jamie Lee, *The Family Law FL-DOORS Handbook*, Attorney General's Department (2012), Canberra, Australia 2012; Jennifer E McIntosh, Yvonne Well, and Jamie Lee 'Development and validation of the Family Law DOORS' in (2016) 28(11) *Psychological Assessment* 1516–1522.

A systemic difference between mothers and fathers was revealed: mothers tended to report indications of child stress and worry more than the fathers.

Data about the health of children and parents coming to the collaboration teams was also gathered from parents and children aged 11 and older through the Strengths and Difficulties Questionnaire (SDQ).[11] This was done at first contact with the teams, and again after approximately four months, and once more after 12 months. The assessment of children's strengths and difficulties indicated that some children had problems at first contact, for example, with emotional problems, behavioural problems, hyperactivity, or problems in peer relationships. This was especially the case for the group of children aged 4–17 years, in which about 40% of the children were reported as having problems (Table 5.3). In addition, in the SDQ, mothers tended to report more problems regarding the child than did fathers.

The follow-up after four months indicated that children's health and wellbeing had tended to improve, but the amount of positive change tended to be small, and for some children, the problems remained at the same level or increased during the period.[12] This pattern of limited improvement can also be interpreted in respect of the information about the services offered by the collaboration teams. In terms of interventions, the most common response was no intervention aimed directly at the child, and if the child did receive an intervention of some kind, the most common was one or two individual sessions. There was no clear link

Table 5.3 Children 4–17 years (n = 86), strengths and difficulties according to parents* at first contact with the team (*fathers: n = 20, mothers: n = 66)

	Number	Percent
Normal or slightly raised level of difficulties	51	59
High level in one area	13	15
Very high level in one area	5	6
Multiple areas with high or very high levels of difficulties	17	20
Total (n)	86	100

[11] See www.sdqinfo.com accessed 18 May 2017.

[12] Eriksson, Bruno and Klingstedt (n 9).

between the level of problems reported at first contact and the type or extent of intervention.

In summary, a significant proportion of children in contact with services aimed at early intervention and prevention of disputes displayed problems regarding health and wellbeing to such an extent that a need for more extensive interventions by social services and/or health services was indicated.

5.2.2 Problems Displayed by Children Involved With 'Cooperation' and Investigation Agencies

Another set of empirical results indicating a need to consider children's health and wellbeing when their parents are engaged in a family-law dispute, comes from a national evaluation study of services for children exposed to violence against their mother.[13] In this study, children who had been exposed to intimate partner violence (IPV) and who had received services aimed at this target group (n = 185) were compared to children receiving 'standard' services within child welfare and child psychiatry ($n = 75$) after exposure to IPV, and to violence-exposed children in contact with a social services family-law unit (*socialtjänstens familjerättsenhet*) (n = 55). In the family-law group, the child's parents had participated in cooperation talks or an investigation by the social services family-law unit into the child's situation that was mandated by the court in a legal dispute between the parents.[14]

The children were followed for 12 months after inclusion in the study, and some important differences were seen between the family-law services study group and the other children in the study. Mothers in the social services family-law unit study group reported ongoing violence

[13] Anders Broberg, Linnéa Almqvist, Ulf Axberg, Kjerstin Almqvist, Åsa K Cater and Maria Eriksson, *Stöd till barn som upplevt våld mot mamma. Resultat från en nationell utvärdering* [Support to Children Who Have Experienced Violence Against their Mothers. Results from a National Evaluation Study] (University of Gothenburg, Department of Psychology 2011).

[14] As mentioned, 'cooperation talks' is a Swedish version of mediation. On this notion, see further Anna Singer, 'Out-of-court custody dispute resolution in Sweden—A Journey without destination' in Anna Kaldal, Agnes Hellner and Titti Mattsson(eds) *Children in Custody Disputes: Matching Legal Proceedings to Problems* (Palgrave 2023).

(76% of the mothers in this group) to a higher degree than mothers in the other groups. This itself is a cause for concern, and even more so with the fact that the children in the social services family-law unit group tended to be younger than those in the other groups. It is also noteworthy that children in the social services family-law unit study group were demonstrating clinical symptoms at the same level as children in contact with other services, including social services child-welfare units (*socialtjänstens enhet för social barnavård*) and child psychiatry.[15] In the latter groups, children could be expected to display clinical levels of symptoms to a higher degree than within, for example, the social services family-law unit group, but that was not the case in this data set. Furthermore, unlike children in the other groups, children in the social services family-law unit study group did not improve over time (defined as a reduction in symptoms). Instead, their health and wellbeing tended to deteriorate (that is, symptoms increased) during the period when these children were followed in the study.

In summary, a significant proportion of the children in contact with the social services family-law unit showed levels of symptoms warranting interventions from child psychiatry. Furthermore, children's health and wellbeing deteriorated during and after the contact with the social services family-law unit that was providing cooperation talks or investigating the child's situation.

5.3 Care and Participation for Vulnerable Children

The empirical examples above demonstrate the need for dissolving boundaries between family-law proceedings and child welfare/child protection policy and practice. Furthermore, there is clearly a need for improving services for children in family disputes, both in terms of early intervention and prevention, and when a dispute has escalated to a court

[15] Ibid.

case or interventions from social services. When trying to improve practice, I would argue that it is vital to connect risk assessments and ways of communicating with children to the matter of children's participation.

5.3.1 A 'Dual Approach' to Children

Since the late 1990s, a growing body of studies—not least in Nordic countries and the United Kingdom—of children and intimate partner violence have included children as informants and explored their views of both the violence and their own situation.[16] This trend can broadly be linked to the influence from the 'new' sociology of childhood/social studies regarding children and childhood that has gained ground within all fields of research concerning children since the early 1990s.[17] Here, children are conceptualized as social actors, and children's competence and participation in research as well as social life are highlighted. This conceptualization of children as social actors, of course, does not exclude the possibility that children might need protection and support from adults. Existing knowledge, for example, about possible consequences of childhood traumas, must be recognized in this context.

As pointed out by researchers involved in 'new' social studies on children and childhood, an ambiguity in current perspectives on children constructs them on the one hand as subjects and as objects on the other.[18] Sometimes these different approaches to children can conflict,

---

[16] Åsa Källström (Carter), '*Negotiating Normality and Deviation – Father's Violence against Mother from Children's Perspectives*' (Örebro University 2004); Inkeri Eskonen, 'Violence in Children's Narration' (2005) 8(1) *The International Journal of Child & Family Welfare* 32–45; Caroline McGee, *Childhood experiences of domestic violence* (Jessica Kingsley 2000); Audrey Mullender *Children's Perspectives on Domestic Violence* (SAGE journals 2002); Katarina Weinehall '"Take my Father Away from Home": Children growing up in the proximity of violence' in Maria Eriksson, Marianne Hester and Suvi Keskinen (eds), *Tackling Men's Violence in Families. Nordic Issues and Dilemmas* (Policy Press 2005) 136–154.

[17] See Allison James, Chris Jenks and Alan Prout, *Theorizing Childhood* (Polity Press 1998); Jens Qvortrup, Marjatta Bardy, Giovanni Sgritta, and Helmut Wintersberger (eds), *Childhood Matters. Social Theory, Practice and Politics (*Avebury 1994); Jens Qvortrup, William A Corsaro, and Michael-Sebastien Honig, *The Palgrave Handbook of Childhood Studies* (Palgrave Macmillan 2009).

[18] Nicki Lee, 'The Challenge of Childhood. Distributions of Childhood's Ambiguity in Adult Institutions' in (1999) 6(4) *Childhood* (SAGE journals) 455–474; Ibid. Qvortrup and others (1994) (n 17).

but they do not necessarily have to. Instead, combining them can be the key to improved practice in relation to children, for example, in family disputes. Thus, a *care principle* based on a needs-oriented perspective on children's views, constructing children as objects of adults' care and control, can be combined with a competence-oriented perspective on children's views,[19] expressed through *the principle of participation*—according to which, children are viewed as citizens and social actors.[20] Participation—for example, to be informed about what is going to happen next, consulted about which contact arrangements will feel sufficiently safe, and to take part in decisions regarding the future—can create possibilities for validation of children's traumatic experiences and thus support children's recovery after violence and abuse.[21]

5.3.2 Participation Enabling a Sense of Coherence

Another way of framing the importance of a dual approach to children in difficult life situations is to claim that a high degree of participation can contribute to children's sense of coherence.[22] According to Antonovsky's framework, health is a movement on a continuum of ease and disease, and depends on a person's ability to comprehend the situation as well as her or his capacity to use available resources. This capacity is a combination of people's ability to assess and understand the situation they are in ('comprehensibility'), to find a meaning for moving in a health-promoting direction ('meaningfulness'), and the capacity to do so ('manageability'). This framework can be linked to the various aspects of

[19] Anna Singer, *Föräldraskap i rättslig belysning [Parenthood According to the Law]* (Iustus 2000).

[20] Maria Eriksson and Elisabeth Näsman, 'Participation in Family Law Proceedings for Children whose Father is Violent to their Mother' (2008) 15(2) *Childhood* 259–275.

[21] Halvard Leira, 'From Tabooed Trauma to Affirmation and Recognition – An Explanatory Model to Understand and Work With Children who have Experienced Violence in the family' in Maria Eriksson, Aili Nenola and Marika Muhonen Nilsen (eds), *Kön och våld i Norden: rapport från en konferens i Køge, Danmark, 23–24 november 2001* [Gender and Violence in the Nordic Countries: Report from a Conference in Køge, Denmark, 23–24 November 2001], Copenhagen (2002): Nordic Council of Ministers, TemaNord no 545 285–295.

[22] Aaron Antonovsky, *Unraveling the Mystery of Health: How people manage stress and stay well* (1 edn, Jossey-Bass 1987).

participation outlined by Roger Hart in his work on the ladder of children's participation[23]—getting *information*, being *consulted*, taking part in *decision-making*, and being able to take the *initiative*.[24] I would argue that, in encounters with professionals working with family disputes, child participation is central to the promotion of children's health and wellbeing. Obtaining information that allows you—the child—to:

- understand what will happen to you.
- express what you think, feel, and know.
- feel that adults (professionals) genuinely listen to what you have to say and how you see things.
- veto situations that frighten you and undermine your sense of security.
- bring issues into the conversations that adults (professionals) did not think to ask about.

All these opportunities can support your sense that the situation is comprehensible, manageable, and meaningful, that is, your sense of coherence.

5.3.3 The Dual Approach and Risk Assessment

The recognition of children's voices is important not only in relation to general knowledge about children and family disputes, but also for understanding the situation of individual children. Risk assessment can illustrate this point.[25] Some commentators have noted that more widely used risk assessment instruments or methods are adapted to, for example, violent perpetrators found in a criminal justice context rather than child

---

[23] Roger A. Hart, *Children's Participation: From Tokenism to Citizenship* in (1992) no 4 *Innocenti Essay*, International Child Development Centre, Florence.

[24] See Eriksson and Näsman (n 20).

[25] Maria Eriksson, 'Children's Voices, Children's agency, and the Development of Knowledge About Children Exposed to Intimate Partner Violence in Marita Husso, Tuija Virkki, Marianne Notko, Helena Hirvonen and Jari Eilola (eds), *Interpersonal Violence: Differences and Connections* (Routledge 2017) 140–152.

protection matters or family disputes.[26] The complexity of these cases, in which both adults and children are at risk, has led some experts to argue that we need step-by-step models for risk assessment—where case workers use a variety of instruments and methods to assess risk to partners and to children, and then integrate the results into an overall conclusion.[27]

My argument is similar, though it brings the issue of children's agency and voices to the fore. Drawing on the dual approach outlined above, a risk assessment model combining the principle of care with the principle of participation would encompass at least four components[28]:

- Immediate danger (including risk of physical and sexual violence against the child).
- The child's strategies to tackle violence.
- The child's perspective (especially the sense of security).
- Developmental/long-term risk and the child's needs in relation to recovery.[29]

Although crucial and an important first step, a focus on, for example, the perpetrator of intimate partner violence, is not enough in a child-centred risk assessment model. Even when a previously violent parent is assessed as no longer posing a danger, the child might still *feel* afraid. In the case of trauma, contact that is experienced as unsafe may re-traumatize the child. Thus, we must also assess the child's sense of

[26] For example, Aron Shlonsky and Colleen Friend, 'Double Jeopardy: Risk Assessment in the Context of Child Maltreatment and Domestic Violence' (2007) 7(4) *Brief Treatment and Crisis Intervention* (Oxford University Press, Cary, NC) 253–274.

[27] Lorraine Radford, Neil Blacklock, and Kate Iwi, 'Domestic Abuse Risk Assessment and Safety Planning in Child Protection—Assessing Perpetrators' in Cathy Humphreys and Nicky Stanley (eds), *Domestic Violence and Child Protection. Directions for Good Practice* (Jessica Kingsley 2006).

[28] See Ulf Axberg, Anders Broberg, Maria Eriksson and Ole Hultmann, *Utveckling av bedömningsmetoder för barn som utsatts för våld i sin familj. Rapport från en fortsättningsstudie* [Development of Assessment Methods for Children Subjected to Violence in their Family. Report from a Continuation Ctudy] (Department of Psychology, University of Gothenburg 2018); Eriksson (n 25).

[29] See also Anna Kaldal, *Parallella processer. En rättsvetenskaplig studie av riskbedömningar i vårdnads- och LVU-mål* [Parallel Processes. A study in Law on Risk Assessment in Custody Cases and Cases of Taking Children into Care] (Jure 2010).

security and needs in relation to recovery.[30] These aspects are key when attempting to be genuinely child-centred, and to ensure children's rights to protection. We must offer support and listen carefully to the child concerned. By including the perspectives and views of the child in the assessment, it can be regarded as both, following the care principle to ensure that the child is protected and supported; and the principle of participation according to which, children have a right to have a say about all matters that concern them. The fact that the situation might become complicated in cases where children do not want what adults think they need (for example, to interact with a parent whom other adults regard as unsafe; or *not* interact with a parent whom other adults regard as safe) does not justify not asking children or listening to what they have to say—especially when it comes to fear and perceived threats from a previously violent parent. Furthermore, research shows that children are not 'passive' victims of situations at home; indeed, they attempt to intervene and manage these situations, sometimes in ways that put them at risk of harm.[31] Children's actions must also be considered just as much as the effects of violence and children's need of recovery. In terms of violence, as focused upon here, key issues to consider include how to avoid re-traumatization and how various care and contact arrangements can aid the child's recovery.

5.3.4 Evidence-Based Ways of Communicating With Children

How then, can we enable children's participation? In recent decades, research on methods to elicit reliable reports from children has increased dramatically and there is now a general agreement on a set of core,

---

30 Ibid; Dagmar Lagerberg and Claes Sundelin, *Risk och prognos iocialt arbete med barn. Forskningsmetoder och resultat* [Risk and Prognosis in Social Work with Children. Research Methods and Results] (Gothia 2000).

31 For example, Jeffrey L Edleson, Amanda L Ellerton, Ellen A Seagren, Staci L Kirchberg, Sarah O Schmidt and Amirthini T Ambrose, 'Assessing Child Exposure to Adult Domestic Violence' 2007 29(7) *Children and Youth Services Review*, 961–971; Jeffrey L Edleson, Narae Shin and Katy K Johnson Armendariz, 'Measuring Childre"s Exposure to Domestic Violence: The Development and Testing of the Child Exposure to Domestic Violence (CEDV) Scale' (2008) 30(5) *Children and Youth Services Review* 502–521.

evidence-based principles for interviewing children.[32] These principles have been derived mainly from experimental research within the forensic field, focusing on cognitive factors related to memory and suggestibility. However, less attention has been paid to children's emotional reactions and the best ways to help them describe these reactions.[33] Within the forensic field, there is a lack of research into how the interviewer can relate to children's emotional experiences. There is a clear need for protocol development and more research investigating exactly how and when evaluative questions should be posed to children, and whether this differs depending on severity of experience as well as the children's ages.[34]

As components derived from the research on forensic interview techniques are disseminated to other fields of practice—possibly including family disputes—protocol development is urgent. I also want to point out that existing research tends to focus more on children as sources of information (about their experiences, feelings, or perspectives), and less on children's rights to participation.[35] We may even ask to what extent there is an evidence base for enabling children's participation in decisions regarding their lives. Some efforts have been made to develop models intended to aid child-guided ways of communicating with children about their situation and views.[36] However, as far as I have been able to ascertain, such methods have not been documented or evaluated to any great extent. This, too, explains why protocol development to enhance child participation is urgently needed.

---

32 Karin Fängström, *'I don't even remember anything': Optimising the Choice of Method when Interviewing Preschoolers* (Uppsala University 2017); Clara Iversen, 'Beyond Accessing Information: Claiming to Understand in Child Social Welfare Interviews' (2019) 58(3) *British Journal of Social Psychology* 550–568.

33 Fängström (n 32); Karin Fängström and Maria Eriksson 'The Feasibility of the In My Shoes Computer Assisted Interview for Eliciting evaluative Content in Interviews with Young Children' (2020) 119 *Children & Youth Services Review*.

34 Karin Fängström, Anna Sarkadi, Steven Lucas, Rachel Calam, and Maria Eriksson, '"And they gave me a shot, it really hurt"—Evaluative Content in Investigative Interviews with Young Children' (2017) 82 *Children and Youth Services Review* 434–443.

35 Cf Kaldal (n 29) on the legal distinction of children as witnesses and children forming an opinion/view.

36 Maria Eriksson, *Användningen av BRA – Barns rätt som anhöriga* [The use of "BRA" – Children's Rights as Next of Kin] (Mälardalen University 2018).

5.3.5 Children's Views on Participation

What then, do children themselves say about participation? In a previous study in Sweden on vulnerable and victimized children in family-law proceedings,[37] children's views on child participation in family-law proceedings were explored in terms of their own participation as well as children's participation in general. The interviewed children in the sample (8–17 years old) tended to place less emphasis on shared decision-making compared to children in other studies[38] and stressed the right to decide 'for yourself'. This tendency can perhaps be linked to the experience of previous violence and/or oppression by parents and/or oppression by professionals, as some children in the sample described it.[39] A similar pattern of children emphasizing a right to make decisions has been described, for example, in a study from the United Kingdom on family life after divorce. The study did not focus on violence per se, but one of the conclusions was that children who had experienced 'neglect or disrespect' from a parent, strongly emphasized children's opportunities to choose where they should live and how contact should be organized.[40] One of the researchers in the team commented: 'In these contexts, specialist support, an independent voice and legal representation were seen as crucial to a child's wellbeing. Children will clearly assert their rights to self-determination where their family relationships are oppressive or abusive'.[41]

Another example comes from a study in Australia where Parkinson and colleagues interviewed children, parents, and judges about judges

[37] Maria Eriksson, 'Participation for Children Exposed to Domestic Violence? Social Workers' Approaches and Children's Strategies' (2012) 15 (2) *European Journal of Social Work* 205–221; Eriksson and Näsman (n 20).

[38] For example, Carol Smart, Bren Neale, and Amanda Wade, *The Changing Experience of Childhood. Families and Divorce* (Polity Press 2001).

[39] Eriksson and Näsman (n 20).

[40] Bren Neale, 'Dialogues with Children. Children, divorce and citizenship' (2002) 9 (4) *Childhood* (SAGE journals, London) 445–475.

[41] Neale (n 40) 469.

speaking to children directly in family-law disputes.[42] As with the case from the UK, children in Australia demonstrated different approaches to the issue of participation. Many children wanted to talk directly to their parents. However, one group of children said it would be best if children could talk to the judge directly instead of talking to their parents. Predominantly, the children in this group had experienced violence. The fact that the principle of participation was expressed quite strongly in the study from Sweden could perhaps be explained by the specificity of this sample, as the interviewees had experienced IPV (their father's violence against their mother) and in some cases also against themselves.

Another interpretation is that children's emphasis on a right to decide is an expression of a competent assessment of what will work, based upon the child's knowledge about (a lack of) parenting capabilities. The pattern emerging in the interviews also seems to be linked to a moral principle of fairness,[43] that is, the one who will have to live with the consequences of the decision—the child—should also have the right to decide:

> ***Bill*** *(11): It is as if you think that they [professionals] decide for me, they decide about my life. What I want and don't want [Interviewer: Mm].*
>
> ***Interviewer****: And you want to be able to decide yourself?*
>
> ***Bill****: Yes [Interviewer: Mm], not anyone else deciding for me [Interviewer: No].*
>
> ***Ali*** *(10): I'm the one who is going to be there.*

When it comes to the issue of violence, children's opportunities to talk about feelings and how conversations with professionals can be a source of help and emotional relief, was a recurring theme in the interviews. Furthermore, some child interviewees explicitly stressed the importance of professionals taking the history of violence and children's feelings of fear into account.[44] It should be noted that a child can deal with the

---

42 Patrick Parkinson, Judy Cashmore, and Judi Single, 'Parents' and Children's Views on Talking to Judges in Parenting Disputes in Australia' (2007) 21(1) *International Journal of Law, Policy and the Family* 84–107.

43 Zlatana Knezevic, 'Amoral, Im/moral and Dis/loyal: Children's Moral Status in Child Welfare' (2017) 24(4) *Childhood* 470–484.

44 Axberg and others (n 28); Kaldal (n 29); Lagerberg and Sundelin (n 30).

experience of further violence and oppression during or after the family dispute investigation process in quite different ways. The two children in the sample that most clearly described problematic professional practice were two boys, both approximately ten years old. Their views on participation, were almost diametrically opposite. While one drew exclusively upon the principle of participation, saying that 'otherwise it doesn't work', and insisted that he wanted to control his life himself (cf. above), the other boy tended to speak from a situation where children are dependent on adults who recognize their vulnerability and are prepared to intervene on their behalf if necessary. For example, when asked whether he thought that children should decide for themselves, such as where they should live and how much they should see the non-resident parent, he stated that 'it depends':

> ***Interviewer:*** *It depends, yes, and on what does it depend, how are you thinking?*
>
> ***Johan***: *If the father understands that he has not got the right to do this, and that, and when he goes to apologize and says that it is ok that you are with your mum for a little while so he can have a think about it [Interviewer: Mm], since of course the child could be afraid and start to cry and run away when the dad is coming to apologize and so.*

Thus, children can deal with very similar experiences in quite different ways. One of the implications of this, of course, is that practitioners who encounter vulnerable children in family disputes should take as their point of departure that these children may need and want a high degree of participation and strong decision-making rights, while at the same time carefully exploring the views and wishes of the individual child.

5.4 Conclusions

As pointed out in the introductory chapter to this anthology, the twenty-first century represents a paradigm shift in terms of how the interests and perspectives of the child are conceptualized in society at large. The editors argue that this ideological transformation is reflected in the adoption of the Convention on the Rights of the Child (CRC), granting children rights to participation as well as protection and provision. The research outlined above demonstrates that, to ensure children are granted rights in practice, and to enhance the health and wellbeing of children who experience a family dispute, there is a need to dissolve boundaries between family-law proceedings and child welfare—boundaries that are currently shaping both law and professional practice in many parts of the Western world.

In this chapter, I have also argued that to reach these objectives, the issue of children's participation must be connected to risk assessments and how to best communicate with children. Adopting a dual view of children entails regarding them both as in need of adult protection and care, and as competent actors with rights to participation. Furthermore, there is an urgent need for interview protocol development, for both children's experiences, and their right to participation, to improve practice in legal disputes concerning custody, contact, or residence.

Children's right to participation, the editors argue, constitutes a challenge with strengthening the child-rights perspective in the context of parental conflicts. In practice, professionals may recognize the views of a particular child only if those views correspond to the professionals' own, and/or with normative constructions of the child's best interests as being identical to contact with both parents.[45] Drawing on the views and experiences of children quoted in this chapter, it can be argued that both policymakers and practitioners must recognize children's own views on participation, including the fact that vulnerable and victimized children—to a greater degree than other children in family-law disputes—tend to emphasize a right to decide for themselves—because, after all, they are the ones 'who are going to be there'.

---

[45] Eriksson and Näsman (n 20).

References

Antonovsky A, *Unraveling the Mystery of Health: How people manage stress and stay well* (1 ed., Jossey-Bass 1987).

Axberg U, Broberg A, Eriksson M and Hultmann O, *Utveckling av bedömningsmetoder för barn som utsatts för våld i sin familj. Rapport från en fortsättningsstudie* (Department of Psychology, Göteborgs University 2018).

Broberg A, Almqvist L, Axberg U, Almqvist K, Cater Å K and Eriksson M, *Stöd till barn som upplevt våld mot mamma. Resultat från en nationell utvärdering* (Department of Psychology, Göteborg University 2011).

D'Onofrio B and Emery R, 'Parental Divorce or Separation and Children's Mental Health' (2019) 18(1) *World Psychiatry* 100.

Danermark B and Englund U, 'Utvärdering av Allmänna Barnhusetsocialt Samverkansteam – stöd till barn med föräldrar i konflikt' in Slutrapport Samverkansteam – för stöd till barn och föräldrar i samband med separation (Children's Welfare Foundation Sweden 2018).

Danermark B and Englund U, 'Samverkan – förutsättningar och utfall – en kompletterande och avslutande analys' in Slutrapport Samverkansteam – för stöd till barn och föräldrar i samband med separation (Children's Welfare Foundation Sweden 2018).

Edleson J L, Ellerton A L, Seagren E A, Kirchberg S L, Schmidt S O and Ambrose A T, 'Assessing Child Exposure to Adult Domestic Violence' 2007 29(7) *Children and Youth Services Review* 961.

Edleson J L, Shin N and Johnson Armendariz K K, 'Measuring Children's Exposure to Domestic Violence: The Development and Testing of the Child Exposure to Domestic Violence (CEDV) Scale' (2008) 30(5) *Children and Youth Services Review* 502.

Eriksson M, 'Participation for Children Exposed to Domestic Violence? Social Workers' Approaches and Children's Strategies' (2012) 15 (2) *European Journal of Social Work* 205.

Eriksson M, 'Children's Voices, Children's agency, and the Development of Knowledge about Children Exposed to Intimate Partner Violence' in Husso M, Virkki T, Notko M, Hirvonen H and Eilola J (eds), *Interpersonal Violence: Differences and Connections* (Routledge 2017).

Eriksson M, Användningen av BRA – Barns rätt som anhöriga [The use of "BRA" – Children's Rights as Next of Kin] (Mälardalen University 2018), available at https://mdh.diva-portal.org/smash/get/diva2:1249659/FULLTEXT02.pdf accessed 4 September 2023.

Eriksson M, Bruno L and Klingstedt M-L, 'Samverksansteam: Barns och föräldrars situation och upplevelser' in Slutrapport. Samverkansteam – för stöd till barn och föräldrar i samband med separation (Children's Welfare Foundation Sweden 2018).

Eriksson M and Gabrielsson M, 'Supporting Children and Parents in Sweden through Collaboration Teams' (2019) 57(3) *Family Court Review* 362.

Eriksson M and Näsman E, 'Participation in Family Law Proceedings for Children whose Father is Violent to their Mother' (2008) 15 (2) *Childhood* 259.

Eskonen I, 'Violence in Children's Narration' (2005) 8(1) *The International Journal of Child & Family Welfare* 32.

Family Law and Parental Support Authority 2021 (Statistics on family law 2020) www.mfof.se accessed 29 September 2021.

Fängström, K 'I Don't Even Remember Anything': Optimising the Choice of Method when Interviewing Preschoolers (Uppsala University 2017).

Fängström K and Eriksson M, 'The Feasibility of the in My Shoes Computer Assisted Interview for Eliciting evaluative Content in Interviews with Young Children' (2020) 119 *Children & Youth Services Review* 1.

Fängström K, Sarkadi A, Lucas S, Calam R and Eriksson M, '"And they gave me a shot, it really hurt"—Evaluative Content in Investigative Interviews with Young Children' (2017) 82 *Children and Youth Services Review* 434.

Hart R A, 'Children's Participation: From tokenism to citizenship' Innocenti Essay, International Child Development Centre Florence (1992) 4.

Iversen C, 'Beyond Accessing Information: Claiming to Understand in Child Social Welfare Interviews' (2019) 58(3) *British Journal of Social Psychology* 550.

James A, Jenks C and Prout A, Theorizing Childhood (Polity Press 1998).

Kaldal A, Parallella processer. En rättsvetenskaplig studie av riskbedömningar i vårdnads-och LVU-mål (Jure 2010).

Knezevic Z, 'Amoral, Im/moral and Dis/loyal: Children's Moral Status in Child Welfare' (2017) 24(4) *Childhood* 470.

Källström (Carter) Å, 'Negotiating Normality and Deviation—Father's Violence against Mother from Children's Perspectives' (Örebro University 2004).

Lagerberg D, and Sundelin C, Risk och prognos iocialt arbete med barn. Forskningsmetoder och resultat (Gothia 2000).

Lee N, 'The Challenge of Childhood. Distributions of Childhood's Ambiguity in Adult Institutions' in (1999) 6(4) *Childhood* 455.

Leira H, 'From Tabooed Trauma to Affirmation and Recognition – An explanatory model to understand and work with children who have experienced violence in the family' in Eriksson M, Nenola A and Muhonen Nilsen M (eds), *Kön och våld i Norden: rapport från en konferens i Køge, Danmark, 23–24 november 2001*, Copenhagen (2002): Nordic Council of Ministers, TemaNord no 545.

McGee C, *Childhood experiences of domestic violence* (Jessica Kingsley 2000).

McIntosh J E, Well Y and Lee J, 'The FL-DOORS Detection of Overall Risk Screen Framework', Attorney-General's Department, Canberra, Australia (2012).

McIntosh J E, Well Y and Lee J, The Family Law FL-DOORS Handbook, Attorney General's Department, Canberra, Australia (2012).

McIntosh J E, Well Y and Lee J, 'Development and validation of the Family Law DOORS' (2016) 28(11) *Psychological Assessment* 1516.

Mullender A, *Children's Perspectives on Domestic Violence* (SAGE journals 2002).

National Board of Health and Welfare 2011, Familjerätten och barnet i vårdnadstvister: uppföljning av hur 2006 års vårdnadsreform slagit igenom i socialtjänstens arbete 2011.

Neale B, 'Dialogues with Children. Children, divorce and citizenship' (2002) 9 (4) *Childhood* (SAGE journals, London) 445.

Parkinson P, Cashmore J and Single J, 'Parents' and Children's Views on Talking to Judges in Parenting Disputes in Australia' (2007) 21(1) *International Journal of Law, Policy and the Family* 84.

Radford L, Blacklock N and Iwi K, 'Domestic Abuse Risk Assessment and Safety Planning in Child Protection—Assessing Perpetrators' in Humphreys C, and Stanley N (eds), *Domestic Violence and Child Protection. Directions for Good Practice* (Jessica Kingsley 2006).

Shlonsky A and Friend C, 'Double Jeopardy: Risk Assessment in the Context of Child Maltreatment and Domestic Violence' (2007) 7(4) *Brief Treatment and Crisis Intervention* 253.

Singer A, Föräldraskap i rättslig belysning (Iustus 2000).

Statistics Sweden 2021 (Child and family statistics 2021) www.scb.se

Statistics Sweden 2013, 'Barn, föräldrar och separationer: Utvecklingen under 2000-talet', Demographic reports 2013:1 2013.

Smart C, Neale B and Wade A, *The Changing Experience of Childhood. Families and Divorce* (Polity Press 2001).

Qvortrup J, Bardy M, Sgritta G and Wintersberger H (eds), Childhood Matters. Social Theory, Practice and Politics (Avebury 1994).

Qvortrup J, Corsaro W A and Honig M-S, *The Palgrave Handbook of Childhood Studies* (Palgrave Macmillan 2009).
Weinehall K, '"Take my Father Away from Home": Children growing up in the proximity of violence' in Eriksson M, Hester M, and Keskinen S (eds), Tackling Men's Violence in Families. Nordic Issues and Dilemmas (Policy Press 2005).

6

Mapping Paths to Family Justice: Resolving Family Disputes Involving Children in Neoliberal Times

Anne Barlow, Rosemary Hunter, and Jan Ewing

6.1 Introduction

As noted in the introduction to this volume, parental conflicts concerning children often lead to major challenges that can jeopardize the wellbeing of all involved.[1] While parents have traditionally turned to the courts to resolve such conflicts, Barton argues that:

[1] See Anna Kaldal, Agnes Hellner and Titti Mattsson, 'Introduction: Matching Legal Proceedings to Problemsin Custody Disputes' in Anna Kaldal, Agnes Hellner and Titti Mattsson (eds), *Children in Custody Disputes: Matching Legal Proceedings to Problems* (Palgrave 2023).

A. Barlow (✉) · J. Ewing
University of Exeter Law School, Exeter, UK

R. Hunter
University of Kent Law School, Canterbury, UK

J. Ewing
Faculty of Law, University of Cambridge, Cambridge, UK

A. Kaldal et al. (eds.), *Children in Custody Disputes*,
https://doi.org/10.1007/978-3-031-46301-3_6

> The demands of child custody issues are so profound that we in the law may be required to transcend our normal understanding of a "legal procedure". Custody arrangements may require lawyers to acknowledge and incorporate different ways of thinking and speaking about rights, relationships, and social environments.[2]

Yet different ways of approaching custody issues must also be subject to scrutiny to determine their impact on children and parents.

Against this background, in England and Wales—where policy-makers have used changes to legal aid to restrict access to lawyers and encourage people to resolve custody and visitation[3] conflicts outside the court system through mediation—research into these developments can provide some important insights. These changes stemmed from a radical, neoliberal shift in thinking about family justice, driven by state cost-saving imperatives. Yet the rhetoric which accompanied them extolled the virtues of mediation (compared with court processes), as a means of reducing parental conflict and improving outcomes for children. This was despite a lack of evidence about experiences of mediation or about outcomes achieved when cases are diverted away from court into mediation. Neither was there any serious consideration of what other out-of-court alternatives may offer or what wider support such as counselling might be needed. Nonetheless, the Legal Aid, Sentencing and Punishment of Offenders Act 2012 was implemented in April 2013, preserving legal aid for family mediation, but withdrawing it for both legal advice and court representation in all custody and visitation cases—except in cases where there was evidence of domestic abuse. This means that only those who can afford to pay can now seek legal advice, and those who cannot, must either mediate (assuming both parties agree to this) or represent themselves in court. As will be discussed, this attempt to remove lawyers and courts from the resolution of parental conflicts

---

[2] See Thomas D Barton, 'Challenges When Family Conflicts Meet the Law—A Proactive Approach' in Anna Kaldal, Agnes Hellner and Titti Mattsson (eds), *Children in Custody Disputes: Matching Legal Proceedings to Problems* (Palgrave 2023).

[3] These terms have been replaced by the deliberately more neutral and collective term 'child arrangements' in the law of England and Wales. See Section 8 Children Act 1989.

concerning children, and to replace them with mediation, has had unintended consequences; many of which risk negatively affecting children's agency and best interests in matters involving them when their parents separate.

In this chapter, we will first draw on research evidence examining whether the interests of the child are of primary concern and the voice of the child is heard when out-of-court dispute resolution processes are used by separating parents. Second, we will discuss whether, in certain types of cases, the interests of the child are better protected by means of in-court procedures, where the guiding legal principle specifically states that the welfare of the child is paramount.[4] Then we will examine growing evidence that many children would like to be consulted in out-of-court family dispute resolution, and evidence that consultation with children involved in court processes is inadequate. In both instances, we reflect on whether current practice corresponds with the rights expressed in Article 12 UN Convention on the Rights of the Child (CRC) and what might be done to improve recognition of those rights.

6.2 The Studies

The chapter uses research evidence from three empirical studies undertaken by the authors in England and Wales. The first, *Mapping Paths to Family Justice*[5] (*Mapping*), was conducted between 2011 and 2014 and was a major study on awareness and experiences of out-of-court family dispute resolution processes. Two smaller follow-up studies focused on how to improve these processes, and in particular mediation, in the light of the *Mapping* findings: *Creating Paths to Family Justice (Creating)* (2015–2016) and the *Healthy Relationship Transitions (HeaRT)* project (2019–2022). Both of the smaller studies, unlike *Mapping*, collected data from young people whose parents had separated.

[4] Children Act 1989 Section 1.

[5] This was funded by the Economic and Social Research Council (ESRC) (grant no ES/1031812/1). See further, Anne Barlow, Rosemary Hunter, Janet Smithson and Jan Ewing, *Mapping Paths to Family Justice: Resolving Family Disputes in Neoliberal Times* (Palgrave Macmillan 2017).

6.2.1 Project Design and Methods

The relevant *Mapping* research objectives were:

1. To provide an up-to-date picture of awareness and experiences of three main out-of-court family dispute resolution processes, namely:
   - ***Family mediation***, where both adult parties attempt to resolve issues, including arrangements for their children, with the assistance of a family mediator.
   - ***Solicitor negotiation***, in which the parties' lawyers engage in a process of correspondence and discussion to broker a solution of the issues on behalf of their clients without going to court.
   - ***Collaborative law***, where each party is represented by their own lawyer and negotiations are conducted face to face in four-way, non-adversarial 'collaborative' meetings between the parties and their lawyers, all committed in a formal contract to reaching agreement without going to court. If no agreement is reached, the parties must instruct new lawyers if they want representation in court.
2. To map which out-of-court processes suited which types of cases and parties.
3. To consider how well children's best interests were served and how, if at all, their voices were heard in out-of-court processes concerning child arrangements.

This study is comprised of three interlinking phases.[6] First, a quantitative, nationally representative survey ($n = 2974$) was conducted, using a structured questionnaire to gauge public awareness of out-of-court dispute resolution options and to collect experiences from the divorced and separated populations who had used out-of-court processes between 1996 and 2011. Second, we used qualitative, semi-structured interviews to gain insights and experiences of the out-of-court processes from 40 practitioners (lawyers, mediators, or both), and also from 95

[6] Research Ethics Approval was obtained from the University of Exeter Social Sciences Research Ethics Committee.

divorced/separated men ($n = 45$) and women ($n = 50$). Our third phase focused on gaining a more in-depth understanding through recording and analysing the transcripts of 13 complete, out-of-court processes relating to children and/or financial disputes. These included five mediation processes, three collaborative law processes, and five first interviews between solicitor and client in which the aim was to reach agreement without going to court.

Relevant findings included:

- Relatively high levels of satisfaction (over 66%) with all three processes among those interviewed, but different out-of-court processes have different strengths which suit different parties and cases.
- Parties must be emotionally ready for any out-of-court process to be successful, particularly mediation, because parties cannot rely on a lawyer for support in the process.
- The main reasons people chose not to mediate were fear of their partner and refusal of their partner to engage.
- Screening for domestic violence in mediation was not consistent and often ineffective.
- The out-of-court procedures all aimed to be child-focused, but the recorded sessions revealed a substantial risk that adult interests could predominate over those of the children.
- Although mediation could extend to be child-inclusive (that is, where a child, with parental agreement, sees the mediator at a separate meeting and their views are fed back sensitively to the parents), this option was rarely used in practice. We found this was due to both parental and mediator reluctance.

Creating[7] involved five themed workshops conducted with policy-makers, practitioners, and professionals. It followed various practical aspects of addressing the *Mapping* findings, in light of the new policy

[7] For further details, see Anne Barlow, Jan Ewing, Rosemary Hunter and Janet Smithson, *Creating Paths to Family Justice: Briefing Paper and Report on Key Finding* (University of Exeter, 2017). The project was funded by the ESRC Impact Accelerator Account. Research Ethics Approval for the workshop was obtained from the University of Exeter Social Sciences Research Ethics Committee.

emphasis on resolving parental disputes through mediation in most circumstances. The final workshop in 2016, focused on children's voices. Participants included five young people aged 9–20, who were members of the Family Justice Young People's Board (FJYPB) and who had themselves experienced conflict between their parents about their post-separation child arrangements. Through their work with the FJYPB (which campaigns to improve family justice for children[8]), these participants were also familiar with other young people's accounts of their experiences. The objective was to understand what information young people needed about in-court and out-of-court procedures, and whether and how children's views could be included in both settings. The conclusion was that a trusted website was needed that covers a range of issues relevant to young people, including parental separation, and that technology should be better harnessed to help guide young people through disputes, including a means for children to contact professionals involved in their parents' case.

The *HeaRT* project[9] considered experiences of child-inclusive mediation (CIM), including the role it might play in promoting paths to better mental health and wellbeing for young people whose parents separate. Here, we interviewed 10 relationship professionals, 20 CIM-trained mediators, 12 parents, and 20 young people who had participated in CIM. We also ran four focus groups (one for those aged 11–15, one for those aged 16+, and two with more mixed age groups) with a total of 22 FJYPB members. We then ran two panels with a wider group of FJYPB members, plus young people from schools and community groups ($n = 24$). The purpose was to gauge their views on learning within the school curriculum about the legal processes

[8] This is a formal consultative group of the Family Justice Board and is supported by the Children and Families Court Advisory Service (Cafcass).

[9] *The Wellcome Centre on Cultures and Environments of Health-funded Healthy Relationships Beacon Project: Healthy Relationship Education (HeaRE) and Healthy Relationship Transitions (HeaRT)* (2019–2022) led by Anne Barlow. Research Ethics Approval for the *HeaRT* project was obtained from the University of Exeter Social Sciences Research Ethics Committee (Grant ref: 203109/Z/16/Z). See further, Anne Barlow, Jan Ewing, Tamsin Newlove-Delgado and Simon Benham-Clarke, *Transforming Relationships and Relationship Transitions with and for the Next Generation: Report and Key Findings* (University of Exeter 2022).

surrounding parental separation, as well as whether children feel they should have a voice within such processes. We found strong support for both more child-inclusive processes and more education.

6.3 Theory and Practice With Children's Voices Out-of-Court

The *Mapping* study exposed how the focus on children's welfare was handled by the practitioners and parents in out-of-court dispute resolution processes. We found little direct child consultation was taking place, despite mediators' high uptake of formal training and accreditation to conduct CIM.[10]

6.3.1 Child-Focused Processes

The practitioners in the *Mapping* study all stressed that the child's best interests were 'fundamental' to out-of-court family dispute resolution. It should be noted that while Section 1(1) Children Act 1989 makes the child's welfare paramount in decisions made by the court, this does not extend to out-of-court dispute resolution processes. However, though the professional codes of conduct governing lawyer and mediator practice are not directly enforceable as a matter of law, they do require these professionals to promote the child's welfare as the paramount consideration.[11] This has helped to make child-focus the norm in all processes. The opening to one of our recorded mediation sessions typifies the approach:

[10] For a fuller discussion see Jan Ewing, Rosemary Hunter, Anne Barlow and Janet Smithson, 'Children's Voices: Centre-Stage or Side-lined in Out-of-Court Dispute Resolution in England and Wales?' (2015) 27(1) *Child and Family Law Quarterly*, 43–61.

[11] Family Law Protocol, 3rd ed, 2010, para. 1.5.1; see also Family Mediation Council Code of Practice, 2018 para. 5.7.1: 'At all times mediators must have special regard to the welfare of any children of the family'. Failure to observe the codes and protocols can found a complaint of professional misconduct but these matters are handled by the professional bodies themselves, not as a matter of law.

> What we are looking for here is a solution that has [child]'s best interests at heart rather than a solution that is specifically geared to either one of you, because that's the most important isn't it? Mediation 209(1)

Most parties we interviewed also agreed that their practitioner had focused on the child's best interests. One party, Kathy,[12] when asked whether the mediator succeeded in getting her and her ex-partner both focused on their child's wellbeing, confirmed:

> Yeah, she did. It were obvious that her main goal was to – I mean, she'd never met my daughter, but her main goal were to get something sorted between the pair of us for her. Kathy, Mediation

Good, child-focused practice where mediators were skilled at reframing issues around children was also noted:

> One of my husband's objectives was to spend as much time with the children as possible and so the mediator said, "Well, why don't we phrase it as 'to be able to build meaningful relationships with the children?'" Tracy, Mediation

> Because you have both accepted that you do want [child] to have a relationship with his dad, so how can we reintroduce contact in a way that would be sensitive for [child]? Mediation 209(1)

However, while the separation of adults and children's needs is encouraged as good practice, children's active involvement in non-court processes is not mandatory—either in law or as a matter of professional conduct.[13] Thus we found a tendency (also observed within court proceedings[14]) for children's voices to be channelled through parental perspectives. Although all processes started child-focused, we found this

---

[12] All participant names have been pseudonymized to preserve anonymity.

[13] Family Law Protocol (n 11); Family Mediation Council Code of Practice (n 11).

[14] See Helen Stalford and Kathryn Hollingsworth, '"This Case Is About You and Your Future": Towards Judgments for Children' (2020) 83(5) MLR 1030–1058, who talk of children's voices being "represented by proxy, adult-filtered accounts" in court.

was often difficult to maintain in competition with the drive for agreement between the adults, so that the interests and voices of young people risked getting lost.[15] As one mother put it:

> It was more "this is what [ex-partner] wants to do, this is what Rebecca wants to do, can you come to an arrangement of what you want?" rather than "this is what is best for the children." Rebecca, Mediation

Time constraints and complexity of other issues could also mean the focus on children could get overlooked in mediation:

> [The mediator] decided that we had a choice between discussing our finances or discussing about the child, and we discussed finances. Sonia, Mediation

The notion of 'child-focus' could also be observed superficially, as parents often used a child-welfare discourse to justify their own position, rather than really thinking about what was best for the child. For example, some fathers thought children had the right to spend half their time with their father, whereas some mothers thought that children needed to be mostly with their mothers—without either parent considering what their child wanted.

Indeed, some parents felt it was inappropriate to consult their children, preferring to shield them from the conflict situation as far as possible. Seth, a father of nine-year-old twins, told them he was moving out only two weeks before it happened, saying:

> So at the time of the mediation they didn't know anything about it, but of course we wanted to protect the children from all that as much as possible.

---

[15] See further, Janet Smithson, Anne Barlow, Rosemary Hunter and Jan Ewing, 'The "Child's Best Interests" as an Argumentative Resource in Family Mediation Sessions' (2015) 17(4) *Discourse Studies* 1–15.

There was certainly no accepted view that children should be consulted, which raises the issue of how well non-court processes accord with children's rights under Article 12 CRC in England and Wales.[16]

There was, however, some evidence that where parents did consult their children, this could break the deadlock. This worked for Sheila, who ended her collaborative law process because she thought the proposed arrangements would not work well for their children:

> I actually spoke to the kids … and I said, "Look, part of the reason things were difficult was because we were about to make these new arrangements. What do you think?" And they said, "Fine, we'll try it".

This confirmed other research[17] that, as well as being beneficial for the child, going beyond a child-focused approach and directly consulting children may be an effective way of dealing with cases where the parents' views on what is best for the children are fixed and incompatible.

6.3.2 Child-Inclusive Practices

CIM involves the child being directly consulted by the mediator, who feeds their views back to the parents at a separate mediation session, in a way agreed between the child and the mediator. In theory, this is available to all who mediate child arrangements in England and Wales. Yet children are likely to discover this option only if their parents tell them. Few of the *Mapping* study practitioners offered CIM routinely, despite two-thirds of the mediators we interviewed (20 of 31) being qualified to undertake it. We found a surprising lack of practitioner confidence.

---

[16] UN Convention on the Rights of the Child (CRC), Article 12: 'States Parties shall assure to the child who is capable of forming his or her own views the right to express those views freely in all matters affecting the child, the views of the child being given due weight in accordance with the age and maturity of the child'.

[17] Jennifer E McIntosh, Yvonne D Wells, Bruce M Smyth and Caroline Long, 'Child-focused and Child-inclusive Divorce Mediation: Comparative Outcomes from a Prospective Study of Post-separation Adjustments' (2008) 46(1) *Family Court Review* 105–124; Jennifer McIntosh, Bruce Smyth, Margaret Kelaher, Yvonne Wells and Caroline Long, 'Post-separation Parenting Arrangements: Patterns of Developmental Outcomes. Studies of Two Risk Groups' (2011) *Family Matters* No 86, Australian Institute of Family Studies.

While many felt it was a good idea, only two practised direct consultation frequently. Around half had only ever conducted one or two cases and some had not taken a single case.

A minority of mediators were very pro-direct consultation. One such example was Molly Turner:

> I am very much about involving the voice of the child, you know. All the research that I have read ... tells me the same common factor; children don't feel heard, they feel lied to and they feel betrayed by the parents because they haven't been told the truth about things ... and ... the decision making quite often ignores the children's wishes.

However, others found that the practical objections to it, such as lack of parental consent or the additional cost, inadequately covered by legal aid, most often prevailed:

> We can offer it in very unusual circumstances, but it is very rare. Melanie Illingworth

In the study, we found very few parents who had consented to CIM. One father, who had successfully used the method to resolve an entrenched dispute about which school his daughter should attend, still had reservations:

> I think it puts [children] in a very difficult position ... I think it has to be managed so very carefully. (Ernest, CIM)

Thus, while we did not interview children in the *Mapping* study, this led us to reflect further on how they could be better consulted or involved in decision-making out-of-court, in line with their ostensible CRC rights, and whether the desire to protect children from consultation should be challenged. We concluded that the issue of children's voice was an area where further research was certainly needed.

6.4 Safeguarding Children and the Role of the Court

Despite the policy emphasis on mediation, it is clear that out-of-court family dispute resolution processes are not always appropriate. They can pose a risk to the safety of both adult participants and children affected by arrangements that are 'agreed' as a result of intimidation, coercion, or continuing control by an abusive parent. Social services have no involvement in cases that do not go to court in England and Wales, and no role in assessing the suitability of agreements about child arrangements made out-of-court. As noted in the description of the project design in the Introduction, part of the objective of the *Mapping* study was to identify which cases and parties were suitable for different dispute resolution processes. We concluded, where there is a significant psychological disparity between the parties, a significant power imbalance between them, or where one party is vulnerable in some way; that party and their children needed the protection at least of a lawyer. In many of these cases, the more powerful party will seek to exploit this imbalance and be unwilling to compromise or offer a fair and just resolution of the dispute, with the result that court proceedings become necessary. Furthermore, with the major cuts to legal aid in 2013, legal representation is now out of reach for many people with family disputes, making recourse to the protection of the court the only safe option in such cases.

One finding of concern in the *Mapping* study, was that screening for domestic abuse and other vulnerabilities that would make mediation unsuitable was not done consistently or effectively. We interviewed a number of women who said they had not been asked about any history of abuse in their relationship, had not felt able to disclose their fear of the other party to the mediator—due to the circumstances in which screening took place—or had been pushed into attempting mediation despite a known history of abuse. In these cases, the failure of screening led to traumatic experiences of mediation and unfair agreements which exposed them and their children to the ongoing risk of abuse.

Direct consultation with children might seem even more important in these cases, given that children's safety is at stake. Yet this was not a consideration raised in our interviews with practitioners in *Mapping*, many of whom appeared to adhere to the (false) belief that violence between adults would have no or minimal effect on the children, and that an abusive partner could still be a good parent. Consultation with children could operate to displace these assumptions. In Tilda's case, for example, there had been threats of violence undisclosed due to poor screening, yet sufficient concerns about her ex's forceful attitude in the mediation intake procedure resulted in the appointment of two mediators to co-mediate the case, rather than the usual one. Despite this, there was no suggestion by the mediators that the children's views on a proposed agreement for equal shared care should be considered. Nor did any practitioners in our interview sample raise children's perspectives as a potentially important consideration in cases where there was a history of domestic abuse.

By contrast, in court proceedings in England and Wales, there is a dedicated agency—Cafcass (the Children and Family Court Advisory and Support Service)—whose role is to promote and safeguard children's welfare. In all cases in which a court application is made concerning post-separation child arrangements, Cafcass undertakes initial safeguarding checks to discover whether the family is known to the police or local children's social services. They also conduct a telephone interview with both parents, inviting them to raise any concerns about their children's welfare. The results of these checks then inform the court throughout the process. It is notable, for example, that a recent pilot study by Cafcass to explore the scope for initial diversion from court, to support parents to agree on arrangements rather than continuing with court proceedings, found that 80–86% of cases raised such serious safeguarding issues that they were not suitable for diversion.[18]

However, while the child focus of the court process may be clearer, direct inclusion of children's voices remains limited. In the majority of cases, the court encourages and assists parents to settle matters between themselves, with no reference to the views of the children. It is only if cases reach a more advanced stage of proceedings that Cafcass may be

[18] Cafcass, 'Support with Making Child Arrangements Programme: Six Month Pilot Evaluation Report', 2019, unpublished, on file with authors.

ordered to provide a report that includes the children's wishes and feelings. And it is only in the most serious cases that the court will appoint a guardian to provide separate representation for the child. Cafcass data indicates that it provides reports in only around one-third of cases, and a guardian is appointed in fewer than 10% of cases.[19] It is also very rare for children to give evidence in family courts and uncommon for them to meet with the judge in their case.[20] Thus, while the court process may pay more direct attention to children's welfare, it is not necessarily better at making good their Article 12 rights.

6.5 Facilitating Children's Voices—The Evolving Picture

Since the *Mapping* study, the mediation community and its regulators have made changes encouraging greater uptake of CIM where appropriate, while ensuring children's safety and wellbeing.[21] This is arguably paving the way for children's voices to be better heard in mediation: according to surveys conducted by the Family Mediation Council, the use of CIM increased from 14% of cases in 2017 to 26% in 2019.[22]

[19] Cafcass annual reports, cited in, Rosemary Hunter, Mandy Burton and Liz Trinder, *Assessing Risk of Harm to Children and Parents in Private Law Children Cases: Final Report* (Ministry of Justice 2020) 69–70. See also, Claire Hargreaves, *Uncovering Private Family Law: What Can The Data Tell Us About Children's Participation?* (Nuffield Family Justice Observatory, Report, 2022). https://www.nuffieldfjo.org.uk/wp-content/uploads/2022/06/nfjo_report_private_law_child_participation_20220615_FINAL-1.pdf, accessed 10 May 2023.

[20] Hunter and others (n 19) 70.

[21] Following the Final Report of the Voice of the Child Dispute Resolution Advisory Group, 2015, The Family Mediation Council (FMC), which sets standards for mediation nationally, amended its 'Standards Framework' in 2018 to require all mediators to attend CIM awareness or update training and explain CIM to prospective clients.

[22] See FMC Survey 2017 https://www.familymediationcouncil.org.uk/wp-content/uploads/2018/01/Family-Mediation-Survey-Autumn-2017.pdf and FMC Survey, 2019 https://www.familymediationcouncil.org.uk/wp-content/uploads/2020/01/Family-Mediation-Survey-Autumn-2019-Results.pdf both accessed 25 February 2023.

Other research indicates that consultation with children is associated with children being more satisfied with arrangements,[23] arrangements lasting longer, better father-child relationships, and more cooperative parenting.[24] However, we wanted to capture children's perspectives on whether the right to be consulted on matters affecting them on parental separation would be welcomed. At the *Creating* workshop[25] in 2016 with the FJYPB members, these participants flagged difficulties encountered by children seeking information about the separation process. They emphasized how unsupported children typically were when parents separate, and unanimously agreed that, as a matter of principle, children of appropriate age should have the right to be consulted, irrespective of whether parents resolved issues in or out-of-court. The participants took the view that consultation should be the child's choice, with children being part of the conversation rather than simply being asked to choose between their parents' preferred options. In the further *HeaRT* study in 2020, during the focus groups, the wider group of FJYPB participants also strongly argued that children should be actively involved in decision-making:

> I think the child ... should be involved as much as they can just because it's their life that's being decided about ... you should [not] ... let your parents decide ... what's going to happen in your life when it's not their life that they are making decisions for. Max

Several young people interviewed in the *HeaRT* study were pragmatic, appreciating how CIM helped to '*get stuff sorted*' (Alex). Most spoke of benefits outside of dispute resolution. Freddy liked that his parents cared about his opinion. Christina felt that being consulted had validated her feelings. Several spoke of anxieties lessened by having a clearer understanding of the process. Many welcomed the opportunity to discuss with

---

[23] Ian Butler, Lesley Scanlan, Margaret Robinson, Gillian Douglas and Mervyn Murch, 'Children's Involvement in Their Parents' Divorce: Implications for Practice' (2002) 16(2) *Children & Society* 89–102.

[24] Janet Walker and Angela Lake-Carroll, in *Report of the Family Mediation Task Force* 2014.

[25] With eight young people aged 9–20 who had experienced the family justice system during parental separation, and other family justice stakeholders, as part of the *Creating Paths to Family Justice* follow-on study. See further, Barlow and others (n 7).

an empathetic third party, things they felt unable to raise with their parents, which Ellie noted gave children *'a sense that somebody is there for them, that they have somebody … to … talk to'*. Alfie felt the process had improved communication with his parents:

> It opened me a lot more and made me a lot more confident to speak to my [parents] about things, which just made a lot of stuff much, much easier and took a lot of stress off my chest.

Most felt empowered by the process, as summed up by Anna:

> [CIM gives young people] … a voice … they are being respected … it's actually quite cathartic for children to be able to kind of explain what's going on to someone and someone to listen to them.

One of the key features of CIM, and children's responses to it, is that children's voices are heard and validated in a non-judgemental way. More recent research suggests that regrettably, this may not be the case when children are consulted as part of court proceedings. In 2019, the Ministry of Justice established an expert panel and issued a public call for evidence on how effectively family courts protect children and adult victims of domestic abuse, child abuse, and other serious offences from harm in family-law cases. The call received over 1,000 submissions, a substantial majority of them from mothers who were victims of domestic abuse and who had attempted to protect their children from abuse through the court process. In addition, there were a small number of responses from young people who had been the subject of court proceedings as children. The experiences recounted in these submissions pointed to serious failings in the court process. In particular, the panel concluded that 'The weight of evidence from both research and submissions suggests that too often the voices of children go unheard in the court process or are muted in various ways'.[26]

Even in those cases where children were consulted by Cafcass for the purposes of reporting their wishes and feelings to the court, the panel

[26] Hunter and others (n 19) 67.

found extensive evidence of 'selective listening', whereby children who said they wanted to have contact with the parent they did not live with were supported, but children who said they did not want to have contact were ignored, disregarded, dismissed, or misrepresented. Children opposed to contact were often considered to be simply reflecting the views of the parent with whom they were living, or to have been brainwashed by that parent or 'alienated' by them from the non-resident parent. Furthermore, the process by which children's views were elicited was also criticized. Children were not given sufficient time to build a relationship of trust with the Cafcass officer or guardian in which they felt safe to disclose their fears. These concerns were compounded for children with learning difficulties or other special needs who were not effectively supported to enable them to communicate their views. At the same time, trusted adults in whom children had confided were either not interviewed or were similarly dismissed. Children found the failure to listen to them (and the resulting court orders which left them with contact arrangements in which they did not feel safe) to be profoundly disempowering.[27] The report concluded that more should be done to accord children the opportunity to be heard in proceedings in accordance with their Article 12 rights.[28] It recommended substantial reforms to the court process to, among other things, incorporate consultation with children of sufficient age in all cases. Systematic consultation would not only have procedural benefits in including children in decision-making in matters affecting them, but also, should have substantive benefits in improving the protection offered by the courts against future abuse and the risk of harm to the child.

6.6 Conclusion

In the context of England and Wales, mediation is seen as a 'good' means of dispute resolution: it is non-adversarial, reduces conflict, and restores autonomy to the parties. It is contrasted with court, which is seen as

[27] Hunter and others (n 19) Chapter 6.

[28] Hunter and others (n 19) 176.

inherently 'bad' and likely to inflame conflict between parents, with lawyers being regarded similarly. In our view, this dichotomy between court (and lawyers) and out-of-court processes is far too simplistic. While we cannot say that one process is always better for children than the other, in some circumstance one or the other will be more appropriate, and we suggest that the focus should be on good practices within ANY process. Above all, there is a need for effective screening to distinguish different types of conflicts and adjust procedures or divert people to the right process for their situation.[29] In all procedures, however, whether in or out-of-court, barriers to hearing the child's voice must be overcome.

The findings of our *Mapping* research indicate that, while out-of-court family dispute resolution processes attempt to focus on children's welfare, that focus can be lost in the details of the adult dispute. Direct consultation with children in out-of-court processes would help to maintain focus on the child's interests and preferences on matters directly affecting them, but the *Mapping* research found that this occurred only rarely, revealing a clear gap between the theory and the practice.

In the mediation context, some of the practical and attitudinal barriers to hearing the child's voice are now being addressed,[30] and although CIM remains a minority practice, enthusiasm for it has grown. Its use is increasing and our subsequent *Creating* and HeaRT research suggests this is in accordance with children's desires to be included in conversations about the custody and visitation arrangements their parents make post-separation. This also resonates with other research findings on this issue in Norway.[31]

---

[29] This finding resonates with Singer's view that 'differentiated and family-specific services are required'.

In Anna Singer, "Out-of-court Custody Dispute Resolution in Sweden—A Journey Without Destination' in Anna Kaldal, Agnes Hellner and Titti Mattsson (eds), *Children in Custody Disputes: Matching Legal Proceedings to Problems* (Palgrave 2023).

[30] See also, recommendations on how these should go further and be holistically approached in the *Report of the Family Solutions Group*, 2020 https://www.familysolutionsgroup.co.uk/, accessed 25 February 2023.

[31] See Thørnblad, R and A Strandbu, 'The Involvement of Children in the Process of Mandatory Family Mediation' in Anna Nylund and others, (eds) Nordic *Mediation Research* (Cham: Switzerland: Springer Open, 2018), 183–208. https://link.springer.com/content/pdf/10.1007/978-3-319-73019-6.pdf.

The *Mapping* research also identified an important role for the court in protecting those vulnerable to abuse, coercion, and control. In such cases, the process and outcomes of mediation can be unsafe and unsatisfactory, while the court is required by law to make the child's welfare its paramount consideration and to consider children's wishes and feelings in its decision-making. Particularly in the absence of lawyers after the Legal Aid, Sentencing and Punishment of Offenders Act 2012, court proceedings appear to be more appropriate than mediation in such cases. Recent evidence suggests, however, that the safeguarding and protection that should be offered by the court is not being effectively delivered in practice. Here, more progress must be made in both consulting children and listening to what they say—but the government's commitment to implementing the expert panel's recommendations,[32] including those on more consistent attention to the voice of the child, gives some hope for future improvement.

Lack of consultation with children whose parents separate, about the arrangements being made for them—either in or out-of-court—would seem to infringe Article 12 CRC, despite the UK having ratified the Convention. While Scotland and Wales are in the process of adopting the CRC into domestic law,[33] England currently has no such plans; thus, children's rights—including the right to express their views freely in matters affecting them—are currently unenforceable. Although improvements are now being seen in out-of-court and in-court procedures, this lack of enforceability must continue to be challenged.

---

[32] Ministry of Justice, *Assessing Risk of Harm to Children and Parents in Private Law Children Cases: Implementation Plan* (2020). See also, Family Procedure Rules, Practice Direction 36Z, which sets out a new investigative procedure in custody and visitation cases, currently being piloted in two court areas, which includes a default of consultation with the child in every case.

[33] The Scottish parliament voted unanimously for the United Nations Convention on the Rights of the Child (Incorporation) (Scotland) Bill to become law in 2021 but was referred to the Supreme Court by the UK government which successfully challenged its constitutionality. See *REFERENCE by the Attorney General and the Advocate General for Scotland - United Nations Convention on the Rights of the Child (Incorporation) (Scotland) Bill* [2021] UKSC 42. The Scottish government has announced the intention to reintroduce a revised Bill. See https://www.thenational.scot/news/19956835.uncrc-bill-come-back-holyrood-supreme-court-defeat/, accessed 10 May 2023. Wales-only legislation incorporated aspects of the CRC into Welsh domestic law through the Rights of Children and Young Persons (Wales) Measure 2011.

References

Barlow A, Ewing J, Hunter R and Smithson J, *Creating Paths to Family Justice: Briefing Paper and Report on Key Finding* (University of Exeter 2017).

Barlow A, Ewing J, Newlove-Delgado T and Benham-Clarke S, *Transforming Relationships and Relationship Transitions with and for the next generation: Report and Key Findings* (University of Exeter 2022).

Barton T, 'Challenges When Family Conflicts Meet the Law—A Proactive Approach' in Kaldal A, Hellner A and Mattsson T (eds), *Children in Custody Disputes: Matching Legal Proceedings to Problems* (Palgrave 2023) 169.

Butler I, Scanlan L, Robinson M, Douglas G and Murch M, 'Children's Involvement in Their Parents' Divorce: Implications for Practice' (2002) 16(2) *Children & Society* 89.

Cafcass, 'Support with Making Child Arrangements Programme: Six Month Pilot Evaluation Report' (2019) unpublished, on file with authors.

Ewing J, Hunter R, Barlow A and Smithson J, 'Children's Voices: Centre-Stage or Side-lined in Out-of-Court Dispute Resolution in England and Wales?' (2015) 27(1) *Child and Family Law Quarterly* 43.

Family Mediation Council Survey, 2017 https://www.familymediationcouncil.org.uk/wp-content/uploads/2018/01/Family-Mediation-Survey-Autumn-2017.pdf accessed 25 February 2023.

Family Mediation Council Survey, 2019 https://www.familymediationcouncil.org.uk/wp-content/uploads/2020/01/Family-Mediation-Survey-Autumn-2019-Results.pdf accessed 25 February 2023.

Family Solutions Group, *Report of the Family Solutions Group*, 2020 https://www.familysolutionsgroup.co.uk/ accessed 25 February 2023.

Hargreaves C, *Uncovering Private Family Law: What Can the Data Tell Us About Children's Participation?* (Nuffield Family Justice Observatory, Report 2022) https://www.nuffieldfjo.org.uk/wp-content/uploads/2022/06/nfjo_report_private_law_child_participation_20220615_FINAL-1.pdf accessed 14 May 2023.

Hunter R, Burton M and Trinder L, *Assessing Risk of Harm to Children and Parents in Private Law Children Cases: Final Report* (Ministry of Justice 2020).

Kaldal A, Hellner A and Mattsson T, 'Introduction: Matching Legal Proceedings to Problems in Custody Disputes' in Kaldal A, Hellner A and Mattsson T (eds), *Children in Custody Disputes: Matching Legal Proceedings to Problems* (Palgrave 2023) 1.

McIntosh J, Smyth B, Kelaher M, Wells Y and Long C, 'Post-separation parenting, Post-separation parenting arrangements: Patterns and developmental outcomes. Studies of two risk groups' (2011) *Family Matters* No 86, Australian Institute of Family Studies.

McIntosh J E, Wells Y D, Smyth B M and Long C M, 'Child-Focused and Child-inclusive Divorce Mediation: Comparative Outcomes from a Prospective Study of Post-separation Adjustments' (2008) 46(1) *Family Court Review* 105.

Singer A, 'Out-of-court Custody Dispute Resolution in Sweden—A Journey Without Destination' in Kaldal A, Hellner A and Mattsson T (eds), *Children in Custody Disputes: Matching Legal Proceedings to Problems* (Palgrave 2023) 129.

Stalford H and Hollingsworth K, '"This Case Is About You and Your Future": Towards Judgments for Children' (2020) 83(5) *Modern Law Review* 1030.

Thørnblad R and Strandbu A, 'The Involvement of Children in the Process of Mandatory Family Mediation' in Anna Nylund et al (eds) *Nordic Mediation Research* (Springer 2018) 183.

Walker J and Lake-Carroll A, in *Report of the Family Mediation Task Force* (2014) https://www.justice.gov.uk/downloads/family-mediation-task-force-report.pdf accessed 10 May 2023.

7

Out-of-Court Custody Dispute Resolution in Sweden—A Journey Without Destination

Anna Singer

7.1 Introduction

The Swedish system for the adjudication of custody disputes[1] was introduced at the beginning of the twentieth century and reflected the views and values of those times regarding children, parenthood, and family. When parents divorced, which at the time was rare, custody was usually granted to the mother.[2] Since then, divorce rates in Sweden have increased dramatically; both the values and understanding of parenthood, parental responsibility, and children have changed. Nowadays, custody is determined in accordance with the child's best interests, which

[1] Swedish law still differentiates between custody—which concerns the child's personal matters—and guardianship—which concerns economic matters. Usually, a child's parents are both custodians and guardians. Throughout this chapter, the term "custody dispute" is used. The dispute between parents could concern custody but also residence and contact.

[2] The child's father retained guardianship. Starting in 1949, mothers could also become guardians.

A. Singer (✉)
Faculty of Law, Uppsala University, Uppsala, Sweden

A. Kaldal et al. (eds.), *Children in Custody Disputes*,
https://doi.org/10.1007/978-3-031-46301-3_7

in a Swedish context, is often defined as having two parents with joint parental responsibility. Joint custody for separated parents is the main rule and can even be decided against the will of both parents if it is considered the best option for the child.[3]

Despite profound changes in the societal view of parenthood, children, and custody, the rules governing court procedure concerning custody disputes have undergone only limited reforms. Instead, alternative methods for dispute resolution have been established to facilitate the fulfilment of the best interests of the child and to keep the parents out of court. This started with the introduction of cooperation talks (*samarbetssamtal*) in the 1970s. Nevertheless, evidence exists that shows cooperation talks have not been able to provide solutions in custody disputes to the desired extent, nor have subsequent reforms proven adequate. As will be discussed, both in and out-of-court alternatives display a number of shortcomings in terms of their procedural organization. It is clear that the current system for resolving custody disputes in Sweden is not the best tool for the task.

This statement prompts several questions: What are the shortcomings? Why has the system not been developed to address them? Are there alternatives to the existing legal framework? These questions will be addressed from a development perspective, through which some of the key historical events and legal amendments will be identified. While the analysis focuses on Swedish law, it also deals with issues and challenges that are common to many countries and legal systems.[4]

---

[3] Swedish Government Bill 2020/21:150 Ett stärkt barnrättsperspektiv i vårdnadstvister [A Strengthened Child Rights Perspective in Custody Disputes].

[4] In her contribution to the present anthology, Anna Nylund, 'Scandinavian Family Mediation: Towards a System of Differentiated Services?' in Anna Kaldal, Agnes Hellner and Titti Mattsson (eds), *Children in Custody Disputes: Matching Legal Proceedings to Problems* (Palgrave 2023), Anna Nylund offers a general overview of the Scandinavian systems for custody-dispute resolution.

7.2 Joint Custody as a Way to Keep Parents Out of Court

It is well documented that, in many cases, the conflicts underlying custody disputes and the associated court proceedings are detrimental to the children involved.[5] Custody disputes are also matters that are inherently difficult for courts to solve. Hence, for the past 50 years, legal development in Sweden concerning the adjudication of custody disputes has focused on how to keep divorcing parents out of the courts by reaching out-of-court agreements on custody-related issues.

One way to achieve this has been continuous reform of the material rules on custody, in order to underline the importance of cooperation between parents after separation, while at the same time emphasizing that the best interests of the child should always come first. Joint custody for parents not living together has been brought forward as a significant step in that direction.

When the first rules on custody were introduced in 1920, it was considered self-evident that only the parent living with the child should have the right to make decisions on the child's behalf and hence should be the sole custodian. As divorce rates increased mid-century, many children stayed with their mothers and often lost contact with their fathers. The only way the fathers could become custodians was through a court decision. In 1976, it became possible for separated (and unmarried cohabiting) parents to agree on joint custody. Joint custody thus became a way to prevent conflicts. The preparatory work states that in many cases, one parent could accept that the other parent would provide physical care for the child if he (*sic*) could remain custodian together with the other parent.[6] The result of the reform of 1976 was that children whose parents had joint custody after separation had better contact with

[5] See for example, Anna Norlén, 'Children's Health Matters in Custody Conflicts—What do we know?'; Maria Eriksson, 'Children's Participation and Perspectives in Family Disputes', all in Anna Kaldal, Agnes Hellner and Titti Mattsson (eds), *Children in Custody Disputes: Matching Legal Proceedings to Problems* (Palgrave 2023).

[6] Swedish Government Bill 1975/76:170 Faderskap och vårdnad [Paternity and Custody] 143; The same reasoning is found in subsequent government bills, for example, Swedish Government Bill 1990/91:8 om vårdnad och umgänge [on Custody and Contact] 32; Swedish Government Bill 1997/98:7 Vårdnad, boende och umgänge [Custody, Residence and Contact] 51.

both parents than children with parents where one had sole custody.[7] Thus, joint custody became a universal solution to several problems—a solution that was also applied in cases where the parents did not agree.

Joint custody for parents living apart, when first introduced, required the consent of both parents.[8] Over the years, this has changed; today the court can order joint custody against the will of both parents if this solution is considered to be in the best interests of the child.[9] However, before deciding on custody, the court should pay particular attention to the parents' ability to put the child's best interests first and take shared responsibility in matters concerning the child.[10] Parents who have joint custody have the same rights and responsibilities to make decisions about the child's personal matters and should come to a mutual decision. The parent living with the child does not have any formal right to decide alone. However, in practice, a parent with whom a child resides must make independent decisions without the consent of the other parent. This is a source of conflict between many parents and results in custody disputes; when parents have joint custody, one of them may want sole custody to be able to make child-related decisions alone, and a parent with no custody may want joint custody to gain the right to participate in the decision-making.[11] There are no possibilities of conflict resolution within joint custody, apart from decisions about with whom the child should reside and time spent with the non-residential parent. Suggestions to give the resident parent certain rights to decide as a way to

[7] Ministry memorandum 1989:52 Vårdnad och umgänge [Custody and Contact] 48–49.

[8] Swedish Government Bill 1975/76:170 Faderskap och vårdnad (n 6); Swedish Government Bill 1981/82:168 om vårdnad och umgänge m.m. [on Custody and Contact etc.], joint custody is the main rule for married parents after divorce, unless one parent is opposed to joint custody; Swedish Government Bill 1990/91:8 om vårdnad och umgänge (n 6), joint custody even if one parent would prefer sole custody; Government Bill 1997/98:7 Vårdnad, boende och umgänge (n 6), joint custody even if one parent is opposed.

[9] Swedish Government Bill 2020/21:150 Ett stärkt barnrättsperspektiv i vårdnadstvister (n 3) 73–76.

[10] Swedish Government Bill 2020/21:150 Ett stärkt barnrättsperspektiv i vårdnadstvister (n 3) 70–73. Before 1 July 2021, the law stated that the court should pay particular attention to the parents' ability to cooperate, Swedish Government Bill 2005/06:99 Nya vårdnadsregler [New custody rules]. The practical effect of this was that in court, parents focused on the other parent's inability to cooperate.

[11] Ann-Sofie Bergman and Annika Rejmer, 'Parents in Child Custody Disputes: Why are they Disputing?' (2017) 14(2–3) *Journal of Child Custody* 134–150, 140, 141.

prevent conflicts have been rejected, based on the argument that doing so would undermine the very idea behind joint custody.[12] From the argumentation, a view emerges of the family, in some sense, as a protected zone, populated by mature, rational individuals who can resolve conflicts on their own—at least if forced to do so. If the parents still cannot reach a solution, the only recourse is for the court to give one parent sole custody. However, the courts are reluctant to do so, with reference to joint custody being in the best interests of the child. The result is repeated court proceedings concerning custody.[13]

7.3 A Growing Number of Custody Disputes in Sweden

In Sweden, the parents of some 40,000–45,000 children separate every year.[14] According to available statistics, most parents agree on custody, residence, and contact after a separation, sometimes with the assistance of the social services (*socialtjänsten*) and cooperation talks. Nevertheless, in some cases parents will not reach a consensus, and they need help from others—and as a last resort, the court—to reach a solution.

In 2021, the parents of 20,931 children in the age group 0–17 years participated in cooperation talks organized by the social services.[15] Approximately, three out of ten children whose parents separate, are the objects of the parents' disputes in court about custody or custody-related matters. In 2021, at least 12,612 children had parents involved in court proceedings since the social services gave courts retrieval orders for these

[12] Swedish Government Official Report 1995:79 Vårdnad, boende och umgänge [Custody, Residence and Contact] 87–88; Swedish Government Bill 1997/98:7 Vårdnad, boende och umgänge (n 6) 53.

[13] Swedish Government Official Report 2017:6 Se barnet! [See the Child!] 149–151.

[14] This only includes children who are living with their legal parents. If separation between an original parent and a stepparent were to be included in the statistics, it is estimated that around 60,000 children experience a separation between the adults in the family. In the latter case, however, the separation will not result in a custody dispute.

[15] Family Law and Parental Support Authority, Statistics on Family Law 2021. This corresponds to 95 children per 10,000 in this age group, which is the same as 2020. Statistics for the last five-year period show that the number of children per 10,000 has decreased in the last two years, www.mfof.se accessed 13 January 2023.

children.[16] The same year, 6,973 children were subject to social-services investigations regarding custody, residence, or contact; these statistics indicate a high conflict level between parents.[17]

It has been estimated that from 2006 to 2015, the number of court custody disputes in Sweden increased by almost 50%.[18] There are several possible explanations for this dramatic increase. Since 2008, the Court of Appeal must grant leave to appeal,[19] and this might have made repeat proceedings more common.[20] An increased incidence of cases with a foreign connection—where one parent is in Sweden and the other is outside the country—is pointed out as another likely reason for the increase in cases.[21] In 2006, a new provision was introduced in the Children and Parent Code. It stated that, when deciding on custody matters, the court should pay particular attention to the parents' ability to cooperate. In practice, this made it easier for one parent to obtain sole custody by demonstrating the other parent's difficulties in cooperating, thus increasing the number of court cases. More equal parenting is another explanation, meaning that fathers are now more interested in taking on their parental role, implying of course that mothers are less inclined to share custody with fathers. It is also believed that a greater propensity for conflict among parents has contributed to the increased number of cases.

[16] Family Law and Parental Support Authority, Statistics on Family Law 2021. This corresponds with 57 children per 10,000 in this age group.

[17] Family Law and Parental Support Authority, Statistics on Family Law 2021, https://www.mfof.se/download/18.e9eaab18120d9a7fa298e5/1655443358465/Statistics%20on%20family%20law%202021_Fact%20sheet.pdf accessed 10 May 2023.

[18] Swedish Government Official Report 2017:6 Se barnet! (n 13) 135–136.

[19] Swedish Government Bill 2007/08:139 En modernare rättegång—några ytterligare frågor [A more modern trial—some additional questions].

[20] Decisions concerning custody-related matters never become *res judicata* because a decision must always be in the best interests of a child; hence, it must be continually possible to adjust to the child's current situation. The 2014 Custody Inquiry found that around 40% of parties had previously been involved in a dispute concerning children, Swedish Government Official Report 2017:6 (n 14) 44.

[21] When a sole parent arrives in Sweden with children and specifies his or her civil status as married, joint custody is registered for the parents. Because of the joint right to decide, it becomes difficult for the parent living with the children in Sweden to take formal decisions concerning the children without the consent of the other. If the whereabouts of the other parent are unknown, the only way to resolve this situation is for the parent in Sweden to apply to the court for sole custody.

Finally, another explanation for the increase in court custody cases could be deficiencies in the preventive work.[22] The help that separating parents need cannot be provided by the court; it must be found elsewhere.

7.4 The Emergence of Alternative Dispute Resolution in Custody Cases

7.4.1 The Inadequacy of Court Proceedings in Custody Cases

The inadequacies of the court as a place for resolving custody disputes, has been known for a long time. Previous research has revealed several shortcomings in the Swedish system.[23] Proceedings in court are typically adversarial. The applicant must prove the claim, which means, for instance, that in principle, anyone who wants sole custody must show that the respondent—the other parent—is unfit in this regard. This automatically promotes conflict, not consensus. Furthermore, the court procedure was established at a time when only one of the separated parents could have custody. Yet today, with joint custody as a starting point, the process is insufficient. A court should settle a legal dispute based on the legal arguments. Lady Justice is blindfolded for a reason; she should not remove her blindfold to become involved in parents' conflicts. Even if it is accepted that the court should promote consensus solutions in the course of its proceedings, the court has very limited means to do so. It should also be noted that, as a legal criterion, the best interests of the child is hardly suitable for judicial review. The courts have very limited knowledge of these children and their living conditions, and one can reasonably question whether courts should or even could have such knowledge. Equally, even if a court *does* know what the 'best'

---

[22] Swedish Government Official Report 2017:6 *Se barnet!* (n 13) 136–142.

[23] See, for example, Annika Rejmer and Anna Singer, Vårdnadstvister och barnets bästa. Alternativa modeller för konfliktlösning på familjerättens område (2003) 26(102) *Retfærd* 63–72.

outcome is for a particular child, its decision-making options to achieve such a solution are very limited. The more recent requirements regarding children's participation cannot be met within the framework of Sweden's current system. Finally, research shows that parents involved in custody disputes often have specific problems.[24] In many cases, the dispute is not really about the child; instead—however inadequate it may be as a solution—parents approach it as a way of dealing with a life crisis.

All of these features have been recognized for a long time. Cooperation talks under the auspices of the social services have been used from as early as the 1970s. In addition to cooperation talks, procedures have been introduced in recent years to facilitate or achieve consensus solutions: the courts are responsible for mediation between the parties and can appoint an independent mediator. The latest innovation is the introduction of obligatory information talks (*informationssamtal*) as a prerequisite in custody cases. There is no lack of initiative, but one may ask: to what avail?

7.4.2 Cooperation Talks Offered by the Social Services

Social services, as mentioned above, have offered cooperation talks since the 1970s as a method for solving custody-related conflicts. From 1991, municipalities were required to provide cooperation talks; after the 1998 reform, these talks can also concern conflicts over the child's residence or maintenance.[25] Today, approximately 50% of separating parents participate in such talks.[26] Any agreement that is reached can be documented in a written contract confirmed by the social services. Contracts are as binding as court decisions and can be executed.

Cooperation talks are usually described as structured talks with parents who disagree over custody, residence, or contact, in connection with or

---

[24] See, for example, Bergman and Rejmer (n 1) 134–150.

[25] Swedish Government Bill 1990/91:8 om vårdnad och umgänge (n 6); Swedish Government Bill 1997/98:7 Vårdnad, boende och umgänge (n 6); Social Services Act [Socialtjänstlagen] (2001:453) Chapter 5, Section 7.3.

[26] Social Services Act Chapter 5 Section 7.3.

after a separation. The purpose is to help parents, with the guidance of a counsellor, to make arrangements for the child based on the child's needs and wishes.[27] The goal is to offer parents cooperation talks as soon as possible, and ideally two to four weeks from the initial contact.[28]

In its follow-up of parents' experiences from participation in mediation talks for 2014–2015, the Family Law and Parental Support Agency (MFoF) analysed and mapped the results of the talks to determine whether these talks contributed to agreements and kept parents out-of-court.[29] The survey showed that many of the parents who participated in the study were, 'very' or 'fairly satisfied' with the talks—even parents who had severe conflicts.[30] A follow-up study indicated that only 10% of the parents had initiated court proceedings or continued their court process four to six months after the conclusion of the talks.[31] The results from the MFoF survey indicated the cooperation talks had helped a large group of parents reach consensus solutions and that court proceedings might thus have been avoided. At the same time, the survey noted a need for continued support for many parents and their children, and it is not clear whether they continued to stay out-of-court.[32]

Unfortunately, knowledge is limited regarding the effects of cooperation talks in the longer term. One aspect of particular interest is to determine the durability of resulting agreements over time and the prerequisites that make it easier for an agreement to be reached. The MFoF survey also indicates that the moderators for cooperation talks lack training and that no specific models, methods, tools, or assessment instruments are used during the talks. The children concerned are seldom

[27] National Board of Health and Welfare, Vårdnad, boende och umgänge [Custody, Residence and Visitation] 155.

[28] Family Law and Parental Support Authority, Regulation and general advice (HSLF-FS) 2017:51, https://www.mfof.se/sarskilda-innehallssidor/foreskrifter-och-allmanna-rad.html accessed 9 May 2023.

[29] Family Law and Parental Support Authority, *Samarbetssamtal. Kartläggning av föräldrars och samtalsledares erfarenheter*, https://www.mfof.se/download/18.7a15f94516e8e25421b18716/1574925630064/samarbetssamtal-kartlaggning.pdf accessed 10 May 2023.

[30] Family Law and Parental Support Authority, *Samarbetssamtal* (n 29) 32.

[31] Family Law and Parental Support Authority, *Samarbetssamtal* (n 29) 32–33. The follow-up included only those parents who agreed to participate and not all parents in the first study.

[32] Family Law and Parental Support Authority, *Samarbetssamtal* (n 29) 7.

involved in the talks. Another possible disadvantage with cooperation talks is, when parents are engaged in a high level of conflict, they have no real incentive to reach an agreement. The option of going to court is always available and the foreseeability of a court decision is limited. There is always a chance for a 'better' solution in court and many want to take that chance.

7.4.3 Court-Initiated Cooperation Talks

Cooperation talks can also be ordered by the court, after the parents have initiated court proceedings. Any previous talks that the parents may have had are not an obstacle. Court-initiated cooperation talks do not require the consent of the parents, but will most likely be in vain if one or both parents object. An order for talks should be given as soon as it can be assumed to serve any purpose; every aspect that parents can agree on is beneficial to the child.

No statistics are available regarding the number of court-initiated cooperation talks that have been ordered; there is reason to believe that the courts have seldom taken this approach. If parents have turned to the court, their conflict level is usually high, and it is less likely that cooperation talks will result in an agreement. Cooperation talks can prolong the conflict between the parents and delay a ruling by the court. Furthermore, as an alternative, the court can try to mediate between the parents.[33]

7.4.4 Mediation in Court

In 2006, the courts were given increased opportunities to promote consensus solutions between parents. A provision in the Code of Judicial Procedure states that in the initial stages of proceedings, the court should clarify the possibilities for the parties to reach a consensus solution; this provision also became applicable in custody cases.[34] Furthermore, a new

[33] Code of Judicial Procedure [Rättegångsbalken] (1942:740) Chapter 42 Section 17.

[34] Ibid Chapter 42 Section 6.

provision states that the court has the duty, if appropriate in view of the nature of the case and other circumstances, to act for the parties to reconcile or for them to otherwise achieve a consensus solution.[35] The methods of doing this varies between the courts.[36] No uniform model is used.

However, a party who does not want to discuss a consensus solution cannot be forced to participate; the parties have a legitimate right to have their dispute resolved and settled by the court if they so wish.[37] It is emphasized that any efforts to reconcile the parties in custody disputes should be exercised with caution. If the court concludes that an agreement between the parties is incompatible with the best interests of the child, that agreement should not be the basis for the court's decision. The court should be particularly careful about accepting—or advocating for—a consensual solution in cases where one parent has committed violence or other abuse against the other parent, the child, or any sibling of the child.[38]

It is worth noting that a majority of custody-related court decisions are based on the parents' agreement.[39] Whether this is the result of the courts' mediation or simply process fatigue is unknown.

7.4.5 Court Appointed Mediator

If the court is unsuccessful in reconciling the parents but believes for some reason that reconciliation could still be possible, the court can appoint a mediator to help the parents reach a consensus solution in the best interests of the child.[40] This possibility was introduced in

[35] Ibid Chapter 42 Section 17.

[36] Swedish Government Official Report 2017:6 Se barnet! (n 13) 219–222.

[37] Swedish Government Bill 2005/06:99 Nya vårdnadsregler (n 10) 104.

[38] Ibid.

[39] In an investigation by the 2014 Custody Inquiry, it was noted that in 256 out of 412 lower court cases (62%) the decision was based on the parents' agreement, Swedish Government Official Report 2017:6 Se barnet! (n 13).

[40] Children and Parent Code [Föräldrabalken] (1949:381) Chapter 6 Section 18 a.

2006 taking inspiration from successful mediation previously used for enforcement of judgements.[41]

The underlying idea is that a special mediator, independent of the court, can go further than a judge in efforts to reconcile the parties. Nevertheless, the prospect of reaching a consensus solution between parents who have already taken a dispute to court, might be limited. Yet in cases where there is even the smallest chance that parents can reach a consensus solution, this approach was considered a desirable way to provide additional support for reaching an agreement.[42]

A prerequisite for success in mediation efforts is that the appointed mediator has experience and/or is appropriately qualified. According to the law, a mediator should have relevant education and professional experience and be suitable for the task.[43] However, no formal educational requirement for mediators has been established. The individual judge who appoints the mediator must ensure that the competence and suitability requirements are met. The mediation procedure is subject to confidentiality because this is typically conducive to achieving a solution.[44] Information that a party has given to a mediator regarding personal or economic matters remains confidential if the party wishes it.[45] The mediator can be heard as a witness about what has been said during mediation, but only when this is allowed by law or with permission of the person who gave the information.

Court-appointed mediators are not frequently used. An investigation by the 2014 Custody Inquiry indicated that mediators had been appointed in 1–3% of custody cases, and this limited data made it difficult to evaluate whether the mediation process had had the desired effect.[46]

---

[41] Ibid Chapter 21 Section 7.2.

[42] Swedish Government Bill 2005/06:99 Nya vårdnadsregler (n 10) 64.

[43] Children and Parent Code Chapter 6 Section 18 a; Swedish Government Official Report 2017:6 *Se barnet!* (n 13) 61–264; Swedish Government Bill 2020/21:150 Ett stärkt barnrättsperspektiv i vårdnadstvister (n 3) 78–79. There is no special education for mediators available in Sweden.

[44] Swedish Government Official Report 2017:6 Se barnet! (n 13) 264.

[45] Public Access to Information and Secrecy Act [Offentlighets- och sekretesslagen] (2009:400) Chapter 36 Section 7.3 a.

[46] Swedish Government Official Report 2017:6 Se barnet! (n 13) 259.

7.4.6 Obligatory Information Meetings to Precede Court Proceedings

The latest (but probably not the last) initiative to help separating parents stay out of court, is the law on obligatory information meetings, in force from 1 March 2022.[47] Again, the objective is to help parents reach an out-of-court settlement concerning custody-related matters. It is believed that some custody disputes taken to court result from the parties' lack of knowledge regarding what can actually be achieved through a court decision.[48] Therefore, as a general rule, before initiating court proceedings concerning custody, residence, or contact, parents must present a valid certificate proving that they have attended an obligatory information meeting. If no certificate is submitted—despite a subsequent court injunction to do so—the court will dismiss the case.

At the meetings, parents who are considering court proceedings concerning a custody-related matter should receive information about finding the best solution for the child—this includes information about the limitations of the court process. When appropriate, parents should also be offered cooperation talks and, unless inappropriate, they should be offered support or given guidance in finding other forms of assistance.

The municipalities are responsible for the information meetings, within the framework of their social-services provision. Information meetings should be held at the earliest opportunity and within four weeks of a request for them. The social welfare committee will issue a certificate to parents who have attended information meetings.

7.5 Conclusions and Further Thoughts

It can be said that there has been no lack of ambition in Sweden to establish an order for custody dispute settlements outside of court. The question is, whether these efforts have borne fruit. Despite long-standing

---

[47] The law entered into force 1 March 2022.

[48] Government Bill 2020/21:150 Ett stärkt barnrättsperspektiv i vårdnadstvister (n 3). The evidence for this assumption is weak and based on anecdotal evidence, Swedish Government Official Report 2017:6 Se barnet! (n 13).

efforts to create systems that can help parents reach an out-of-court settlement on issues related to custody, residence, or visitation, too many parents still go to court—often to the detriment of the children involved.[49] The problems identified above are not unique to the Swedish system. While out-of-court procedures differ between legal systems, it appears they all have similar challenges that must be dealt with.[50]

Several intersecting features explain why the current system for handling parental custody conflicts out-of-court has not enjoyed the success that was hoped for. One is the unclear purpose of alternative solutions. The primary function of Sweden's system of alternative dispute resolution is to keep parents out of court, and not necessarily to *resolve* their conflict, illustrated by the recent addition of obligatory information meetings.

Furthermore, the possibilities to follow up the results of alternative dispute resolution are notably limited. This is exacerbated by what can be described as a clear lack of interest in investigating the extent that, for example, cooperation talks really lead to sustainable solutions or even determining whether a conflict remains out of court. Therefore, cooperation talks seemingly appear to be sufficient in themselves and disconnected from custody conflict resolution. Even if the ambition for cooperation talks is to help the parents reach an agreement, it is unclear how this can be achieved. The methods for cooperation talks and especially for mediation are undeveloped and lack a scientific basis.

It is notable that Lady Justice also seems to be blindfolded when it comes to out-of-court handling of custody disputes. A clear approach to solving these problems, using the various methods referred to here, is often absent. The system of alternative custody-dispute procedures is based on the assumption that parents are rational and, when given sufficient information about child-related needs, laws, and procedures, they will resolve their differences out-of-court. Some parents will certainly fit this model, but not all; parents who do not fit this pattern—owing to

[49] See for example, Swedish Government Official Report 2017:6 Se barnet! (n 13) 229–234.

[50] See for example, Nylund (n 4); Anne Barlow, Rosemary Hunter and Jan Ewing 'Mapping paths to family justice: Resolving family disputes involving children in neoliberal times' in Anna Kaldal, Agnes Hellner and Titti Mattsson (eds), *Children in Custody Disputes: Matching Legal Proceedings to Problems* (Palgrave 2023).

the custody conflict, the overarching life crisis of separation, or other problems—are not served by this model for conflict resolution.

We know from research that parents in custody disputes have problems that do not fit with the image of parents that formed the basis of the design for the custody dispute process.[51] The system lacks what could be described as diagnostic tools. We simply know too little about those whom we are supposed to help. The Swedish out-of-court processes are too rigid in the sense that they only fit some of the families targeted, and are not sufficiently adapted to the varying and often complex needs of the specific family. As Anna Nylund points out in her contribution to this anthology, a more nuanced understanding and consideration of the specific needs of different families would contribute to a more balanced, well-functioning system of out-of-court procedures.

Finally, the children concerned do not have a given place in the proceedings. If giving children a place is considered desirable, then the current arrangement is not satisfactory. Ensuring the child's right to participation in the context of the complex legal structure described in this chapter is a challenge that the Swedish legal system shares with other countries.[52]

As long as we strive to help parents achieve a cooperative state with equal responsibility for the child, and joint custody is the goal, it can be questioned whether court decisions are at all relevant in instances other than when one parent is deemed unfit and should not have custody responsibility. While the possibility remains for parents to take their dispute to court, measures to keep custody disputes out-of-court by providing information, ordering cooperative talks, and appointing mediators will have little impact. The ability to predict the outcome of a case is limited when the matter involves custody—it is always possible to win. Even more important is the fact that many separating parents are in a life crisis; cooperation or obligatory information meetings cannot necessarily help them resolve this problem.

---

[51] See, for example, Annika Rejmer, *Vårdnadstvister: En rättssociologisk studie av tingsrätts funktion vid handläggning av vårdnadskonflikter med utgångspunkt från barnets bästa* (Lund University 2003).

[52] Barlow, Hunter and Ewing (n 50).

If we want to help parents reach a lasting solution to their conflict and protect the rights of the child, different methods are called for. In short, differentiated and family-specific services are required.

References

Bergman A-S and Rejmer A, 'Parents in Child Custody Disputes: Why are they Disputing?' (2017) 14(2–3) *Journal of Child Custody* 134.

Barlow A, Hunter R and Ewing J, 'Mapping paths to family justice: Resolving family disputes involving children in neoliberal times' in Kaldal A, Hellner A and Mattsson T (eds), *Children in Custody Disputes: Matching Legal Proceedings to Problems* (Palgrave 2023) 107.

Eriksson M, 'Children's Participation and Perspectives in Family Disputes' in Kaldal A, Hellner A and Mattsson T (eds), *Children in Custody Disputes: Matching Legal Proceedings to Problems* (Palgrave 2023) 85.

Norlén A, 'Children's Health Matters in Custody Conflicts—What do we know?' in Kaldal A, Hellner A and Mattsson T (eds), *Children in Custody Disputes: Matching Legal Proceedings to Problems* (Palgrave 2023) 21.

Nylund A, 'Scandinavian Family Mediation: Towards a System of Differentiated Services?' in Kaldal A, Hellner A and Mattsson T (eds), *Children in Custody Disputes: Matching Legal Proceedings to Problems* (Palgrave 2023) 41.

Rejmer A, *Vårdnadstvister: En rättssociologisk studie av tingsrätts funktion vid handläggning av vårdnadskonflikter med utgångspunkt från barnets bästa* (Lund University 2003).

Rejmer A and Singer A, Vårdnadstvister och barnets bästa. Alternativa modeller för konfliktlösning på familjerättens område (2003) 26(102) *Retfærd* 63.

Swedish Ministry Memorandum 1989:52 Vårdnad och umgänge.

Swedish Government Bill 2007/08:139 En modernare rättegång – några ytterligare frågor.

Swedish Government Bill 1975/76:170 Faderskap och vårdnad.

Swedish Government Bill 1981/82:168 om vårdnad och umgänge m.m.

Swedish Government Bill 1990/91:8 om vårdnad och umgänge.

Swedish Government Bill 1997/98:7 Vårdnad, boende och umgänge.

Swedish Government Bill 2005/06:99 Nya vårdnadsregler.

Swedish Government Bill 2020/21:150 *Ett stärkt barnrättsperspektiv i vårdnadstvister* [A Strengthened Child Rights Perspective in Custody Disputes].

Swedish Government Official Report 1995:79 Vårdnad, boende och umgänge.
Swedish Government Official Report 2017:6 Se barnet!

8

Children's Health Matters in Custody Conflicts: Best Interests of the Child and Decisions on Health Matters

Trude Haugli and Randi Sigurdsen

8.1 Introduction

A conflict between parents can cause both psychological and physical health problems for their children.[1] It can also lead to a situation where the parents are unable to cooperate on decision-making in the best interests of the child—irrespective of whether the child's health problems result from the family conflict or other sources. Ultimately, conflicts concerning the healthcare of a child can result in a custody dispute, where parents file for sole custody.[2] With this in mind, our main

[1] Cf Anna Norlén, 'Children's Health Matters in Custody Conflicts—What Do We Know?' in Anna Kaldal, Agnes Hellner and Titti Mattsson (eds), *Children in Custody Disputes: Matching Legal Proceedings to Problems* (Palgrave 2023).

[2] See for example, Annika Rejmer, 'Custody Disputes from a Socio-Legal Perspective' in Anna Kaldal, Agnes Hellner and Titti Mattsson (eds), *Children in Custody Disputes: Matching the Legal Proceedings to Problems* (Palgrave 2023).

T. Haugli (✉) · R. Sigurdsen
UiT The Arctic University of Norway, Tromsø, Norway

A. Kaldal et al. (eds.), *Children in Custody Disputes*,
https://doi.org/10.1007/978-3-031-46301-3_8

question is: how should legal instruments be used to reach a decision concerning a child's health when the parents disagree?

In this article, we present current Norwegian legislation and discuss how children's and parents' rights are balanced when the parents are in conflict and the child needs healthcare. This situation presents different scenarios depending on:

- the severity of the medical intervention and its potential consequences;
- the child's age and maturity;
- the consistency of the child's view regarding the medical intervention; and
- the nature of the family conflict.

Therefore, we present four scenarios and explore current legal challenges using these examples. There is an underlying question of whether current legislation is more family-oriented than child-oriented and, if so, whether the child's right to healthcare, under Article 24 of the Convention on the Rights of the Child (CRC), is challenged.[3]

These questions are rarely presented before the Norwegian courts or any other conflict-resolving bodies, due to the character of Norway's decision-making system in healthcare situations.[4] The overall purpose of this article is to visualize the complexity of the legislation in this area, and to emphasize that these are difficult legal questions. Further, the intention is to show how little attention is paid in legislation to differing opinions between parents about health matters concerning their children, and to highlight the fact that parents and children do not necessarily have concurrent interests and views. Consequently, this system may have harmful effects for children.

[3] UN Convention on the Rights of the Child (CRC) adopted by the General Assembly 20 November 1989. Committee on the Rights of the Child, *General Comment No. 15 (2013) on the Right of the Child to the Enjoyment of the Highest Attainable Standard of Health (Art. 24)* (17 April 2013) CRC/C/G/15.

[4] For more details, see Karl Harald Søvig, 'Reviewing Medical Decisions Concerning Infants within the Norwegian Healthcare System; A Public Law Approach' in Imogen Goold, Cressida Auckland and Jonathan Herring (eds), *Medical Decision-Making on Behalf of Young Children. A Comparative Perspective* (Hart Publishing 2020) 259–268.

8.2 Method Used, Structure of the Contribution, and Main Findings

The article begins by presenting current Norwegian legislation on health matters. The interpretation is based on the wording of the provisions, the preparatory works, relevant literature, and basic principles in child law (the best interests of the child), Article 3 CRC; the right to life and development, Article 6 CRC; participation rights, Article 12 CRC), and health law (availability, accessibility, acceptability, equality, agency, accountability, and quality).[5] The nature of the Norwegian system means that there is a lack of relevant case law for reference in this area.

The remainder of the chapter is structured as follows: After an introduction to the legal system and relevant legal provisions, is a discussion of our main questions based on the scenarios. These are arranged according to the seriousness of the health matters involved. Using the example scenarios, the article analyses the main findings in the light of the general principle of participation rights. The main finding is that the set of rules is complicated, and partly inaccessible; top legal competence is needed to comprehend the rules, yet it is health personnel, children, and parents who are supposed to apply them. The lack of a suitable conflict resolution system can cause harm or unnecessary risk to children's health, and ultimately, escalate parental conflicts.

[5] World Health Organization, 'Advancing the Right to Health: the Vital Role of Law' (2016) http://www.who.int/iris/handle/10665/252815 accessed 25 February 2023; Asbjørn Kjønstad, "Twelve main Principles in Norwegian Health Law" (2010) Retfærd 60–78.

8.3 Relevant Norwegian Legislation

Article 104 of the Norwegian Constitution[6] is intended to safeguard children's human rights. It includes the four principles from the CRC and a reference to an obligation to ensure that children receive necessary healthcare.[7] The European Convention on Human Rights (ECHR) and CRC are incorporated into Norwegian law; consequently, the state has undertaken clear obligations to secure both the rights of the child and the parents' right to respect for their privacy and family life, Article 8 ECHR.[8] Until the child reaches the age of maturity, the parents have the right and duty to make decisions in personal matters on the child's behalf.[9] Still, Norwegian law is built upon the principle of the evolving capacity of the child. According to the Norwegian Act Related to Children and Parents (Children's Act), the child has a right to co-determination: parents shall, as and when the child becomes able to form their own point of view on matters that concern them, consider the child's opinion before deciding on the child's personal situation.[10] Importance is attached to the opinion of the child according to their age and maturity. The same applies to other persons with custody of the child or who are involved with the child.

Children aged seven and younger, who are able to form their own points of view, must be provided with information and opportunities to express their opinions before decisions are made concerning personal matters affecting the child, including parental responsibility, custody, and contact rights. The opinions of the child shall be given due weight

[6] Constitution of the Kingdom of Norway [Kongeriket Norges Grunnlov] 17 May 1814.

[7] Report from the Human Rights Commission to the Presidium of the Parliament on Human Rights in the Constitution, 19 December 2011 (Dokument 16) Sections 32.5.2–32.5.6; Trude Haugli, 'Constitutional Rights for Children in Norway' in Trude Haugli, Anna Nylund, Randi Sigurdsen and Lena R L Bendiksen (eds), *Children's Constitutional Rights in the Nordic Countries* (Brill/Nijhoff 2019) 39–57. The wording is 'health security' in the Norwegian Constitution 104.

[8] European Convention on Human Rights and UN Convention on the Rights of the Child.

[9] Norwegian Act related to Children and Parents (Children's Act) [Barneloven] Section 30 Subsection 1.

[10] Children's Act Section 31 Subsection 1.

according to their age and maturity, thus the opinions of children aged 12 and above, carry significant weight.[11]

Regarding children's right to decide for themselves, parents shall steadily extend the child's right to make their own decisions as they get older and until they reach the age of 18.[12] Specific age limits have been set for self-determination in various areas, including education, religious matters, using the internet and social media, and for the child as a consumer. Health is one area where there is a specific regulation, and this is the topic for the following text. However specific such rules may be, they must be read in the light of the general principles stated in the Children's Act.

In health matters, with a few exceptions, the age of maturity in Norwegian law is 16 years.[13] Even if children younger than 16 have reached a sufficient level of maturity to decide for themselves, the competence to decide lies with the parents. However, the child's maturity is a factor to be considered when parents or health personnel determine the weight of the child's opinion. In this text, we concentrate on children younger than 16; there is a potential conflict for this group between the child's right to the highest attainable standard of health, Article 24 CRC and Patient and Service User Rights Act (PRA),[14] and the parents' right and duty to make decisions on the child's behalf, keeping in mind the principle of the evolving capacity of the child, Article 5 CRC.

The parental right to consent to or refuse healthcare on behalf of their child deviates from the general rule in Norwegian legislation, which stipulates that the individual who is to receive healthcare shall provide informed consent before receiving this care. This principle[15] is linked to ethical and legal aspects, including the right to respect for human dignity and bodily integrity and the right to respect of private life—all

[11] Children's Act Section 31 Subsection 2.

[12] Children's Act Section 33.

[13] Norwegian Patient and Service User Rights Act [Pasient- og brukerrettighetsloven] Section 4-3 Subsection 1.

[14] Patient and Service User Rights Act Section 2-1 b Subsection 2.

[15] Patient and Service User Rights Act Section 4-1.

core values in human-rights legislation.[16] Moreover, healthcare is easier to provide and often more efficient when the patient is well informed and wishes to receive the treatment.

For children to be able to express their view and have an influence in these matters, it is crucial for them to receive information adapted to their age and maturity. Children's general right to participate may be constrained by the fact that, in Norwegian legislation, their right to information is not very clear. The main problem is linked to the law's ambiguity regarding who is responsible for informing the child: is it the parents or health personnel? Another challenge is the lack of an official system to ensure that children have their say.

In Norway, most parents have joint parental responsibility, even if they are not living together. Thus, both have the right to receive relevant information from health personnel and, as a rule, the right to give their consent to medical treatment.[17] Even if the parents are in conflict, they are generally expected to be able to set aside their personal conflicts and act in the best interests of the child regarding health matters.[18]

8.4 Four Scenarios

8.4.1 Scenario 1: Healthcare as a Part of Daily Care—Consent From Only One Parent

Maria is six years old and has lived with her mother since her parents divorced two years earlier. Her parents have a high conflict level. Maria stays with her father every second weekend. During one such stay, she has an accident and sustains a deep cut on her knee.

---

[16] Jonathan Herring, *Medical Law and Ethics* (3rd edn, Oxford University Press 2010) Chapter 1, Item 6 and 7; Henriette Sinding Aasen, *Pasientens rett til selvbestemmelse ved medisinsk behandling* (Fagbokforlaget 2000) 43–44.

[17] Patient and Service User Rights Act Section 4-4 Subsection 1.

[18] The relationship between the child and the parents is generally not questioned, except in cases requiring intervention into the family's life in the interest of the child. The parents are expected to have a key role in realization of children's rights; see Jaap E Doek, "The Human Rights of Children: An Introduction" in Ursula Kilkelly and Ton Liefaard (eds), *International Human Rights of Children* (Springer 2019) 3, 4, 14–15.

Consent from both parents is not required in all situations. If the child needs healthcare that is regarded as a part of the daily care of the child, consent from one parent is sufficient.[19] Whether the parents have joint parental responsibility is not at issue here. When Maria stays with her father, he is obliged to provide for her wellbeing.[20] Accordingly, when the decision cannot be postponed, Maria's father must act; he must decide whether the cut requires medical assistance and, if so, he must take Maria to a medical facility. Consent from the father is sufficient for further medical treatment in this case, and the law does not require that consent is obtained from the mother or that she is informed of the matter. The law requires that Maria shall be listened to, even if her view is not decisive. The father and health personnel are obliged to make a decision based on the best interests of the child.

As the wound is very deep and there is a risk of infection, the doctor recommends a course of antibiotics. The father knows that Maria's mother vehemently opposes treatment with antibiotics except in life-threatening situations. This scenario must be viewed as a common situation that a parent must address as part of the daily care responsibility. Thus, in accordance with the same provision, the decision rests with Maria's father.

The preparatory work gives no indication that the provision is in place to prevent parental conflict in health matters; rather, the provision's purpose is to provide an easy way to ensure that the child, at any given time, shall receive adequate healthcare related to daily life. A precondition is that the parent who gives consent will follow the medical advice given by qualified health personnel. Consequently, this precondition could have a moderating effect on the potential conflict between the parents. The provision may help parents who are in conflict about other matters regarding the child to avoid conflict in health situations, even though this outcome is not the legislator's intention with the provision.

However, because the authority to decide on behalf of the child lies with the parent in whose custody the child resides at the time of the decision, consent to ongoing medical treatment given by one parent

[19] Patient and Service User Rights Act Section 4-4 Subsection 2.

[20] Children's Act Section 42.

might subsequently be withdrawn by the other. In Maria's case, her mother might stop the antibiotics treatment when Maria returns to her home, contrary to medical advice. Hence, within day-to-day care, the residing parent is free to turn down treatment, irrespective of the advice of medical authorities.

8.4.2 Scenario 2: Need of Significant Healthcare—Both Parents Refuse

> **Peter,** 14, is depressed due to the high level of conflict between his parents. Over the past few months, he has skipped school several times and has stayed at home instead of participating in his usual activities. He has had a few talks with the school nurse, who is of the opinion that Peter needs specialized psychiatric treatment. As Peter is below the age of 16, his parents must give their consent; moreover, in a case of referral to a specialist health service, both must consent. However, Peter's parents refuse to give their consent.

Peter has a right to receive treatment but needs consent from both of his parents.[21] Although the parents are in conflict, they might agree not to consent to psychiatric treatment for Peter. It is conceivable that parental conflict with an obvious negative effect on the child's right to healthcare could occur even when parents live together. In addition, parents' resistance might stem from a desire to avoid illuminating domestic problems. Especially in cases of sexual abuse, or where parents struggle with their own health issues, addiction problems, or domestic violence, at least one parent may be reluctant to let the child receive medical or psychiatric treatment. In the current scenario, the parental conflict is putting Peter's right to healthcare at risk.

As a rule, when parents refuse to consent, health personnel are obliged to respect this refusal. Still, an alternative is available in situations where parents deny their child healthcare, even when health personnel have strongly advised it. In these cases, health personnel are obliged

[21] Patient and Service User Rights Act Section 2-1 b Subsection 2.

to consider carefully whether the child has a significant need for the healthcare.[22] Even if health personnel are bound by a strict duty of confidentiality, in some situations they have a right and a duty to inform the child-welfare services (*Barnevernstjenesten*) in order to help secure the child's rights.[23] A prerequisite for sharing information is that the health personnel have a *reason to believe* that the child has a *life-threatening* or other *serious* medical condition for which the child is not currently receiving sufficient treatment.[24]

The threshold for giving information to child-welfare services without the parent's agreement is quite high. In Peter's case, health personnel must consider whether his condition is serious enough to involve child-welfare services. If health personnel conclude that the law does *not* permit them to give information to welfare services, they must either wait to see whether Peter's health condition meets the requirements in the law; or try to give the parents more information to persuade them to consent. For health personnel, this can be a challenging situation. The legal text confers a degree of discretion with respect to determining whether to inform the child-welfare services. When health personnel are in doubt about whether they are free to involve child-welfare services without the parents' permission, some will choose to hold to the rule of confidentiality as a way out of the dilemma. Whether information is to be given or not, implies difficult assessments and consequences; thus, when health personnel are aware of the high conflict level between the parents, they may refrain from alerting child-welfare services to avoid escalating the conflict. In such a case, children in Peter's situation would have their right to healthcare violated.

On the other hand, if child-welfare services are informed, they are obliged to investigate the case.[25] If the conditions stated in the act seem to be fulfilled, child-welfare services may bring the case before the child protection and health board (*barneverns- og helsenemnda*), which is an

---

22 Søvig (n 4) 263.

23 Norwegian Health Personnel Act [Lov om helsepersonell] Section 33.

24 Health Personnel Act Section 33 Subsection 2 Litra b. See also Norwegian Child Welfare Act Section 33 Subsection 2 Litra b.

25 Child Welfare Act Section 2-2.

administrative body, and has much in common with a court of law.[26] The board is competent to decide whether the child shall receive healthcare if he or she is suffering from a life-threatening illness or other profoundly serious illness or injury, even if the parents do not cooperate.[27] If an order to start healthcare is issued, parental rights are limited; for example, they are obliged to bring the child to hospital for medical examination and treatment. If they do not respond to the order, their parental responsibility may be questioned, and the next step could be a care order and placement of the child in foster care, if the other conditions for such an order are fulfilled.[28]

Case law shows the above possibilities are very seldom applied.[29] If health matters are mentioned in a child-welfare order, they are usually related to maltreatment or serious neglect by the parents. This begs the question of whether the threshold in Norwegian legislation to secure adequate medical services for children is too high. The preparatory works do not discuss the possibility that a parental conflict might be the cause of the reluctance to consent to medical treatment for children.[30] Nor do the preparatory works address how a child might influence a parental decision to refuse him or her medical treatment. A right follows for children older than 12 to have party rights in cases related to healthcare.[31] However, the contents of the provision are unclear; there is no presentation in the preparatory works and the provision is barely discussed in the literature.[32]

Peter's own voice could be a crucial factor in a case like this. Even if his right to complain was limited, it might have helped him nevertheless, but this is an unresolved question. As long as Peter has no right to complain and the school nurse finds that she must respect the rule of confidence, no official organ will be informed of Peter's need for psychiatric assistance. Peter's right to healthcare is at risk.

---

[26] Child Welfare Act Section 14-1.

[27] Ibid. Section 3-7.

[28] Ibid. Section 5-1.

[29] Ibid. Section 3-7.

[30] Proposition to the Odelsting (Ot.prp.) nr 12 (1998–1999).

[31] Patient and Service User Rights Act.

[32] Aslak Syse, *Pasient- og brukerrettighetsloven* (4th edn, Gyldendal 2015) 548–549.

The CRC does not directly address the possible conflict of interest between children and parents in health matters.[33] In the above scenario, Peter wants help, and the parents are obliged to give considerable weight to his view; still, the final decision rests with the parents, unless the rather serious conditions specified in the Child Welfare Act are present. Since the threshold is so high, one can argue that in these situations, the rights and interests of the parents prevail over the best interests of the child.

8.4.3 Scenario 3: Need of Significant Healthcare—Parents with Differing Opinions

> **David** is twelve years old and has long suffered from leukaemia. His parents live together but have had periods of living apart due to cohabitation difficulties. Both parents have supported David during his long period of cancer treatment. After the COVID-19 vaccine was introduced, David's principal doctor at the hospital recommended that the parents should consent to vaccination for David, and they accepted. However, when David heard about this, he said no. In his opinion, there was too little information about the vaccine, especially regarding long-term effects. After hearing what David had to say, his father changed his mind. The mother continues to uphold her decision to consent to the vaccination.

When medical treatment is given within the specialist healthcare system, it cannot be characterized as a part of the child's daily care. Therefore, the starting point in this case is a requirement on consent from both of David's parents. David's mother agrees, but the father declines vaccination. In a situation like this, we might use an exception in the law (PRA Section 4-4 ss. 3) stating that if only one parent gives consent, the considered opinion of qualified health personnel is decisive for whether

[33] John Tobin, 'Fixed Concepts but Changing Conceptions: Understanding the Relationship Between Children and Parents' in Martin D Ruck, Michele Peterson-Dadali and Michael Freeman (eds), *Handbook of Children's Rights: Global and Multidisciplinary Perspectives* (Routledge 2017) 53–67.

healthcare should be provided. In other words, the opinion of qualified health personnel is crucial.

A prerequisite is that the treatment is *necessary* to avoid any *injury* to the child, which is a medical question. There are no further qualification terms for the concept of *injury*. This provision is a result of experience gained in situations where children did not receive necessary medical treatment due to one parent's refusal to consent.[34] Parental conflict was pointed out as one explanation. A decisive factor here is how 'qualified' health personnel are identified to determine whether the treatment is necessary to avoid injury. In most cases, the opinion of a medical doctor is needed, perhaps a doctor with special qualification in a medical field. In David's case, a medical doctor must decide whether David needs the vaccination. If after professional consideration qualified health personnel give an opinion that the child's condition meets the criteria set in the Patient and Service User Rights Act,[35] and examination and/or treatment is in the child's best interest, this treatment can start when one of the parents has given her/his consent.[36] To a certain degree, the decision to give or refrain from giving medical treatment can be regarded as taken out of the hands of the parents, as health personnel's assessment is essential. This might be a positive factor in a conflict situation between the parents.

But how can the child's own opinion be included here? The parents have an obligation to inform the child.[37] This might be difficult when they are of different opinions, as in this case, with a newly introduced vaccine. There is a risk that their information is affected by their attitude to the vaccine. Whether health personnel have any obligations to inform the child when parents are unable to give the child factual and objective information is not clear in Norwegian *health* legislation. Still, the child's right to be heard follows clearly from the Norwegian Constitution, CRC, and the Children's Act, and indirectly from the principle of due diligence in healthcare. According to the principle of the best interests of the child,

[34] Norwegian Official Report 2008:9 Med barnet i fokus [Whit the child in focus] 49.

[35] Section 4-4 Subsection 3.

[36] Norwegian Official Report 2008:9 Med barnet i fokus 51 and Proposition to the Odelsting nr 104 (2008–2009) 63.

[37] Patient and Service User Rights Act Section 4-4 Subsection 5.

and the right to the highest attainable standard of health, there are several reasons to impose obligations on health personnel. Another reason is the respect for the child's right to participate. For David, it might be easier to talk to a professional, thus involving as little emotion as possible. In our opinion, if David still refuses to get the vaccine, even after being informed, he must have the right to have his view respected and to refuse the treatment. However, current law in this respect is unclear.[38]

The preparatory works emphasize that both parents shall be informed and heard when they have joint parental responsibility.[39] The law does not discriminate between the parents. This brings us back to Peter's story.

8.4.4 Scenario 4: Parents' Right to Information

Peter, now age 15, suffers from serious depression. His parents have separated; he lives with his mother and has no contact with his father. The parents still have joint parental responsibility, and Peter's mother has given her consent to psychiatric treatment. Because healthcare professionals strongly advise healthcare for Peter, the consent of only one parent is needed.[40] Peter's father abuses alcohol and has outbursts of anger. The challenge in this case is the main rule stating that both parents shall be informed and can speak out, even if their consent is not required. However, the mother will withdraw her consent if the father is informed, because she is afraid of the father's reaction and she believes that Peter's treatment will reveal the father's problems. The relevant question then becomes: Are the health personnel obliged to inform the father?

If the parents have joint parental responsibility, both parents have the right to be heard, which implies a right to information. The right of both parents to receive information and express their views is normally of essential value, even in a conflict situation. By receiving comments

[38] Marit Hellebostad, Aslak Syse and Reidun Førde, 'Når en mindreårig pasient nekter livreddende behandling' (2017) 137(14–15); *Tidsskrift for den norske legeforening*; Stephen Gilmore and Jonathan Herring, '"No" is the Hardest Word: Consent and Children's Autonomy' (2011) 23(1) *Child and Family Law Quarterly* 3–28.

[39] Proposition to the Odelsting nr 104 (2008–2009) 63.

[40] Patient and Service User Rights Act Section 4-4 Subsection 3.

from both parents on all aspects of the wellbeing of the child, healthcare personnel will be able to evaluate the severity of the child's condition.

However, in Peter's situation, the father's right to information conflicts with Peter's right to healthcare, because his mother will withdraw her consent to treatment if the father is informed. This type of conflict is not given attention in the preparatory works. Indeed, it seems that parental rights are given more weight than the child's rights.

The strength of parental rights is also demonstrated in the declining parent's right to bring the decision about healthcare to the County Governor's office for appeal. This opportunity is illusory without information. However, the right to information may be limited according to the wording 'as far as possible'.[41] The wording indicates a reservation concerning the duty to inform both parents, and this is the intention according to the preparatory works.[42] There is no absolute obligation to inform both parents, but there must be legitimate reasons for *not* doing so. The preparatory works point out various practical aspects as obstacles (for example, a lack of time or ability to consult the other parent).[43]

In the case of Peter, there are no practical obstacles. Instead, the reason for not informing the father is to shield Peter from an escalation of the conflict between the parents and perhaps to shield Peter from his father's temper. In our opinion, there are legal reasons not to inform the father based on the principles of best interests of the child and the child's right to participation.[44] Peter is 15 and has no contact with his father, and the parental conflict has caused him serious health problems. If Peter's mother withdraws her consent to avoid escalating the conflict, Peter's right to healthcare will be jeopardized. Moreover, the law gives Peter no opportunity to bring the question of whether his father shall be informed to the County Governor's office for appeal, as this right is reserved for the

---

[41] Patient and Service User Rights Act Section 4-4 Subsection 3.

[42] Proposition to the Odelsting nr 104 (2008–2009) 63.

[43] Proposition to the Odelsting nr 104 (2008–2009) 63.

[44] E Kay M Tisdall, 'Challenging Competency and Capacity?' (2018) 26(1) *International Journal of Children's Rights* 159–182; David Archard and Marit Skivenes, 'Balancing a Child's Best Interests and Child's Views' (2019) 17(1) *The International Journal of Children's Rights* 1–21; Jaap E Doek, 'Children's Rights in Health Care and the General Principles of the CRC', in Jozef Dorscheidt, H H M and Jaap E Doek (eds), *Children's Rights in Health Care* (Brill/Nijhoff 2019) 48–70.

parents.[45] Still, health personnel should ask Peter about the involvement of his father in the matter.

This scenario exemplifies the fact that although core child human-law principles are not communicated in the Patient and Service User Rights Act, they must be included in the assessment of whether a parent shall be informed.[46] Not taking these principles into account may result in a violation of the Norwegian Constitution, 'Children have the right to respect for their human dignity'.[47] They have the right to be heard in questions that concern them, and due weight shall be attached to their views in accordance with their age and development' and 'For actions and decisions that affect children, the best interests of the child shall be a fundamental consideration'.[48]

8.5 Concluding Observations

Our main question was: how should legal instruments be used to reach a decision concerning a child's health when the child's parents disagree? By presenting different scenarios, we have shown, in current Norwegian legislation, how children's and parents' rights are balanced when the parents are in conflict and the child needs healthcare. Even if the purpose here is not to provide broader and more general considerations relating to children's capacity to decide for themselves, we will add a few comments regarding this broader view—because both social and family-law aspects might become relevant in the scenarios we have analysed.

There is no doubt about the child's right to participate in decision-making according to human-rights instruments and domestic Norwegian

---

45 Ursula Kilkelly and Mary Donnelly, 'Participation in Healthcare: The Views and Experiences of Children and Young People' (2011) 28(1) *International Journal of Children's Rights* 107–125.

46 Aoife Daly, 'No Weight for "Due Weight"? A Children's Autonomy Principle in Best Interests Proceedings' (2018) 26(1) *International Journal of Children's Rights* 61–92; Aoife Daly, 'Children, Autonomy and the Courts: Beyond the Right to Be Heard' (2018) 26(4) *International Journal of Children's Rights* 843–847.

47 Section 104 Subsection 1.

48 Haugli and others (n 7).

law.[49] This right is clearly stated in the Constitution, the CRC, the Children's Act, and the Child Welfare Act. However, several challenges emerge when the right of the child is supposed to be exercised within the family sphere.[50] One of those relates to the topic we have discussed: when the parents have different opinions about health issues concerning the child, or the child and his or her parent have different views. Another challenge is the lack of children's agency, and the lack of bodies or institutions to which children can direct a complaint about violations of their right to participate.[51] If the child has the right to co-determination in personal matters, and is not heard before authorities make decisions, this will be a violation of the rules of procedure and may influence the lawfulness of the decision. However, in health matters, there are no such decision-making bodies. Hence, the decisions are more informal and made in cooperation with the parents, medical personnel, and ideally, also in cooperation with the child. This raises concerns with respect to the child's access to justice.

The legislation presented above is based on an assumption that parents will act in a responsible way.[52] Yet, we have seen that conflicting parents' actions may harm their children's health. Some steps have been taken

---

[49] Henriette Sinding Aasen, 'Barns rett til selvbestemmelse og medbestemmelse i beslutninger om helsehjelp' (2008) *Tidsskrift for familierett, arverett og barnevernrettslige spørsmål* 3–26; Kirsten Sandberg, 'Children's Right to Participate in Health Care Decisions' in Henriette Sinding Aasen, Antonio Barbosa da Silva, Rune Halvorsen and Bjorn Hvinden (eds), *Human Rights, Dignity and Autonomy in Health Care and Social Services: Nordic Perspectives* (1st edn, Intersentia 2009) Chapter 3; Kristin Skjørten, 'Mellom beskyttelse og selvbestemmelse' in Ingunn Ikdahl and Vibeke Blaker Strand (eds), *Rettigheter i velferdsstaten. Begreper, trender, teorier* (Gyldendal Oslo 2016) 167–182; Anna Nylund, 'Children's Right to Participate in Decision-Making in Norway: Paternalism and Autonomy' in Haugli and others (n 7); Kristin Skjørten, 'Normer i endring. Barns rettigheter og domstolspraksis i foreldretvister med påstander om vold' in Reidun Førde, Morten Kjelland and Ulf Stridbeck (eds), *Cand.mag., cand.med., cand.jur., cand.alt Festskrift til Aslak Syse* (Gyldendal 2016) 421–434; Syse (n 32).

[50] Caroline Adolpsen, *Mindreåriges retsstilling i relation til behandling* (Jurist- og Økonomforbundets Forlag 2013); Priscilla Alderson, 'Giving Children's View "Due Weight" in Medical Law' (2018) 26(1) *International Journal of Children's Rights* 16–37; Marianne K Bahus, Pål Friis and Terje Mesel, 'Pasientautonomi – en rettighet med moralske implikasjoner' (2018) *Kritisk Juss* 56–78.

[51] Irma Hein, 'Children's Competence in Medical Care Decision-Making' in Joseph H H M Dorscheidt and Jaap E Doek (eds), *Children's Rights in Health Care* (Brill/Nijhoff 2019) 150–172.

[52] Lucinda Ferguson, 'The Jurisprudence of Making Decisions Affecting Children: An Argument to Prefer Duty to Children's Rights and Welfare' in Alison Diduck, Noam Peleg and Helen

by the legislator to try and avoid this consequence—as we have seen in Scenario 1 about daily care, and in Scenario 3 about the need for significant healthcare. The purpose is to make healthcare available and accessible for children. Even if the child does not have the right to self-determination, there could be other agency rights available, such as the right to refuse and the right to complain.[53]

The situation where both parents deny healthcare for their child, thus posing the risk of harm to the child, is complicated (Scenario 2). Healthcare will not be available for the child unless the situation is of a rather serious nature. The parents have a clear right to decide for their child and to be involved (Scenario 4). The duty of health personnel and the health authorities to influence which decisions the parents make is rather weak, perhaps out of respect for the family's privacy and respect for the basic principle of autonomy; however, in this perspective, there is no autonomy for the child. Any underlying conflict between the parents or a threatening situation for any of the parents, or even the child, risks remaining unresolved.

The scenarios presented here show that lawmakers designing health legislation have not always directed their attention to potential conflicts between parents' and children's rights and interests. The right of the parents is based on a presumption that they will act in the best interests of the child, and that the parents are best suited to make decisions on behalf of their children who are under 16 years of age.[54] The family shall be effectively protected as a fundamental unit in society, and this is reflected in several CRC provisions and the ECHR.[55] As we have shown, one cannot rely on the assumption that parents will always act in the interests of their children, particularly when there is a high level of conflict between the parents. The current Norwegian health-law legislation is, in our opinion, more family-oriented than child-oriented, and

---

Reece (eds), *Law in Society: Reflections on Children, Family, Culture and Philosophy: Essays in Honour of Michael Freeman* (Brill/Nijhoff 2015) 141–189.

[53] Ursula Kilkelly and Mary Donnelly, 'Child-Friendly Healthcare: Delivering on the Right to be Heard' (2011) 19 *International Journal of Children's Rights* 27–54; Rosalind Dixon and Martha C Nussbaum, 'Children's Rights and a Capabilities Approach: The Question of Special Priority' (2012) 97 *Cornell Law Review* 549–593.

[54] See e.g. Proposition to the Odelsting nr 104 (2008–2009) 63.

[55] Tobin (n 33) 53–67, 56.

consequently, several conflict situations are not given any attention in the founding documents. Thus, the right to respect for family life and the child's right to healthcare do not fully coincide. Furthermore, this can provide a parent with a dichotomy: either choose to file for sole custody or submit to the other parent's will. This conflict requires further investigation.[56]

Even if children younger than 16 are not free to give their own consent to healthcare, the right to participation should be respected. To fulfil this right, children have a right to relevant information that is provided in an individually adapted way. In general, health personnel are obliged to give adapted information to each patient individually, and then listen to their views and decisions.[57] However, in the case of children younger than 16, the main obligation seems to be placed on the parents—another sign of family-oriented legislation.[58] The position of co-parenthood, joint custody, or even shared residence after divorce is well established in Norwegian family law. It is built upon the rights and principles of gender equality, but also on the idea that parents will take a common responsibility for their child, acting in the child's best interests. In those situations where this is not the case, there is a lack of services to help the parents solve their conflict and reach a decision in the best interests of the child.

It should be remembered that parents may have factual, unbiased disagreements on health questions, even if they are not in any conflicting situation. It could be the vaccination of children, for example, in cases such as COVID-19 vaccination, where the vaccine is not established as a standard offering to all children in child-vaccination programmes. There could be good arguments both for and against. In these situations,

[56] E Kay M Tisdall, 'Conceptualising Children and Young People's Participation: Examining Vulnerability, Social Accountability and Co-production' (2017) 21(1) *The International Journal of Human Rights* 59–75.

[57] Health Personnel Act Section 10.

[58] Patient and Service User Rights Act Section 4-4 Subsection 5.

upholding the status quo is in accordance with the legislator's intention, and could be a good solution.[59]

References

Aasen H S, *Pasientens rett til selvbestemmelse ved medisinsk behandling* (Fagbokforlaget 2000).

Aasen H S, 'Barns rett til selvbestemmelse og medbestemmelse i beslutninger om helsehjelp' (2008) *Tidsskrift for familierett, arverett og barnevernrettslige spørsmål* 3.

Adolpsen C, *Mindreåriges retsstilling i relation til behandling* (Jurist- og Økonomforbundets Forlag 2013).

Alderson P, 'Giving Children's View "Due Weight" in Medical Law' (2018) 26(1) *International Journal of Children's Rights* 16.

Archard D and Skivenes M, 'Balancing a Child's Best Interests and Child's Views' (2019) 17(1) *The International Journal of Children's Rights* 1.

Bahus M K, Pål Friis and Terje Mesel, *Pasientautonomi – en rettighet med moralske implikasjoner* (Kritisk Juss 2018).

Committee on the Rights of the Child, *General Comment No. 15 (2013), on the Right of the Child to the Enjoyment of the Highest Attainable Standard of Health (Art. 24)* (17 April 2013) CRC/C/GC/15.

Daly A, 'No Weight for "Due Weight"? A Children's Autonomy Principle in Best Interests Proceedings' (2018) 26(1) *International Journal of Children's Rights* 61.

Daly A, 'Children, Autonomy and the Courts: Beyond the Right to Be Heard' (2018) 26(4) *International Journal of Children's Rights* 1.

Dixon R and Nussbaum M C, 'Children's Rights and a Capabilities Approach: The Question of Special Priority' (2012) 97 *Cornell Law Review* 549.

Doek J E, 'The Human Rights of Children: An Introduction' in Kilkelly U and Liefaard T (eds), *International Human Rights of Children* (Springer 2019) 1.

[59] John Eekelaar, 'The Importance of Thinking that Children Have Rights' (1992) 6(1) *International Journal of Family Law* 221–235; Jane Fortin, *Children's Rights and the Developing Law* (Cambridge University Press 2009); John Tobin, 'Taking Children's Rights Seriously: Need for a Multilingual Approach' in Alison Diduck, Noam Peleg and Helen Reece (eds), *Law in Society: Reflections on Children, Family, Culture and Philosophy: Essays in Honour of Michael Freeman* (Brill/Nijhoff 2015) 127–140; Njål Høstmælingen, Elin S Kjørholdt, and Kirsten Sandberg, *Barnekonvensjonen, barns rettigheter i Norge* (4th edn, Universitetsforlaget 2020).

Doek J E, 'Children's Rights in Health Care and the General Principles of the CRC', in Dorscheidt J H H M and Doek J E (eds), *Children's Rights in Health Care* (Brill/Nijhoff 2019) 48.

Ferguson L, 'The Jurisprudence of Making Decisions Affecting Children: An Argument to Prefer Duty to Children's Rights and Welfare' in Diduck A, Peleg N and Reece H (eds), *Law in Society: Reflections on Children, Family, Culture and Philosophy: Essays in Honour of Michael Freeman* (Brill/Nijhoff 2015) 141.

Fortin J, *Children's Rights and the Developing Law* (Cambridge University Press 2009).

Gilmore S and Herring J, '"No" Is the Hardest Word: Consent and Children's Autonomy' (2011) 23(1) *Child and Family Law Quarterly* 3.

Haugli T, 'Constitutional Rights for Children in Norway' in Haugli T, Nylund A, Sigurdsen R and Bendiksen L R L (eds), *Children's Constitutional Rights in the Nordic Countries* (Brill/Nijhoff 2019) 39.

Haugli T, Nylund A, Sigurdsen R and Bendiksen L R L, *Children's Constitutional Rights in the Nordic Countries* (Brill/Nijhoff 2019).

Hein I, 'Children's Competence in Medical Care Decision-Making' in Dorscheidt J H H M and Doek J E (eds), *Children's Rights in Health Care* (Brill/Nijhoff 2019) 150.

Hellebostad M, Syse A and Førde R, 'Når en mindreårig pasient nekter livreddende behandling' (2017) Tidsskrift for den norske legeforening.

Herring J, *Medical Law and Ethics* (3rd edn, Oxford University Press 2010).

Høstmælingen N, Elin S Kjørholdt E S and Sandberg K, *Barnekonvensjonen, barns rettigheter i Norge* (4th edn, Universitetsforlaget Oslo 2020).

Kilkelly U and Donnelly M, 'Participation in Healthcare: The Views and Experiences of Children and Young People' (2011) 28(1) *International Journal of Children's Rights* 107.

Kilkelly U and Donnelly M, 'Child-Friendly Healthcare: Delivering on the Right to be Heard' (2011) 19 *International Journal of Children's Rights* 27.

Kjønstad A, 'Twelve main Principles in Norwegian Health Law' (2010) Retfærd 60.

Norwegian Official Report 2008:9 Med barnet i fokus.

Nylund A, 'Children's Right to Participate in Decision-Making in Norway: Paternalism and Autonomy' in Haugli T and others (eds), *Children's Constitutional Rights in the Nordic Countries* (Brill/Nijhoff 2019) 201.

Proposition to the Odelsting (Ot.prp.) nr 12 (1998–1999) Lov om pasientrettigheter (pasientrettighetsloven).

Proposition to the Odelsting (Ot.prp.) nr 104 (2008–2009) Om lov om endringer i barnelova mv. (flytting, delt bosted, samvær, vold mv.).

Report from the Human Rights Commission to the Presidium of the Parliament on Human Rights in the Constitution, 19 December 2011 (Document 16).

Sandberg K, 'Children's Right to Participate in Health Care Decisions' in Sinding Aasen H, Barbosa da Silva A, Halvorsen R and Hvinden B (eds), *Human Rights, Dignity and Autonomy in Health Care and Social Services: Nordic Perspectives* (1st edn Intersentia 2009).

Skjørten K, 'Mellom beskyttelse og selvbestemmelse' in Ingunn Ikdahl and Vibeke Blaker Strand (eds), *Rettigheter i velferdsstaten. Begreper, trender, teorier* (Gyldendal Oslo 2016) 167.

Skjørten K, 'Normer i endring. Barns rettigheter og domstolspraksis i foreldretvister med påstander om vold' in Førde R, Kjelland M and Stridbeck U (eds), *Cand.mag., cand.med., cand.jur., cand.alt Festskrift til Aslak Syse* (Gyldendal 2016) 421.

Søvig K H, 'Reviewing Medical Decisions Concerning Infants within the Norwegian Healthcare System; A Public Law Approach' in Goold I, Auckland C and Herring J (eds), *Medical Decision-Making on Behalf of Young Children. A Comparative Perspective* (Hart Publishing 2020) 259.

Syse A, Pasient- og brukerrettighetsloven (4th edn, Gyldendal 2015).

The Constitution of the Kingdom of Norway, LOV-1814–05–17.

Tisdall E K M, 'Conceptualising Children and Young People's Participation: Examining Vulnerability, Social Accountability and Co-production' (2017) 21(1) *The International Journal of Human Right* 59.

Tisdall E K M, 'Challenging Competency and Capacity?' (2018) 26(1) *International Journal of Children's Rights* 159.

Tobin J, 'Taking Children's Rights Seriously: Need for a Multilingual Approach' in Alison Diduck, Noam Peleg and Helen Reece (eds), *Law in Society: Reflections on Children, Family, Culture and Philosophy: Essays in Honour of Michael Freeman* (Brill/Nijhoff 2015) 127.

Tobin J, 'Fixed Concepts but Changing Conceptions: Understanding the Relationship Between Children and Parents' in Martin D Ruck, Michele Peterson-Dadali and Michael Freeman (eds), *Handbook of Children's Rights: Global and Multidisciplinary Perspectives* (Routledge 2017) 53.

World Health Organization, 'Advancing the Right to Health: the Vital Role of Law' (2016) http://www.who.int/iris/handle/10665/252815 accessed 25 February 2023.

9

Challenges When Family Conflicts Meet the Law—A Proactive Approach

Thomas D. Barton

9.1 Introduction

Child custody arrangements caused by parental separation present fearsomely difficult problems for parents, courts, and the children themselves. They regularly include: establishing ongoing residence patterns, visitation and contact rights; child support and other payments; decision-making rights about education and other significant developmental issues. The challenges of custodial and relational management often overwhelm social institutions and methods, precisely when the parents' coping skills and resilience are at their weakest. Consequently, children's health, wellbeing, and life prospects can be jeopardized.[1]

[1] Maria Eriksson, 'Children's Health, Participation and Perspectives in Family Disputes', in Anna Kaldal, Agnes Hellner and Titti Mattsson (eds), *Children in Custody Disputes: Matching Legal Proceedings to Problems* (Palgrave 2023).

T. D. Barton (✉)
California Western School of Law, San Diego, CA, USA

A. Kaldal et al. (eds.), *Children in Custody Disputes*,
https://doi.org/10.1007/978-3-031-46301-3_9

Interpersonal skills of the parents, while vital, are not always equal to the task of negotiating either immediate custodial arrangements, or the ongoing environments of their children. Initial structural questions about children's welfare and development come at a time of almost unparalleled stress and emotional turbulence for the parents—the undoing of a personal relationship they typically had expected to be lifelong and mutual in its commitments. Anger, fear, disappointment, and feelings of betrayal understandably challenge the wisdom of immediate decisions. All relationships are in constant flux; over time they shift between the parents, and among the children and their parents, grandparents, siblings, stepparents, stepsiblings, friends, and teachers—all in a variety of contexts, histories, needs, and uncertain futures that compound the complexity of the issues.

As described by the editors in their Introduction to this volume,[2] child custody arrangements are deeply intimate, strongly emotional, and intertwined in complex, dynamic, and often unpredictable relationships. The issues are potentially explosive as well as intensely important to both society and particular individuals. Little wonder, then, that for decades we have looked to the legal system to configure and oversee child custody following parental separations.

Yet relying so heavily on legal institutions has proven problematic. The issues require flexibility even while ensuring stability; the procedures must offer access and immediacy to all affected parties but without overly intruding in daily life. The professionals rendering custody decisions must respect the intimacy of parent/child relationships yet also acknowledge their destructive potentials. Such conversations do not easily proceed in traditional courts, even when their formalities are supplemented by social workers and evaluators. Significant structural reforms are needed. Somehow, we must prudently, but more successfully invoke the power of the state to protect children and society in the risky and sometimes volatile circumstances of parental separation.

[2] See Anna Kaldal, Agnes Hellner and Titti Mattsson, 'Introduction: Matching Legal Proceedings to Problems in Custody Disputes' in Anna Kaldal, Agnes Hellner and Titti Mattsson (eds), *Children in Custody Disputes: Matching Legal Proceedings to Problems* (Palgrave 2023).

What can be done? How can we structure conversations and empathic understanding within a legal framework that will best facilitate the well-being of children and their parents? What combination of constraints and freedom, rationality and emotion, supervision and trust can offer the best chances for successful transition of parents into their new lives, and their children into adulthood?

The demands of child custody issues are so profound that we in the law may be required to transcend our normal understanding of a 'legal procedure'. Custody arrangements might require lawyers to acknowledge and incorporate different ways of thinking and speaking about rights, relationships, and social environments. We must adopt methods and mentalities that challenge some of the underlying assumptions about our historic systems of justice.

In the sections below, I use problem-solving and prevention principles derived from Preventive and Proactive Law (PPL) to explore these issues.[3] Part I considers the mismatch between the structural demands made by custody problems and the procedural tools for resolutions traditionally available through the courts. Part II reflects on alternatives for examining and discussing custody issues and goals. Part III posits ideas for new institutional legal tools and ways of speaking about child custody. Part IV concludes that traditional legal methods should be supplemented by specific practices seeking to strengthen parental cooperation, child development education, and community involvement, and we should consciously broaden the moral and cultural language that courts use to reflect upon children's wellbeing and social integration.

[3] See for example, Thomas D Barton, *Preventive Law and Problem-Solving: Lawyering for the Future* (Vandeplas Publishing 2009); Gerlinde Berger-Walliser, 'The Past and Future of Proactive Law: An Overview of the Development of the Proactive Law Movement' in Gerlinde Berger-Walliser and Kim Østergaard (eds), *Proactive Law in a Business* Environment (DJØF Publishing 2012).

9.2 Matching Problems and Procedures

Social problem-solving—of which the law offers a particularly significant and distinctive example—suffers from several ongoing breakdowns of imagination[4]:

- First, failing to realize that not all problems are alike in the demands they make on procedures for their resolution.
- Second, failing to fully appreciate that every human procedure is limited in its capabilities.
- Finally, failing to see when certain problems have been stuffed into unsuitable procedures that are at best clumsy, but at worst, counter-productive and discourage efforts towards procedural innovation.

In brief, this is what has happened with the problem of child custody arrangements and the procedures of the law: structurally, courtrooms are not well-suited to take on a problem with the attributes of child custody. And yet the problem continues to be decided and managed inside legal institutions. In part, this is legitimate caution—an awareness that violence or moral extortion could follow if we do not employ state power to oversee child custody. But the persistence of child custody proceedings in courtrooms might also have less thoughtful explanations: perhaps we lack alternative institutions, or we have used legal procedures for so long, that we now intuitively frame custody issues according to the structural needs of the legal procedures rather than the relational needs of the children and their parents.

However expedient it might be to send child custody matters to the law, they just do not fit well. As a result, the law has resorted to using an improvised standard to substitute for rules—the 'best interests of the child'—a way of speaking that challenges clear criteria, predictability, or review.[5] This standard arguably glosses over the social complexity of the issues; further, it is articulated in a non-rule format largely devoid of

[4] Lon L Fuller, 'Irrigation and Tyranny' (1965) 17(6) *Stanford Law Review* 1026–1037.

[5] See Lynne Marie Kohm, 'Tracing the Foundations of the Best Interests of the Child Standard in American Jurisprudence' (2008) 10 *J L & Fam Stud* 337.

provable elements and almost immune to falsification—both hallmarks of traditional rule-of-law ideals.

And yet I feel the standard itself is appropriately protective and child-centred. As a guide for legal outcomes, it should be retained. The best-interests standard seems a historically sincere effort by a host of legal professionals to responsibly address a set of problems for which the legal system lacks adequate tools—or even well-articulated goals. The standard is not to blame. It provides a vital moral foundation by focusing attention first and foremost where it should be: on the wellbeing of the child rather than the demands or convenience of either parent. Further, it retains the possibility of state-imposed protections against egregious or exploitive behaviours.

Yet as applied inside traditional legal structures, the best-interests standard oversimplifies the problems and emotions surrounding child custody arrangements.[6] The operations of the legal system thus may be stifling our imaginations and incentives to invent something better. We need a broader repertoire of methods to refine and apply the standard, and stronger, clearer objectives for assessing the outcomes of legal decision-making. In the sections below, I identify better tools as well as more refined and transparent goals.

9.3 New Tools and Goals for Addressing Child Custody Issues

The discussion below seeks to broaden the range of structures and problem-solving tools by which the law approaches child custody arrangements. While acknowledging a continuing background need for state power to intervene when necessary to prevent exploitation or cruelty, it also pursues mechanisms that appeal more broadly to relationships, community values, and independent professional support. These

[6] Cf Anna Singer 'Out-of-court Custody Dispute Resolution in Sweden – A Journey without Destination' in Anna Kaldal, Agnes Hellner and Titti Mattsson (eds), *Children in Custody Disputes: Matching Legal Proceedings to Problems* (Palgrave 2023).

measures would no doubt impose significant financial costs and challenges of staffing, organization, and coordination. I urge, however, that such expenses be placed side by side with the enormous long-term financial, social, and psychological costs of neglecting the developmental needs of children and the wellbeing of their parents.

My suggestions below focus on structures and practices that:

- rely less exclusively on state power, bringing alternative problem-solving mechanisms, such as the willing accommodation of the parties to adjust to changes in their relationships.
- articulate a moral or cultural vocabulary in addition to a 'rights' and 'evidence' legal way of speaking.
- provide modelling or support from community members engaged in day-to-day contact with the parties.

In dealing with the intimate, but also profoundly social problems of child custody, each of these considerations should guide procedural design. They are cumulative rather than exclusive or antagonistic. Taken together, they are humbler about finding an infallible truth.[7] The challenge is to find viable institutions that can realistically and competently harness the diversity of these methods.

9.3.1 State Power

State power, rationally and fairly applied, is the traditional domain of legal problem-solving. Inside courtrooms, power speaks through judging: measuring human behaviour against authoritative norms and pronouncing blame or required action, making little use of emotion or relationships.[8] Notwithstanding its narrow focus, we should never dispense with legal power and judgement, for at least three reasons:

[7] See James Boyd White, 'What Can a Lawyer Learn from Literature?' (1989)102(8) *Harv L Rev* 2014.

[8] Thomas D Barton, 'Therapeutic Jurisprudence, Preventive Law, and Creative Problem Solving: An Essay on Harnessing Human Emotion and Connection' (1999), 5(4) *Psychology, Public Policy, and Law* 921–943, 926–927.

- First, if the parental relationship is formalized by a marriage now requiring divorce, these are state-recognized statuses. The state must have formal mechanisms for conferring and dissolving marital status.
- Second, cruel and exploitative people will sadly always be among us. The courts must provide enforceable public means to prevent physical and mental abuses of children and family members.[9]
- Third, courts and the law provide at least an indirect moral voice. They articulate basic social values through their institutions and practices—which is why this book examining child custody is so important.

9.3.2 Party Accommodation

As I have suggested, formal legal power as traditionally exercised through the courts is necessary, yet insufficient when considering the problems of child custody and domestic relations. But power can readily be supplemented by consensual, mutual accommodation[10]—the primary tool of mediation, cooperative talks, and the willing agreement of the parties.

Still, party 'agreement' is not completely reliable.[11] Often the accommodation of parents comes about through reciprocity, in which the parties come to a fair bargain about the duties and expectations of their relationship and towards their children. At other times, however, the 'accommodation' is basically unjust, the result of exhaustion or an underlying capitulation to superior economic power, fear of physical threat, or moral blackmail. It is not truly 'willing', but instead reflects power imbalance or ulterior motives.[12]

---

[9] Anna Nylund 'Nordic family mediation: towards a system of differentiated services?' in Anna Kaldal, Agnes Hellner and Titti Mattsson (eds), *Children in Custody Disputes: Matching Legal Proceedings to Problems* (Palgrave 2023).

[10] Ibid.

[11] Singer (n 6).

[12] Anne Barlow, Rosemary Hunter and Jan Ewing, 'Mapping paths to family justice: Resolving family disputes involving children in neoliberal times' in Anna Kaldal, Agnes Hellner and Titti Mattsson (eds), *Children in Custody Disputes: Matching Legal Proceedings to Problems* (Palgrave 2023).

9.3.3 Beyond Power and Accommodation: Unconventional Tools and Goals

The limitations of power and accommodation in addressing child custody issues suggest that a broader institutional system should be constructed, moving beyond merely establishing courtroom and private parental agreements. In designing a broader system, newly developed legal structures could focus on unconventional tools and systemic goals.

Alternative tools might be:

- Cognitive depth and restructuring.
- Moral and psychological sentiments such as, forgiveness, apology, respect, empathy, and grace.
- Community peer pressure.
- Support systems emphasizing friendships and finances.

Alternative systemic goals could include:

- Emphasizing and strengthening the long-term relationships of parents to one another, and of each with their children.
- Taking specific measures to avoid parental conflict that clearly jeopardizes child welfare and adjustment.
- Providing 'safety triggers' that signal signs of child abuse, neglect, or poor parenting and can cycle back to stronger state power mechanisms.
- Finding the proper combination of overall stability with the obvious need for flexibility and adaptation to changes in the family environment and children's development.

In the concluding section below, I propose four ideas that attempt to institutionalize a combination of traditional legal tools of power and party accommodation, with the alternative tools and goals outlined above: (A) a beginning *relational contract*; (B) easily accessed, web-viewable videos or other *educational materials* about parenting and post-separation relationships[13]; (C) periodic *mandatory reviews* by the court of problems and progress; and (D) *'court friends'* for every child—community members who would operate like a big sister/big brother or aunt/uncle, but who could also provide early warning in the event of trouble or need.

9.4 Ideas for New Institutions

9.4.1 Create a Relational Contract as a Condition for Obtaining a Formal Separation

The first suggestion is that in every formal decision involving child custody, the court decree is conditioned on the parents committing to a *relational contract* that sets out a framework for cooperative behaviours towards maintaining a stable environment and basic support for their children. They can be used in many settings and are particularly appropriate for longer-term, unpredictable contexts—and thus are especially useful for the volatile course of child custody arrangements as they unfold through the years.

In a relational contract, the parties do not attempt to establish a firm 'legal future' with mutual promises. Instead, the parties acknowledge the unknowability of the future, but also commit to dialogue and fairness in dealing with it. Presenting the separating parents with a formal agreement that they promise to uphold helps identify and underscore their commitment towards specific goals for themselves and their children and provides a permanent touchstone by which they and the courts can measure their progress or backsliding.

Relational contracts to structure and adjust child custody arrangements employ cognitive awareness and restructuring, supplemented by emotional and moral appeal. They can clearly set out the relational goals for both parents and children and specify behaviours that will be expected or prohibited.

[13] Nylund (n 9).

Relational contracts have been used successfully in relationship termination settings through formal 'Collaborative Lawyering' arrangements,[14] but such contracts can be used more broadly and informally. They are particularly appropriate for longer-term, unpredictable contexts like child custody. Relational contracts set out a starting framework of arrangements and responsibilities, and then seek ongoing communication, flexibility, and fairness as ways to address risks of uncertainty and loss of trust.[15]

The International Association of Contract and Commercial Managers (IACCM, now the World Contract and Commerce Association or WorldCC) produced a White Paper[16] identifying the following five design steps for a relational contract. The authors write in the context of commercial relationships, but the principles are the same when the parties are parents creating child custody arrangements:

- Focus on the relationship, not the deal.
- Establish a partnership instead of an arm's-length relationship.
- Embed social norms in the relationship.
- Avoid and mitigate risks by alignment of interests.
- Create a fair and flexible framework.

Here are some sample 'preamble' clauses that I suggest might be inserted at the beginning of a relational contract. They illustrate the kind of cooperative commitment to be made by the parties. One or more of these pledges should be included, specifically signed by the parties, and emphasized by any mediator or court official when faced with any subsequent disagreement concerning custody arrangements:

---

14 Forrest S Mosten, *Collaborative Divorce Handbook: Helping Families Without Going to Court* (Jossey-Bass 2009).

15 Ibid 21.

16 David Frydlinger and others, 'Unpacking Relational Contracts: The Practitioner's Go-To Guide for Understanding Relational Contracts' in International Association of Contracts and Commercial Management White Paper (2016).

1. We agree to work towards arrangements that share risks in a balanced way, striving for maximal realization of *both* parties' interests, and those of the children.
2. We agree to communicate in regularly scheduled meetings about the progress and quality of our arrangements and performances as parents.
3. We agree, when needed, to cooperate and perhaps even provide affirmative assistance towards another party's performance of its contractual duties.
4. We agree to work towards understanding and accommodating the needs of one another in response to changes, and to be open to modifying terms where conditions suggest the need for adjustment.
5. We agree that in the event of a dispute, to negotiate in good faith and to seek mediation and other alternative dispute resolution methods where initial efforts at negotiation fail.
6. We agree that, in the event of litigation, we should not limit the interpretation of the agreement to its explicit language. Instead, all interpretations of the commitments and understandings of the parties should be augmented by the collaborative spirit in which the agreement was entered.[17]

9.4.2 Parenting and Relationship Educational Videos

The idea behind this second suggestion is that when parties understand more deeply the goals of relationships and parenting, and have better skills, they will be able to prevent problems from arising—or de-escalate tensions if they do arise. These videos should be web-based so they are immediately accessible at all times. Each should address a specific topic or context that frequently causes difficulties throughout child custody.[18]

---

[17] Thomas D Barton, 'Collaborative Contracting as Proactive/Preventive Law' in Gerlinde Berger-Walliser and Kim Ostergaard (eds), *Proactive Law in a Business Environment* (DJØF Publishing 2012).

[18] Anna Norlén, 'Children's health matters in custody conflicts – What do we know?' in Anna Kaldal, Agnes Hellner and Titti Mattsson (eds), *Children in Custody Disputes: Matching Legal Proceedings to Problems* (Palgrave 2023).

They would employ cognition and skill-building, combined with a sense of empathy and moral responsibility, to promote better problem-solving by the separating parents.

In producing these videos, the courts could engage expert family and relationship counsellors, plus child developmental psychologists, to create content that alerts separating parents to the types of stress they and their children are likely to encounter, and then communicate skilled, thoughtful ways of dealing with the difficulties. Anticipating the risks to parents and children, and then offering early intervention possibilities, can reduce the eruption of more troublesome problems.

The web videos could be used across the years of changing circumstances, with specific topics such as:

- New partnering or remarriage.
- The interactions of blended families.
- Geographic relocation of one parent.
- Visitation schedules and suggestions for successful interactions following prolonged absence.
- Financing special needs or occasions for the children.
- The possibility of a parent experiencing depression or addiction.

Generally, the web videos could address vital goals, like the need to avoid poisoning a child's relationship or feelings towards the other parent; warning against the dangers of a parent's external financial or emotional stress being brought into co-parenting arrangements, with the child becoming a pawn; and the possibility that the child will feel personal responsibility or guilt for the parental breakup.

9.4.3 Mandatory Periodic Reviews by the Court

For the first couple of years following the creation of a child custody arrangement, the separating parents should appear before the court every six months. This promotes accountability and acts as a reminder of what the community (in the form of the judge) expects from them regarding their children. The idea of a periodic reappearance in court is often adopted in problem-solving courts, and to good effect.[19] With time, and if the parties seem capable of managing their relationships properly, these sessions can be reduced to once every year or even once every two years.

When directing these periodic reappearances, the judge should be encouraged to speak in 'non-legal' as well as 'legal' ways, as appropriate, to effectively impress various issues upon the parents. Moral or psychological sentiments like forgiveness, apology, and grace activate different parts of our psyche—parts that acknowledge our inherent connections with others and the need for transcendence of the self. At one time, such moral reflections were prompted by spiritual leaders and readings. In a more secular world, the influence of religious role-players has been reduced, but the thoughts or sentiments about human connection remain important and powerful. These ideas are not the monopoly of religious figures. They can be used to great effect by any respected persons within a society. Judges are therefore excellent candidates to fill the role of moral or normative counsellors, as are the mediators who might help with creation of the initial relational contract or re-negotiations as circumstances change.

9.4.4 Use of a 'Court Friend'

The need for different sorts of speaking, or relating as people, is also a part of the fourth and final idea for new child custody problem-solving: the creation of formal 'court friends': persons designated by a judge to become a small, but regular, part of every child's life following a parental separation. Securing even an institutionalized friendship could be especially important for children of separating parents, since it is plausible that these children will often find themselves in new schools and having to make new friends just at the time they might feel most vulnerable. The idea is that children, like their parents, need modelling of ideas about cooperation, respect, empathy, and forgiveness.

---

[19] See Paul Holland 'Lawyering and Learning in Problem-Solving Courts' (2010) 34 Wash U J L & Pol'y 185–238.

The court friends could be community volunteers or trained social workers. They could be of any age; indeed, senior citizens could be well-suited to the role, especially if paired with a second, much younger court friend.

- The purpose of the court friend is simply to be a contact for the child—not for the parents—with one or more adults from the community. The intention would be that this person would act in the same capacity as a friend, mentor, aunt/uncle, or godparent—someone with the best interests of the child at heart and a trusted source of conversation and advice.
- The court friend could also provide early warning for the court if abuse or neglect is suspected. The court friends would make periodic contact with the children assigned to them by the court. This could be by a monthly, in-person visitation or, if the children are old enough, a video call. There need be no agenda or script—the court friends would simply talk to the children.
- Conceivably the court friends could convene group online sessions to allow the children to talk within a group of other children in similar circumstances. The same could be done in person once every couple of months; the court friend could take a small group of children on some sort of outing, thus facilitating formation of children's friendship networks.

9.5 Conclusions

The demands of child custody problems outstrip the capabilities of traditional legal procedures. Rather than artificially squeezing the problem into insufficient frameworks, the legal system should supplement its traditional problem-solving methods with unconventional tools and goals, seeking stronger personal relationships and community involvement: willing mutual accommodation of the parties, formalized in a relational contract; improved parenting and relationships with problem anticipation through educational web-based videos; expansion of the moral or cultural vocabulary that court personnel use to speak with parents in meetings at regular intervals; and an increased presence and modelling of community members in the lives of the children. By combining these innovations, it could help the legal system gain the procedural sophistication it needs to meet and overcome the challenges of child custody arrangements.

References

Barton, T D, 'Therapeutic Jurisprudence, Preventive Law, and Creative Problem Solving: An Essay on Harnessing Human Emotion and Connection' (1999) 5(4) *Psychology, Public Policy, and Law* 921.

Barton, T D, *Preventive Law and Problem-Solving: Lawyering for the Future* (Vandeplas Publishing 2009).

Barton, T D, 'Collaborative Contracting as Proactive/Preventive Law' in Berger-Walliser G, and Ostergaard K (eds), *Proactive Law in a Business Environment* (DJØF Publishing 2012).

Berger-Walliser, G, 'The Past and Future of Proactive Law: An Overview of the Development of the Proactive Law Movement' in Berger-Walliser G and Østergaard K (eds), *Proactive Law in a Business Environment* (DJØF Publishing 2012) 13.

Eriksson M, 'Children's Participation and Perspectives in Family Disputes' in Kaldal A, Hellner A and Mattsson T (eds), *Children in Custody Disputes: Matching Legal Proceedings to Problems* (Palgrave 2023) 85.

Fuller, L L, 'Irrigation and Tyranny' (1965) 17(6) *Stanford Law Review* 1026.

Holland. P, 'Lawyering and Learning in Problem-Solving Courts' (2010) 34 *Washington University Journal Law and Policy* 185.

Kaldal A, Hellner A and Mattsson T, 'Introduction: Matching Legal Proceedings to Problems in Custody Disputes' in Kaldal A, Hellner A and Mattsson T (eds), *Children in Custody Disputes: Matching Legal Proceedings to Problems* (Palgrave 2023) 1.

Kohm, L M, 'Tracing the Foundations of the Best Interests of the Child Standard in American Jurisprudence' (2008) 10 *Journal of Law and Family Studies* 337.

Mosten, F S, *Collaborative Divorce Handbook: Helping Families Without Going to Court* (Jossey-Bass 2009).

Singer A, 'Out-of-court custody dispute resolution in Sweden – A Journey without destination' in Kaldal A, Hellner A and Mattsson T (eds), *Children in Custody Disputes: Matching Legal Proceedings to Problems* (Palgrave 2023) 129.

White, J B, 'What Can a Lawyer Learn from Literature?' (1989)102(8) *Harvard Law Review* 2014.

10

Beyond the Horizon: Matching Legal Proceedings to Problems in Custody Disputes

Agnes Hellner and Anna Kaldal

10.1 Introduction

Finding a good match between legal proceedings and the problems they will be used to address, is by no means a new challenge.[1] The complexity of custody disputes—the variations in underlying factors, the child's individual needs, experience, and views, and the health and life circumstances of the parents—can make the challenge seem overwhelming. Therefore, rather than diving into the details of the law applicable to custody

[1] Several contributions to the present edited volume point to the repeated efforts by legislatures to ensure the best interests of the child in custody disputes. See for example, Anna Singer 'Out-of-court Custody Dispute Resolution in Sweden—A Journey Without Destination'; Anna Nylund 'Scandinavian Family Mediation: Towards a System of Differentiated Services?'; Anne Barlow, Rosemary Hunter, and Jan Ewing 'Mapping Paths to Family Justice: Resolving Family Disputes Involving Children in Neoliberal Times', all three in Anna Kaldal, Agnes Hellner, and Titti Mattsson (eds), *Children in Custody Disputes: Matching Legal Proceedings to Problems* (Palgrave 2023).

A. Hellner (✉) · A. Kaldal
Faculty of Law, Stockholm University, Stockholm, Sweden
e-mail: agnes.hellner@juridicum.su.se

A. Kaldal et al. (eds.), *Children in Custody Disputes*,
https://doi.org/10.1007/978-3-031-46301-3_10

disputes, the present anthology seeks to address broader perspectives, and look for new ways forward, perhaps beyond those set out in current laws.

Specifically, the contributions to this edited volume have explored how legal proceedings, in and out-of-court, can be matched to the complex problems underlying custody disputes, or resulting from legal proceedings aimed at solving them. In fulfilling its aim, this anthology illuminates aspects of both, the reality facing children whose parents are in conflict, and legal responses to family conflicts. The varying chapters illustrate that the topic has many faces, but as the pieces are brought together, it is possible to draw several conclusions.

The first such conclusion is that *the specific nature and the underlying causes of custody conflicts are often not sufficiently considered in legal proceedings* (further addressed in Sect. 10.2). In various ways, the chapters of Norlén, Eriksson, Rejmer, Singer, and Barton, each emphasize how parent–child relationships, children's health, risk factors, and other aspects that could be described as characterizing custody conflicts, must be understood and considered in legal proceedings, whether they take place in or out-of-court.[2]

The second conclusion is that *there are tensions between a private-law understanding of custody disputes and an understanding of custody disputes that relies on the best interests of the child as a starting point* (Sect. 10.3). Rejmer and Singer, in particular, point out the historical development of the Swedish law on custody, and the shift that has taken place with regard to seeing the child as a rights-bearer. Singer's mapping of the stepwise development of the law helps us to understand current challenges.[3] These and other contributions suggest that tensions exist between the

---

A. Kaldal
e-mail: anna.kaldal@juridicum.su.se

[2] Anna Norlén, 'Children's health matters in custody conflicts—What do we know?'; 'Annika Rejmer, Custody disputes from a socio-legal perspective'; Maria Eriksson, 'Children's participation and perspectives in family disputes', all three in Anna Kaldal, Agnes Hellner and Titti Mattsson (eds), *Children in Custody Disputes: Matching Legal Proceedings to Problems* (Palgrave 2023); Singer (n 1) and Thomas D Barton, 'Challenges when family conflicts meet the law—A proactive approach' in Anna Kaldal, Agnes Hellner, and Titti Mattsson (eds), *Children in Custody Disputes: Matching Legal Proceedings to Problems* (Palgrave 2023).

[3] Singer (n 1).

legal structures which have been conserved, despite numerous legislative amendments, and the more recently introduced legal objectives.

The third conclusion is that *challenges associated with guaranteeing the child's own procedural rights, particularly the right to participation, persist* (Sect. 10.4). Respecting the child's right to participation is a means of ensuring that the child is treated as a rights-bearer and active agent, with thoughts and ideas worthy of consideration in decision-making. However, several of the authors contributing to the anthology, point out that the implementation of the right to participation is lacking in several respects.

With the fourth and final conclusion, we draw from the discussions in the preceding chapters, that *fragmentation shapes the law governing custody disputes and proceedings in various ways* (Sect. 10.5). One way in which fragmentation shapes the law lies in *how* and *from where* it derives its normative content. Today, the best interests of the child is an international legal standard, applicable in custody disputes, but it has been criticized for being vague and difficult to apply. At the same time, national laws define the more precise content of the best interests of the child, both with respect to the substantive and procedural law. The normative content of the law is thus defined at several levels of government. It can be argued that the procedural law structures and other legal responses in place to tackle custody disputes are themselves fragmented: they take very different shapes and involve a wide range of agencies and courts. In this legal landscape—which spans several areas of law and multiple agencies with different mandates and investigational powers—the principle of the best interests of the child requires an individualized and knowledge-based assessment, which necessitates competence from several disciplines and professionals. In the following, we draw on the findings of the previous chapters of the anthology and elaborate on the above-outlined conclusions.

10.2 The Importance of Considering the Nature of Custody Conflicts in Legal Proceedings In and Out-of-Court

When considering how to implement legal proceedings that minimize the negative effects of custody disputes and optimize positive outcomes for children and their families, a basic starting point is to examine the nature of the conflicts underlying such disputes. This may appear evident, and perhaps even a superfluous point to make, but as the contributions to this edited volume clearly illustrate, it is in fact a challenging and complex task. As Barton describes, the substance matter of a custody dispute has an intimate and emotional character. It affects the parties' most important personal relations—relations that will continue long after the parties leave court.[4] Norlén and Singer point out that we know too little about the needs of the parents and their children and the problems they have.[5] Nevertheless, Norlén gives an overview of the knowledge that *is* available. Several factors characterize families that are going through separations and custody disputes. One such factor is emotional stress and parental worries about their and their children's future. Another factor is the negative effects that custody disputes have on the child's life and health.[6] There is also an overrepresentation of underlying causes, such as domestic violence, neglect, or abuse, and a great deal of underlying problems such as health concerns, unemployment, and substance abuse.[7]

---

[4] Barton (n 2).

[5] Norlén (n 2); Singer (n 1).

[6] Søren Sander, Jenna Marie Strizzi, Camilla S Øverup, Ana Cipric and Gert Martin Hald, 'When Love Hurts—Mental and Physical Health Among Recently Divorced Danes' (2020) 11 *Frontiers in Psychology*; Maria Eriksson 'Children's Participation and Perspectives in Family Disputes' in Anna Kaldal, Agnes Hellner and Titti Mattsson (eds), *Children in Custody Disputes: Matching Legal Proceedings to Problems* (Palgrave 2023).

[7] Annika Rejmer 'Custody Disputes from a Socio-legal Perspective' in Anna Kaldal, Agnes Hellner and Titti Mattsson (eds) *Children in Custody Disputes: Matching Legal Proceedings to Problems* (Palgrave 2023); Eriksson (n 6).

The idea of adapting procedural mechanisms to the substantive-law context in which they will be applied is not new.[8] Rules of procedure affect how substantive law is applied, and therefore the extent to which it succeeds in reaching its objectives.[9] A very basic example of how procedural law has been designed to reflect substantive law, is private-law proceedings. In short, a traditional understanding of a commercial private-law dispute is that the primary aim of the dispute is to resolve a conflict between the parties. Since substantive law leaves it to the individual to freely enter into a contract, or otherwise reach an agreement, procedural law should also not interfere. In Swedish civil procedure, the basic point of departure is that the claims of the parties define the boundaries of the procedure, and the court has no mandate to investigate the substance matter of the case on its own motion; rather, the judge should remain passive.[10] In other words, the court has no duty to decide in accordance with what it considers is in the best interests of the parties or even a third party. This also explains why solving private-law issues out of court has a long tradition, especially in commercial-law disputes; the benefits are numerous, such as avoiding expensive legal proceedings and negative publicity or preserving a business relation.[11]

Similarly, as illustrated by Rejmer and Singer, Barlow, Hunter, and Ewing as well as Nylund, adjustments in existing private-law proceedings have been made to handle the specific character of custody disputes.[12] However, such amendments have often been made without previous research or follow-up evaluation. It seems clear that procedural mechanisms, whether in or out-of-court, remain insufficiently geared to the situations in which they are to be applied.

---

[8] Per Henrik Lindblom'Progressive Procedure. The Courtroom Process and Societal Development' in Per Henrik Lindblom (ed) *Progressive Procedure Twelve Essays 1985–2015* (Iustus 2017) 17, 20.

[9] Per Henrik Lindblom 'Processen—bara en formsak?' in Per Henrik Lindblom (ed) *Studier i processrätt* (Norstedts juridik 1993) 17, 23.

[10] Swedish Judicial Code [Rättegångsbalken] Chapter 17 Section 3.

[11] Julian D M Lew, Loukas A Mistelis and Stefan M Kröll, 'Arbitration as a Dispute Settlement Mechanism' in Julian D M Lew, Loukas A Mistelis and Stefan M Kröll (eds), *Comparative International Commercial Arbitration* (Kluwer Law International 2003). See also Barton (n 2).

[12] Singer (n 1); Rejmer (n 7).

Both in and out-of-court custody proceedings aim to achieve an outcome according to the best interests of the child. However, this assessment is individual and must take all aspects of the child's situation into account. The variations of underlying problems and individual circumstances related to the child and his or her parents, require the availability of a variety of approaches and procedures. The importance of having thorough knowledge about the needs of parents and children in custody disputes, in order to develop efficient dispute resolution models, is echoed among the authors of the present anthology.

In some cases, in-court proceedings could be the most fitting way of handling the dispute.[13] Where there are indications of domestic violence, abuse, or other risk factors, these aspects must be properly investigated in a manner that fulfils due-process requirements. In such cases, the court decision might limit parental rights and fundamental rights to privacy and family. As pointed out by Barlow, Hunter, and Ewing, power imbalances between parents resulting from violence or threats must also be investigated and considered.[14] To be able to address the custody conflict in question, the court must have a nuanced picture of the specificities of the individual case.

In addition, where out-of-court dispute resolution appears to be an option, the nature of the conflict must be properly considered to be able to navigate between different procedures and other approaches that are available. As argued by Nylund, it is crucial to examine whether parents need therapeutic treatment or other types of support, rather than mediation, in the individual case.[15] Different approaches and procedures might be suitable at different points in time, or it might be helpful to combine several approaches. A conscious and careful match between a specific approach or procedure and the nature of the conflict in the individual case, could potentially reduce negative effects of custody disputes on the parents and children involved.

---

[13] Barlow, Hunter and Ewing (n 1).

[14] Barlow, Hunter and Ewing (n 1).

[15] Nylund (n 1).

10.3 Tensions Between a Private-Law Understanding of Custody Disputes and an Understanding That Relies on the Best Interests of the Child as a Starting Point

In line with the shift to viewing children as individuals with their own rights, the principle of the best interests of the child is the standard according to which custody disputes must be decided.[16] The principle includes several aspects: acknowledging that the child's right to both parents, right to protection, and right to participation are paramount in custody disputes.[17] Applying the principle of the best interests of the child requires that both short- and long-term consequences for the child

[16] According to the Committee on the Rights of the Child (CRC), *General Comment no. 14 on the Right of the Child to have his or her Best Interests Taken as a Primary Consideration* (art. 3, para. 1) (1 February 2013) CRC/C/GC/14, the principle is a dynamic concept that requires an assessment appropriate to the specific context. See for example, Michael Freeman, 'Article 3. The Best Interests of the Child' in André Alen, Johan Vande Lanotte, Eugeen Verhellen, Fiona Ang, Eva Berghmans and Mieke Verheyde (eds), *A Commentary on the United Nations Convention on the Rights of the Child* (Brill/Nijhoff 2007); Wouter Vandenhole, Gamze Erdem Türkelli, and Sara Lembrechts, *Children's Rights: A Commentary on the Convention on the Rights of the Child and Its Protocols* (EE 2019) 31. Interpretating the substantive meaning of the best interests of the child, when applied, is described from two (sometimes overlapping) perspectives; one when the best interests of the child is balanced (weight) with another interest (another child, group, and so on), or the best outcome regarding the individual child. See, for example, John Eekelaar, 'The Role of the Best Interests Principle in Decisions Affecting Children and Decisions about Children' (2015) 23(1) *The International Journal of Children's Rights* 3–26. The latter meaning is normally the case in custody disputes, where the best interest of the child prevails other interests, such as the parents' interest.

[17] In its General Comment no. 14 (n 16) para. 67, the Committee states that the best interests of the individual child be the sole criterion when determining parental responsibility, taking into consideration the child's right to maintain his or her relationship and that shared parental responsibilities are generally in the child's best interest. There are several articles that address the child's relation to his or her parents, such as Article 5 addressing the child's family's responsibility for the child, Article 9 preventing the child from separation from his or her parents unless it is necessary for the best interest of the child, and Article 18 stating that parents have common responsibilities for the child. According to the Committee the interpretation of the best interests of the child as a substantive right, includes the child's rights according to the Convention as a whole. General Comment no. 14, para. 4. The articles in the convention are sometimes divided into three themes: the right to provision, protection, and participation (the three Ps). The three Ps are themes under which the articles of the conventions can be subsumed. See, for example, Michael Freeman, 'The future of children's rights' (2000) 14(4) *Children & Society* 277–293; David Reynaert, Maria Bouverne-de-Bie and Stijn Vandevelde, 'A review of children's rights

are considered, and a qualitative and individualized investigation of all relevant elements.[18] Against the backdrop of the great public interests at stake, one could actually find it surprising that custody, residence, and contact for children are generally matters governed by private law and that disputes are resolved under rules of civil procedure.[19]

Much as a result of the shift in how children are perceived, custody disputes can now be described as 'atypical' private-law procedures. Unlike other private-law proceedings, the main aim of a court proceeding concerning custody, is not to decide what is proven according to the claims of the parties or to settle the dispute between the parties, but to reach an outcome that is in the best interests of the child.[20] Arguably, this standard, reflective as it is of a general public interest, adds a public-law dimension to the dispute. This in turn motivates a court proceeding that is not strictly accusatory, but one that has inquisitory traits, such as the judge's extended responsibility for investigating and even deciding beyond the claims of the parties/parents.[21] Ultimately, this can mean investigative measures that go far beyond what would otherwise be expected from a judge in private-law disputes. Furthermore, an outcome according to the best interests of the child is a prospective assessment and therefore differs from retrospective assessments that otherwise dominate private-law proceedings.[22]

---

literature since the adoption of the United Nations Convention on the Rights of the Child' (2009) 16(4) *Childhood* 518–534.

[18] CRC, General comment no. 14 (n 16) para. 6 (c), 16 (c) and 46–49. Para. 29 states that the principle applies to civil cases such as procedures concerning custody. The courts must provide for the best interests of the child to be considered in all such situations and decisions, whether of a procedural or substantive nature, and must demonstrate that they have effectively done so.

[19] See for example, Taylor N, Freeman M, Bruning, M and Schrama W, 'Introduction to the International Handbook' in Marilyn Freeman, Nicola Taylor and Mariëlle Bruning (eds), *International Handbook on Child Participation in Family Law* (1st edn, European Family Law, Intersentia 2021); Anna Nylund, 'A Dispute Systems Design Perspective on Norwegian Child Custody Mediation'; Kirsikka Linnanmäki, 'Mediation and the Best Interests of the Child from the Child Law Perspective' both in Anna Nylund, Kaijus Ervasti and Lin Adrian (eds), Nordic *Mediation Research* (Springer 2018).

[20] Rejmer (n 7); Singer (n 1).

[21] Rejmer (n 7).

[22] Applying the principle of the best interests of the child is an assessment of a future development, in both the short and long terms, CRC, General Comment no. 14 (n 16). See also Anna Kaldal, Parallella processer. En rättsvetenskaplig studie av riskbesömningar i vårdnads-

Contradictory court proceedings, such as those applicable to private-law disputes, come with certain consequences. First, as brought to the fore by both Rejmer and Singer, the applicant must prove the claim, which in custody disputes means that the parents must show that the respondent—the other parent—is unfit.[23] Consequently, the court proceeding lacks incentives for parents to be open about their problems. The dichotomic character of the ruling—one party wins and the other loses—also risks not only prolonging the conflict but intensifying and deepening it. It also involves a risk of working against a transparent and robust investigation.[24] In addition to this, Rejmer argues that, unlike parties in other private-law disputes, parents in custody disputes most often do not fight over resources that can be divided between them. The contested matter typically relates to a question of values concerning a parent's ability or suitability. Such deeply personal and emotional matters conflict with the basic idea behind private-law disputes, according to Rejmer.[25]

In Nordic countries, co-parenting is put forward as an aim of family law.[26] The aim of co-parenting when parents live apart interacts well with the child's right to both parents. This aim is mirrored by procedures seeking to keep parents out of court, and promoting agreements between them, typically regarding co-parenting and shared custody.[27] However, doing so places significant demands on parents' negotiation skills and capacity for cooperation, and requires society to provide

och LVU-mål [A legal study of risk assessments in custody- and child protection cases] (Jure 2010).

[23] Rejmer (n 7); Singer (n 1).

[24] The Committee of the Rights of the Child points out that the flexibility of the concept of the best interests of the child leaves room for manipulation by parents to defend their own interests in custody disputes, General Comment no. 14 (n 18) 34.

[25] Rejmer (n 7). Even if, for example, spending time with a child could be considered a conflict of interest, where the time could be divided between the parents, this is not a solution in high-conflict cases, for instance, when one parent accuses the other of being a risk for the child.

[26] Nylund (n 1).

[27] Singer (n 1); Jay Lebow, 'Integrative Family Therapy for Disputes Involving Child Custody and Visitation' (2003) 17(2) *Journal of family psychology* 181–92; Jessica J Sauer, 'Mediating Child Custody Disputes for High Conflict Couples: Structuring Mediation to Accommodate the Needs & Desires of Litigious Parents' (2007) 7 *Pepperdine Dispute Resolution Law Journal* 501–533.

adequate support. But if this support is lacking, then both legislation where co-parenting is the goal, and social and legal institutions' approaches, risk worsening the situation by leaving the family and the child without adequate support or imposing a decision that is not in the child's best interests.[28]

In Nordic countries, but also in England and Wales, resolving parents' conflicts out of court seems to be a shared ideal and generally considered to be in the best interests of the child.[29] However, also with respect to out-of-court dispute resolution, the understanding of custody disputes as private-law disputes appears to involve certain risks. First, out-of-court dispute resolution runs the risk of being seen as 'the good' method for dispute resolution, if it is simply contrasted with (dysfunctional) court proceedings, because of its non-adversarial nature that reduces conflict and restores autonomy to the parties.[30] As already argued above in Sect. 10.2, court proceedings are the preferable means of resolving a dispute where there are indications of violence, abuse, or other risk factors. Second, it is worth considering that out-of-court dispute resolution mechanisms were often originally developed for commercial legal disputes, that is, private-law disputes of a very different nature than custody disputes. Most out-of-court dispute resolution models are primarily constructed to handle problem-solving with two rational parties, possessing good parenting capacity and the ability to agree on outcomes that are in the best interests of the child.[31] Considering the deeply intimate, personal emotional nature of custody conflicts and the causes underlying them, to assume rationality, negotiating skills, and an ability to agree, might be expecting too much of parents.[32] At worst, the ambition to reach an amicable settlement might be in direct conflict with the best interests of the child.

---

[28] Eriksson (n 6); Norlén (n 2); Nylund (n 1); Barlow, Hunter, and Ewing (n 1). See also, Johanna Schiratzki, 'Barnrättsperspektivet I vårdnadstvister—från domstolsförhandling till föräldraförhandling. Vad händer med barnets bästa?' 2022/23 249.

[29] Nylund (n 1); Barlow, Hunter and Ewing (n 1).

[30] Barlow, Hunter and Ewing (n 1).

[31] Nylund (n 1); Singer (n1); Rejmer (n 7).

[32] Nylund (n 1); Rejmer (n 7).

Mediation is the most established form of out-of-court procedure in the context of custody disputes. It is designed to allow parties to reach an amicable settlement of the dispute with the assistance of a third person. The mediator has no authority to impose a solution upon the parties, and the process lacks a system for gathering information and for enabling the parties to argue their cases. In other words, mediation differs sharply from the inquisitory court proceeding. In contrast to the judge in a court proceeding, the mediator lacks a mandate to investigate the case or go beyond what the parties agree on; suggestions by the mediator might well be based on erroneous assumptions.[33] A dispute resolution model based on a drive to reach an agreement can result in decisions that are neither sustainable, nor in the best interests of the child. If the parents are incapable of reaching an agreement that is in the best interests of the child, then a mediation proceeding does not fit. This dilemma has not always been taken into consideration during the development of legislation or out-of-court models, with the consequence that out-of-court dispute resolution has not been as effective as expected.[34] Access to alternative methods, of a more or less therapeutic character, led by a lawyer, a therapist, or a social worker, could be a solution when choosing a proceeding. Doing this, however, would require a diagnostic tool to identify the nature of the problem.

However attractive out-of-court dispute resolution might seem from the perspective of the child's right to both parents, it is crucial that risk factors are not left unidentified. Similarly, although private-law experiences of out-of-court dispute resolution provide valuable insights that have informed the emergence of out-of-court solutions in the context of custody disputes, it is important not to forget that custody disputes have a public-law dimension that commercial private-law disputes typically lack. The will to promote an agreement between the parties should not be allowed to overshadow the best interests of the child.

---

33 Nylund (n 1).

34 Singer (n 1); Barlow, Hunter and Ewing (n 1); Nylund (n 1).

There are challenges with the out-of-court resolutions, such as, *whether* and *how* the child should be included in the proceeding.[35] This point will be addressed further in the next section.

10.4 Ensuring the Right to Participation Remains a Challenge

One understanding about the introduction of the CRC, is that it reflects a shift towards increasingly recognizing children as autonomous individuals and rights holders.[36] The right to participation, enshrined in Article 12 CRC, is one means by which the respect for the child as an active agent can be ensured.[37] Furthermore, according to the principle of the best interests of the child, state parties are obliged to introduce means of hearing the child and that their view is given due weight in accordance to the child's age and maturity.[38]

Several chapters of the present anthology show that the implementation of the right to participation presents challenges in the context of custody disputes, both in and out-of-court.[39] Even if children are increasingly being heard in custody disputes in Sweden and other Nordic countries, several studies show that children are not always heard, or their view has not informed the decision.[40] For example, there is research that indicates the child's view is not given weight in the decision if it doesn't

---

[35] Barlow, Hunter and Ewing (n 1).

[36] Vandenhole, Erdem Türkelli and Lembrechts (n 16).

[37] Kristin Skjørten and Kirsten Sandberg, 'Children's Participation in Family Law Proceedings' in Malcolm Langford, Marit Skivenes and Karl Harald Søvig (eds), *Children's Rights in Norway: An Implementation Paradox?* (Universitetsförlaget, 2019); Vandenhole, Erdem Türkelli and Lembrechts (n 16) 144.

[38] CRC, *General comment no. 12, The right of the child to be heard* (25 May–12 June 2009) CRC/C/GC/12 e.g. paras. 70–74. See also CRC, General Comment no. 14 (n 18) 43–45.

[39] Barlow, Hunter and Ewing (n 1); Nylund (n 1); Eriksson (n 6).

[40] Maria Eriksson, 'Tackling Violence in Intimacy: Interacting Power Relations and Policy Change' (2013) 61(2) *Current Sociology* 171–189; Linnéa Bruno, 'Contact and Evaluations of Violence: An Intersectional Analysis of Swedish Court Orders' (2015) 29(2) *International Journal of Law, Policy and the Family* 167–182; Maria Eriksson, 'Tackling violence in intimacy: Interacting Power Relations and Policy Change' (2013) 61(2) *Current Sociology* 171–189.

coincide with the aim of a close contact with both parents.[41] There are several reasons why children are not heard, or why their views are not given consideration in custody disputes. Judges or other decision-makers might seek to avoid the child's exposure to the parents' conflict, undue influence from one parent over the child, or a situation where the child feels pressure to choose one parent over the other.[42] Studies show, however, that children want to be heard and taken seriously in custody disputes, even if they do not always want to decide the outcome.[43] As Eriksson points out, the desire to have a say in a custody conflict seems even stronger among children who have experienced violence.[44] The challenges with respect to guaranteeing the right to participation could be the reason why the Committee of the Rights of the Child argues in favour of independent legal representation for the child in relation to the child's custodian, when a potential conflict of interest exists between the child and their parents.[45]

So far, child participation in out-of-court-proceedings has been addressed in research only to a limited extent. Indeed, ensuring the right to participation seems to be especially challenging in mediation, and the child's view is rarely reflected in the decision.[46] One explanation for this could be that an agreement between the parents is presumed to be in the best interests of the child; therefore, including the child's view is not necessary. At other times, involved parties may believe that excluding the

---

[41] Eriksson (n 40); Henrik Ingrids, 'Dilemmas in Child Custody Disputes: the Child's Best Interest in Courtroom Discourse' (Stockholm: Department of Child and Youth Studies, Stockholm University 2014); Bruno (n 40).

[42] Kay Tisdall, 'Challenging Competency and Capacity?' (2018) 26(1) *International Journal of Children's Rights* 159–182; Maria Heimer, Elisabeth Näsman and Joakim Palme, 'Vulnerable Children's Rights to Participation, Protection, and Provision: The Process of Defining the Problem in Swedish Child and Family Welfare' (2018) 23(2) *Child & Family Social Work* 316–323.

[43] Barlow, Hunter and Ewing (n 1).

[44] Eriksson (n 6). See Anna Kaldal, 'Children's Participation in Legal Proceedings—Conditioned by Adult Views of Children's Capacity and Credibility?' in Rebbeca Adami, Anna Kaldal and Margareta Aspan (eds), *The Rights of the Child; Political, Ethical and Legal Challenges* (Brill Nijhoff 2023).

[45] CRC, General comment no. 14 (n 16) para. 96.

[46] Barlow, Hunter and Ewing (n 1); Nylund (n 1); Skjørten and Sandberg (n 37).

child's view protects the child from unnecessary investigative measures.[47] This, however, conflicts with Article 12 CRC. It also seems to conflict with an understanding of the child as a person able to comprehend and process the complex situation.[48] On top of that, as shown in research, many children would like to be consulted both in custody disputes, and out-of-court family dispute resolution. Inclusion (where appropriate and safe) can have a positive effect on children's wellbeing.[49] Furthermore, a high degree of participation can contribute to a more sustainable outcome.[50] The child's age does have implications, but even if children might not always have the capacity to grasp complex situations, they have the right and are often able to contribute thoughts, opinions, and ideas about how their everyday life should be arranged.[51]

One possible explanation for the difficulties of implementing the child's right to participation, is that this carries with it a childhood image not yet fully reflected in the national private law applicable to custody disputes. Further, the procedural-law consequences of understanding the child as a person with thoughts and ideas worth considering in decision-making does not yet seem to have taken a clear and tangible shape. If this is indeed the case, it is a criticism that is similar to some of the findings presented in Sect. 10.2, such as that of Rejmer, suggesting that current procedural-law settings are not sufficiently adapted to the nature of custody conflicts—rather, they suit more typical private-law disputes.

Children's right to participate raises specific demands on any legal proceeding, in or out-of-court, which deal with parents' conflicts regarding children. In addition, the child's experiences and thoughts about alternative outcomes are crucial pieces of information for assessing what is in the best interests of the child; and are noted as a requirement for fulfilling the child's substantive right according to Articles 3 and 12

[47] Barlow, Hunter and Ewing (n 1); Nylund (n 1).

[48] Nylund (n 1); Barlow, Hunter and Ewing (n 1).

[49] Barlow, Hunter and Ewing (n 1); Eriksson (n 6).

[50] Eriksson (n 6); Heimer, Näsman and Palme (n 42).

[51] Norlén (n 2); Eriksson (n 6).

CRC.[52] The legal proceeding, therefore, must balance the interests in protecting the child from being drawn into their parents' conflict, while giving the child the opportunity to express their view and influence the decision. One concrete way of facilitating such a balancing of interests is to develop protocols for interviewing the child.[53]

10.5 Fragmentation Shapes the Law Governing Custody Disputes and Proceedings

The fourth conclusion we draw from the discussions in the foregoing chapters, builds on themes that are less articulated and more difficult to grasp, yet nevertheless are reflected in the contributions to the present work: fragmentation shapes the law governing custody disputes and proceedings. First, the law governing custody disputes can itself be described as fragmented, in the sense that it is derived from both international law and national law. It involves complex factual assessments that sometimes require expert knowledge from other authorities. Second, the law and legal decision-making processes that come into play when parents are in conflict, can be described as fragmented in the sense that they involve various branches of law (for example, family law, social law, procedural law, and public law) and multiple agencies and courts. These two aspects of fragmentation are discussed below.

The first aspect of fragmentation relates to the structure of the law applicable to custody disputes. The principle of the best interests of the child is now the international standard applicable in custody proceedings at national level. Due to its open-ended, vague, and flexible character, the standard leaves scope for implementation and interpretation. Its more precise normative content is derived from legal sources at different levels of government.

---

[52] CRC, General Comment no. 12 (n 38); CRC, General Comment no. 14 (n 18) paras. 43–45; Skjørten and Sandberg (n 37); Vandenhole, Erdem Türkelli and Lembrechts (n 16).

[53] Eriksson (n 6).

The principle of the best interests of the child is not only a rights-based substantive principle but also a rule of procedure. The Committee on the Rights of the Child does not elaborate on this aspect of the principle in custody disputes, but states that applying the principle requires a qualitative and individualized investigation of all relevant elements and, if possible, by a multi-professional team, and includes the child's own view.[54] The principle is therefore an *individualized and knowledge-based assessment* that requires information about the individual child.[55] The Committee emphasizes the importance of research when assessing what is in the best interests of younger children, and giving older children influence in the decision.[56]

The vagueness of the principle of the best interests of the child has been criticized for not giving enough guidance with respect to how it should be applied in individual cases, and for leaving scope for a paternalistic approach.[57] As a consequence of the indeterminate meaning of the principle, the line between ideological aspects and a knowledge-based assessment of a situation is at risk of being blurred.[58] Available research, and knowledge of what is in the best interests of the child in terms of custody, residence, and contact, can be both complex and confusing. The variations in underlying factors, the child's individual needs, experience, and views, and the health and life circumstances of the parents can be manifold.[59] The more vague the aim of the substantive law, combined with the complexity of the factors that come into play in the

---

[54] CRC, General comment no. 14 (n 18) para. 6 (c) and 46–47.

[55] See further discussion on the principle as a procedural rule concerning *the quality of the best interest assessment* in, for example, Milka Sormunen, 'Understanding the Best Interests of the Child as a Procedural Obligation: The Example of the European Court of Human Rights' (2020) 20(4) *Human Rights Law Review* 745–768.

[56] CRC, *General comment no. 7 (2005): Implementing Child Rights in Early Childhood* (20 September 2006) CRC/C/GC/7/Rev.1, for example, para. 4; CRC, General Comment no. 12 (n 38) paras. 32, 33, 51 and 52.

[57] Nigel Cantwell, 'Are "best interests" a Pillar or a Problem for Implementing the Human Rights of Children?' In Ton Liefaard and Julia Sloth-Nielsen (eds*), The United Nations Convention on the Rights of the Child: Taking Stock After 25 Years and Looking Ahead* (Brill/Nijhof 2016); Robert H Mnookin, 'Child-Custody Adjudication: Judicial Functions in the Face of Indeterminacy' (1975) 39 *Law and Contemporary Problems*, 226–293.

[58] Kaldal (n 44).

[59] Norlén (n 2).

individual case, the greater the effort needed to develop proceedings for how to achieve the aim of the law. As a result, assessing the best interest can require competence from several disciplines and professionals. This brings us to the second aspect of fragmentation in the context of custody disputes and proceedings.

The need for support and protection when parents are in conflict can come in different forms. Due to the complexity of problems underlying custody conflicts, the legal responses to them take different shapes. In Nordic countries, the law also allocates responsibility to various agencies and courts, in such a way that parents and children may think that the support offered is fragmented. The Committee of the Rights of the Child states that when the substance matter concerns physical or psychological abuse from a parent, any judicial involvement should be coordinated and based on an integrated approach across sectors, facilitating access to the full range of caregiving and protection services available.[60]

In Nordic countries, child protection is normally regulated in the field of social law and handled by child protection agencies.[61] In custody disputes where the situation implies a risk to the child—typically high-conflict cases where there are indications of violence or abuse—legislation in several areas of law is supposed to interact, ensuring protection of the child. In the Swedish example, this means that, whereas family law regulates custody, residence, and contact, social law is intended to ensure the child's right to protection and support. It has been pointed out, that the legislation and allocation of administrative responsibility regarding family-law matters and child protection are fragmented and uncoordinated.[62] The consequence is, not only that the definition of violence, abuse, and maltreatment, the standard of proof, and the investigative

---

[60] This judicial involvement can consist of differentiated and mediated responses, such as family group conferencing, alternative dispute resolution mechanisms, restorative justice and kith and kin agreements. Committee on the Rights of the Child (CRC), *General comment no. 13, The right of the child to freedom from all forms of violence* (18 April 2011) CRC/C/GC/13, paras. 54 and 55.

[61] Susanna Johansson, Kari Stefansen, Elisiv Bakketeig and Anna Kaldal,'Implementing the Nordic Barnahus Model: Characteristics and Local Adaptions' in Susanna Johansson Kari Stefansen, Elisiv Bakketeig and Anna Kaldal (eds), *Collaborating Against Child Abuse Exploring the Nordic Barnahus Model* (Palgrave Macmillan, 2017).

[62] Eriksson (n 6); Schiratzki (n 28).

tools vary, but that the child can be subjected to several investigations with different aims that subsequently lead to different outcomes.[63] From a strictly legal point of view, application of the law may be technically correct, but from a child-oriented perspective, the outcomes can be confusing and unclear, and in the worst case, they can put the child at risk. Risk assessment concerning a child's situation in their family also places stringent requirements on investigative tools to obtain sufficient information, expertise to assess the child's situation, and means of fulfilling the child's need for protection and support. In Sweden, this is normally the responsibility of the social services, who have the legal means to investigate, give support, and if needed, intervene in the life of the child or the family. Different definitions of violence and risk in the different legal contexts, as well as different investigative legal tools and methods, can lead to outcomes and parallel processes that are not only confusing for parents and children, but also affect the child's rights to protection.[64] Eriksson has emphasized the need for coordination and softening of legal and organizational bonds between these proceedings.[65]

Fragmentation in law and agency responsibility has an impact on the preventive out-of-court resolution models. Eriksson has emphasized the need for coordination and softening of legal and organizational bonds

---

63 Eriksson (n 6); Kaldal (n 22).

64 Eriksson (n 6); Rejmer (n 7); Kaldal (n 22); Schiratzki (n 28). The following practical example illustrates the problems related to fragmentation in law and legal decision-making in situations where parents find themselves in a deep conflict. According to Swedish social law, a child can be separated from his or her custodian *only* when the situation in the parents' home poses a serious risk for the child's health and development. Similarly, in a custody dispute, some situations may ultimately come down to choosing one parent over the other and denying one parent contact with the child. Indeed, limiting the child's contact with a parent does not necessarily have anything to do with protecting the child from violence and/or maltreatment. Instead, parents' inability to cooperate, distance between the parents' homes and/or the child's view can be the reason for giving a parent sole custody over a child. However, when questions of violence and maltreatment arise in a custody dispute, the similarities to child protection cases are obvious. The ethical, legal, and knowledge-based dilemmas related to claims or indicators of violence and other maltreatment in the child's life are a major challenge in parental conflicts.

In these cases, questions arise such as how to investigate the claims or indicators of violence, the burden and standard of proof, how dangerous the situation is in relation to custody, residence, and contact, and the extent to which the child should be allowed to influence the decision.

A system of diverse responsibility and investigation creates a risk for unqualified investigations and decisions.

65 Eriksson (n 6); Rejmer (n 7).

between social law and family law in order to adequately meet the needs of children and their families.[66] Similarly, Nylund has underlined the importance of differentiating between various out-of-court resolution models, to adjust the services to the needs of the individual family, and to provide processes and outcomes that are in the best interests of the child.[67] Enhanced collaboration between responsible social service agencies and courts involved could make this possible.

10.6 Final Words: Beyond the Horizon

Matching proceedings to problems in custody disputes is a complex endeavour. This anthology represents one step towards broadening the perspectives on the issue. A lot remains to be said and done. As the contributions to the volume show, further research and development, concerning both the problem underlying proceedings, and how new models work out in practice, is necessary. The needs of children and their parents will not adapt to the proceedings. Rather, procedural law must be adapted and institutional boundaries overcome, to meet their needs. Any reform, whether it relates to in or out-of-court proceedings, must be followed up and evaluated. Such work must integrate all the relevant disciplines and actors, avoiding one-sided and unsupported approaches. Coordination—both in terms of knowledge, professional skills, and legal fields—can foster individualized, proactive solutions, more likely to benefit the best interests of the child. As a scholar, there is a risk of reproducing existing arguments and following established patterns, even when aiming to reach beyond them. We would like to encourage further study on how proceedings can be matched to problems in custody proceedings, which—no matter the discipline—approaches

[66] Eriksson (n 6); Rejmer (n 7).

[67] Nylund (n 1).

the issue itself as both historically created and complex in the sense described in this final chapter, and illustrated throughout this book.

References

Barlow A, Hunter R and Ewing J, 'Mapping Paths to Family Justice: Resolving Family Disputes Involving Children in Neoliberal Times', in Kaldal A, Hellner A and Mattsson T (eds), *Children in Custody Disputes: Matching Legal Proceedings to Problems* (Palgrave 2023) 107.

Barton T D, 'Challenges when Family Conflicts Meet the Law—A Proactive Approach,' in Kaldal A, Hellner A and Mattsson T (eds), *Children in Custody Disputes: Matching Legal Proceedings to Problems* (Palgrave 2023) 169.

Bruno L, 'Contact and Evaluations of Violence: An Intersectional Analysis of Swedish Court Orders' (2015) 29(2) *International Journal of Law, Policy and the Family* 167.

Cantwell N, 'Are 'best interests' a Pillar or a Problem for Implementing the Human Rights of Children?' in Liefaard T and Sloth-Nielsen J (eds), *The United Nations Convention on the Rights of the Child: Taking Stock After 25 Years and Looking Ahead* (Brill/Nijhof 2016) 61.

Committee on the Rights of the Child, *General comment no. 5 General measures of implementation of the Convention on the Rights of the Child* (27 November 2003) CRC/GC/2003/5.

Committee on the Rights of the Child, *General comment no. 7 (2005): Implementing Child Rights in Early Childhood* (20 September 2006) CRC/C/GC/7/Rev.1.

Committee on the Rights of the Child, *General comment no. 12 The right of the child to be heard* (para. 15) (25 May–12 June 2009) CRC/C/GC/12.

Committee on the Rights of the Child, *General comment no. 13 The right of the child to freedom from all forms of violence* (18 April 2011) CRC/C/GC/13.

Committee on the Rights of the Child, *General comment no. 14 on the right of the child to have his or her best interests taken as a primary consideration* (para. 1) (1 February 2013) CRC/C/GC/14.

Eekelaar J, 'The Role of the Best Interests Principle in Decisions Affecting Children and Decisions about Children' (2015) 23(1) *The International Journal of Children's Rights* 3.

Eriksson M, 'Tackling Violence in Intimacy: Interacting Power Relations and Policy Change' (2013) 61(2) *Current Sociology* 171.

Eriksson M, 'Children's Participation and Perspectives in Family Disputes' in Kaldal A, Hellner A and Mattsson T (eds), *Children in Custody Disputes: Matching Legal Proceedings to Problems* (Palgrave 2023) 85.

Freeman M, 'Article 3. The Best Interests of the Child', in Alen A, Vande Lanotte J, Verhellen E, Ang F, Berghmans E and Verheyde M (eds), *A Commentary on the United Nations Convention on the Rights of the Child* (Brill/Nijhoff 2007).

Freeman M, 'The Future of Children's Rights' (2000) 14 (4) *Children & Society* 277.

Goldsmith J C, Ingen-Housz A and Pointoin G, *ADR in Business: Practice and Issues Across Countries and Cultures* (Kluwer Law International 2006).

Heimer M, Näsman E and Palme J, 'Vulnerable Children's Rights to Participation, Protection, and Provision: The Process of Defining the Problem in Swedish Child and Family Welfare' (2018) 23(2) *Child & Family Social Work* 316.

Ingrids H, *Dilemmas in Child Custody Disputes: The Child's Best Interest in Courtroom Discourse* (Department of Child and Youth Studies, Stockholm University 2014).

Jaffe P G, Johnston J R, Crooks C V and Bala N, 'Custody Disputes Involving Allegations of Domestic Violence: Toward a Differentiated Approach to Parenting Plans' (2008) 46(3) *Family Court Review* 500.

Jämställdhetsmyndigheten, *Uppgifter om våld är inget undantag. Redovisning av kartläggning av uppgifter om våld eller andra övergrepp i mål om vårdnad, boende och umgänge*, Rapport 2022:1.

Johansson S, Stefansen K, Bakketeig E and Kaldal A, 'Implementing the Nordic Barnahus Model: Characteristics and Local Adaptions' in Johansson S, Stefansen K, Bakketeig E and Kaldal A (eds), *Collaborating Against Child Abuse Exploring the Nordic Barnahus Model* (Palgrave Macmillan 2017) 1.

Kaldal A, *Parallella processer. En rättsvetenskaplig studie av riskbesömningar i vårdnads- och LVU-mål* (Jure 2010).

Kaldal A, 'Children's Participation in Legal Proceedings—Conditioned by Adult Views of Children's Capacity and Credibility?' in Adamin R, Kaldal A and Aspan M (eds), *The Rights of the Child; Political, Ethical and Legal Challenges* (Brill/Nijhoff 2023) 61.

Lew J D M, Mistelis L A and Kröll, S M, 'Arbitration as a Dispute Settlement Mechanism' in Lew J D M, Mistelis L A and Kröll, S M (eds), *Comparative*

International Commercial Arbitration (Kluwer Law International 2003) 1–15.
Lebow J, 'Integrative Family Therapy for Disputes Involving Child Custody and Visitation' (2003) 17(2) *Journal of Family Psychology* 181.
Lindblom P H, 'Processen—bara en formsak?' in Lindblom P H (ed) *Studier i processrätt* (Norstedts juridik 1993) 17.
Lindblom P H, 'Progressive Procedure. The Courtroom Process and Societal Development' in Lindblom P H (ed), *Progressive Procedure Twelve Essays 1985–2015* (Iustus 2017) 17.
Mnookin R H, 'Child-Custody Adjudication: Judicial Functions in the Face of Indeterminacy' (1975) 39 *Law and Contemporary Problems* 226.
Norlén A, 'Children's Health Matters in Custody Conflicts—What do we know?' in Kaldal A, Hellner A and Mattsson T (eds), *Children in Custody Disputes: Matching Legal Proceedings to Problems* (Palgrave 2023) 21.
Nylund A, 'A Dispute Systems Design Perspective on Norwegian Child Custody Mediation' in Nylund A, Ervasti K and Adrian L (eds), *Nordic Mediation Research* (Springer 2018) 9.
Nylund A, 'Scandinavian Family Mediation: Towards a System of Differentiated Services?' in Kaldal A, Hellner A and Mattsson T (eds) *Children in Custody Disputes: Matching Legal Proceedings to Problems* (Palgrave 2023) 41.
Rejmer A, 'Custody Disputes from a Socio-legal Perspective' in Kaldal A, Hellner A and Mattsson T (eds), *Children in Custody Disputes: Matching Legal Proceedings to Problems* (Palgrave 2023) 41.
Reynaert D, Bouverne-de-Bie M and Vandevelde S, 'A Review of Children's Rights Literature since the Adoption of the United Nations Convention on the Rights of the Child' (2009) 16(4) *Childhood* 518.
Rossi F S, Holtzworth-Munroe A and Rudd B N, 'Intimate Partner Violence and Child Custody' in Leslie Drozd, Michael Saini and Nancy Olesen (eds), *Parenting Plan Evaluations: Applied Research for the Family Court* (Oxford University Press 2016) 346.
Salminen K, 'Mediation and the Best Interests of the Child from the Child Law Perspective' in Nylund A, Ervasti K and Adrian L (eds), *Nordic Mediation Research* (Springer 2018) 209.
Sander S, Strizzi J M, Øverup C S, Cipric A and Hald G M, 'When Love Hurts—Mental and Physical Health Among Recently Divorced Danes' (2020) 11 *Frontiers in Psychology* 1.
Sauer J J, 'Mediating Child Custody Disputes for High Conflict Couples: Structuring Mediation to Accommodate the Needs & Desires of Litigious Parents' (2007) 7(3) *Pepperdine Dispute Resolution Law Journal* 501.

Schiratzki J, *Barnrättsperspektivet i vårdnadstvister—från domstolsförhandling til föräldraförhandling. Vad händer med barnets bästa?* (2022/23) 1 *Juridisk Tidskrift*.

Singer A, 'Out-of-court Custody Dispute Resolution in Sweden—A Journey Without Destination', in Kaldal A, Hellner A and Mattsson T (eds), *Children in Custody Disputes: Matching Legal Proceedings to Problems* (Palgrave 2023) 129.

Skjørten K and Sandberg K, 'Children's Participation in Family Law Proceedings' in Langford M, Skivenes M and Søvig K H (eds), *Children's Rights in Norway: An Implementation Paradox?* (Universitetsförlaget 2019).

Sormunen M, 'Understanding the Best Interests of the Child as a Procedural Obligation: The Example of the European Court of Human Rights' (2020) 20(4) *Human Rights Law Review* 745.

Taylor N, Freeman M, Bruning M and Schrama W, 'Introduction to the International Handbook', in Taylor N, Freeman M, Bruning, M and Schrama W (eds), *International Handbook on Child Participation in Family Law* (1st edn, European Family Law, Intersentia 2021).

Tisdall K, 'Challenging Competency and Capacity?' (2018) 26(1) *International Journal of Children's Rights* 159.

Vandenhole W, Erdem Türkelli G and Lembrechts S, *Children's Rights: A Commentary on the Convention on the Rights of the Child and Its Protocols* (EE 2019).

Index

A. Kaldal et al. (eds.), *Children in Custody Disputes*,
https://doi.org/10.1007/978-3-031-46301-3

The manufacturer's authorised representative in the EU is Springer Nature Customer Service Centre GmbH, Europaplatz 3, 69115 Heidelberg, Germany. If you have any concerns regarding our products, please contact ProductSafety@springernature.com

Printed and bound by CPI Group (UK) Ltd, Croydon, CR0 4YY
30/09/2026
02225311-0004